Digital Strategy for the Department of the Air Force

PROCEEDINGS OF A WORKSHOP SERIES

Linda Casola, *Rapporteur*

Planning Committee on Digital Strategy for the Department of the Air Force: A Workshop Series

Air Force Studies Board

Division on Engineering and Physical Sciences

The National Academies of
SCIENCES • ENGINEERING • MEDICINE

THE NATIONAL ACADEMIES PRESS
Washington, DC
www.nap.edu

THE NATIONAL ACADEMIES PRESS   **500 Fifth Street, NW**   **Washington, DC 20001**

This activity was supported by Contract No. FA9550-16-D-0001/FA8650-21-F-9308 with the U.S. Air Force. Any opinions, findings, conclusions, or recommendations expressed in this publication do not necessarily reflect the views of any organization or agency that provided support for the project.

International Standard Book Number-13: 978-0-309-68646-4
International Standard Book Number-10: 0-309-68646-6
Digital Object Identifier: https://doi.org/10.17226/26531

Additional copies of this publication are available from the National Academies Press, 500 Fifth Street, NW, Keck 360, Washington, DC 20001; (800) 624-6242 or (202) 334-3313; http://www.nap.edu.

Copyright 2022 by the National Academy of Sciences. All rights reserved.

Printed in the United States of America

Suggested citation: National Academies of Sciences, Engineering, and Medicine. 2022. *Digital Strategy for the Department of the Air Force: Proceedings of a Workshop Series.* Washington, DC: The National Academies Press. https://doi.org/10.17226/26531.

The National Academies of
SCIENCES · ENGINEERING · MEDICINE

The **National Academy of Sciences** was established in 1863 by an Act of Congress, signed by President Lincoln, as a private, nongovernmental institution to advise the nation on issues related to science and technology. Members are elected by their peers for outstanding contributions to research. Dr. Marcia McNutt is president.

The **National Academy of Engineering** was established in 1964 under the charter of the National Academy of Sciences to bring the practices of engineering to advising the nation. Members are elected by their peers for extraordinary contributions to engineering. Dr. John L. Anderson is president.

The **National Academy of Medicine** (formerly the Institute of Medicine) was established in 1970 under the charter of the National Academy of Sciences to advise the nation on medical and health issues. Members are elected by their peers for distinguished contributions to medicine and health. Dr. Victor J. Dzau is president.

The three Academies work together as the **National Academies of Sciences, Engineering, and Medicine** to provide independent, objective analysis and advice to the nation and conduct other activities to solve complex problems and inform public policy decisions. The National Academies also encourage education and research, recognize outstanding contributions to knowledge, and increase public understanding in matters of science, engineering, and medicine.

Learn more about the National Academies of Sciences, Engineering, and Medicine at **www.nationalacademies.org**.

The National Academies of
SCIENCES · ENGINEERING · MEDICINE

Consensus Study Reports published by the National Academies of Sciences, Engineering, and Medicine document the evidence-based consensus on the study's statement of task by an authoring committee of experts. Reports typically include findings, conclusions, and recommendations based on information gathered by the committee and the committee's deliberations. Each report has been subjected to a rigorous and independent peer-review process and it represents the position of the National Academies on the statement of task.

Proceedings published by the National Academies of Sciences, Engineering, and Medicine chronicle the presentations and discussions at a workshop, symposium, or other event convened by the National Academies. The statements and opinions contained in proceedings are those of the participants and are not endorsed by other participants, the planning committee, or the National Academies.

For information about other products and activities of the National Academies, please visit www.nationalacademies.org/about/whatwedo.

PLANNING COMMITTEE ON DIGITAL STRATEGY FOR THE DEPARTMENT OF THE AIR FORCE: A WORKSHOP SERIES

MICHAEL A. HAMEL, *Co-Chair*, USAF (ret.), Independent Consultant
DEBORAH L. WESTPHAL, *Co-Chair*, Toffler Associates
TED F. BOWLDS, USAF (ret.), IAI North America
CHARLES BROOKS, Georgetown University
RAMA CHELLAPPA, Johns Hopkins University
DOUGLAS D. DeMAIO, Alabama Air National Guard
PAMELA A. DREW, Independent Corporate Director
ANNIE GREEN, George Mason University
JAMES M. HOLMES, USAF (ret.), The Roosevelt Group
MARV LANGSTON, USN (ret.), Independent Consultant
ALDEN V. MUNSON, JR., Potomac Institute for Policy Studies
PAUL D. NIELSEN, NAE,[1] USAF (ret.), Carnegie Mellon University
JULIE J.C.H. RYAN, Wyndrose Technical Group
JAY G. SANTEE, USAF (ret.), The Aerospace Corporation
JAMES D. SYRING, USN (ret.), USAA Property and Casualty Insurance Group

Staff

GEORGE COYLE, Senior Program Officer, Air Force Studies Board, *Workshop Director*
ELLEN CHOU, Director, Air Force Studies Board
EVAN ELWELL, Research Associate
MARGUERITE SCHNEIDER, Administrative Coordinator
AMELIA GREEN, Senior Program Associate
DONAVAN THOMAS, Finance Business Partner

---

[1] Member, National Academy of Engineering.

AIR FORCE STUDIES BOARD

ELLEN M. PAWLIKOWSKI, *Chair,* NAE,[2] USAF (ret.), Independent Consultant
KEVIN G. BOWCUTT, NAE, The Boeing Company
CLAUDE CANIZARES, NAS,[3] Massachusetts Institute of Technology
MARK F. COSTELLO, Georgia Institute of Technology
WESLEY L. HARRIS, NAE, Massachusetts Institute of Technology
JAMES E. HUBBARD, JR., NAE, University of Maryland
LESTER L. LYLES, NAE, USAF (ret.), Independent Consultant
WENDY M. MASIELLO, USAF (ret.), Independent Consultant
LESLIE A. MOMODA, HRL Laboratories, LLC
OZDEN OCHOA, Texas A&M University
F. WHITTEN PETERS, Williams and Connolly, LLP
HENDRICK RUCK, Edaptive Computing Inc.
JULIE J.C.H. RYAN, Wyndrose Technical Group
MICHAEL SCHNEIDER, Lawrence Livermore National Laboratory
GRANT STOKES, NAE, Massachusetts Institute of Technology Lincoln Laboratory

Staff

ELLEN CHOU, Director
GEORGE COYLE, Senior Program Officer
RYAN MURPHY, Program Officer
EVAN ELWELL, Research Associate
MARGUERITE SCHNEIDER, Administrative Coordinator
AMELIA GREEN, Senior Program Associate
DONAVAN THOMAS, Finance Business Partner

---

[2] Member, National Academy of Engineering.
[3] Member, National Academy of Sciences.

Acknowledgment of Reviewers

This Proceedings of a Workshop Series was reviewed in draft form by individuals chosen for their diverse perspectives and technical expertise. The purpose of this independent review is to provide candid and critical comments that will assist the National Academies of Sciences, Engineering, and Medicine in making each published proceedings as sound as possible and to ensure that it meets the institutional standards for quality, objectivity, evidence, and responsiveness to the charge. The review comments and draft manuscript remain confidential to protect the integrity of the process.

We thank the following individuals for their review of this proceedings:

James M. Holmes, The Roosevelt Group,
Paul D. Nielsen, NAE,[1] Software Engineering Institute, and
Michael I. Yarymovych, NAE, Sarasota Space Associates.

Although the reviewers listed above provided many constructive comments and suggestions, they were not asked to endorse the content of the proceedings, nor did they see the final draft before its release. The review of this proceedings was overseen by Lt. Gen. (Ret.) Robert J. Elder, Jr., USAF. He was responsible for making certain that an independent examination of this proceedings was carried out in accordance with standards of the National Academies and that all review comments were carefully considered. Responsibility for the final content rests entirely with the rapporteur and the National Academies.

---

[1] Member, National Academy of Engineering.

Contents

INTRODUCTION		1
1	WORKSHOP ONE, PART ONE	2
2	WORKSHOP ONE, PART TWO	16
3	WORKSHOP TWO, PART ONE	31
4	WORKSHOP TWO, PART TWO	48
5	WORKSHOP THREE, PART ONE	63
6	WORKSHOP THREE, PART TWO	81

APPENDIXES

A	Statement of Task	101
B	Workshop Agendas	102
C	Biographical Information for Planning Committee Members	108
D	Chief of Staff of the Air Force Strategic Studies Group Project and Study Ideas	115
E	Workshop Series Recap Meeting	118

Introduction

The Air Force Studies Board of the National Academies of Sciences, Engineering, and Medicine hosted a three-part workshop series to examine the risks associated with the technical, programmatic, organizational, and governance challenges facing the Department of the Air Force (DAF) in its pursuit of enterprise-wide digital transformation strategies. Senior representatives from government, military, industry, and academia considered the DAF's strategic-level decision-making process as well as how it could achieve unity of effort across all of its digital agencies. Workshop participants discussed organizational and management gaps and weaknesses, as well as technical shortfalls associated with the DAF's digital transformation strategies—for example, the issue of cybersecurity within the context of the DAF's proposed digital strategies. Organizational and management practices from both the public and private sectors were also discussed in light of their potential for adaptation and adoption within the DAF.

Sponsored by the U.S. Department of Defense, the three 2-day workshops of the series were held virtually on September 1–2, 2021, September 8–9, 2021, and September 23–24, 2021 (see Appendix A for the workshop series Statement of Task and Appendix B for the agendas from each workshop). Panelists at the first workshop explained and discussed the DAF's digital transformation strategy—in particular, the proposed digital architectures and the systems, programs, organizations, and missions to be supported. The second workshop featured panels of information systems experts and managers from industry and other government agencies who discussed their experiences with digital transformations and shared their views of best practices. The third workshop focused on the potential applicability of these lessons learned to the DAF's digital transformation strategy and architecture.

This proceedings is a factual summary of what occurred during the workshop series. The planning committee's role was limited to organizing and convening the workshops (see Appendix C for biographical sketches of the planning committee members). The views expressed in this proceedings are those of the individual workshop participants and do not necessarily represent the views of the participants as a whole, the planning committee, or the National Academies of Sciences, Engineering, and Medicine.

1

Workshop One, Part One

OPENING REMARKS

As the first day of the workshop series opened, workshop series co-chairs Lt. Gen. Michael Hamel (USAF, ret.), independent consultant, and Ms. Deborah Westphal, chairman of the board, Toffler Associates, welcomed participants and thanked the planning committee; National Academies of Sciences, Engineering, and Medicine staff; and workshop presenters for their contributions to this endeavor to examine the Department of the Air Force's (DAF's) approach to digital transformation. Lt. Gen. Hamel described digital transformation as a critical effort for all 21st century organizations; however, while the rate of change of technology is remarkable, the available resources and talent to devote to it are limited.

He referenced National Academies efforts over the past several years that serve as a foundation to the topic of digital transformation, including a workshop on multi-domain command and control,[1] a workshop series on the time value of decision making,[2] and a study on energy needs at the tactical edge.[3] All of these efforts relate to and raise questions about the DAF's overarching digital transformation strategy. Lt. Gen. Hamel expressed his hope that, during this workshop series, the DAF could learn from others who have

---

[1] National Academies of Sciences, Engineering, and Medicine, 2018, *Multi-Domain Command and Control: Proceedings of a Workshop–in Brief*, The National Academies Press, Washington, DC, https://doi.org/10.17226/25316.

[2] National Academies of Sciences, Engineering, and Medicine, 2021, *Adapting to Shorter Time Cycles in the United States Air Force: Proceedings of a Workshop Series*, The National Academies Press, Washington, DC, https://doi.org/10.17226/26148.

[3] National Academies of Sciences, Engineering, and Medicine, 2021, *Energizing Data-Driven Operations at the Tactical Edge: Challenges and Concerns*, The National Academies Press, Washington, DC, https://doi.org/10.17226/26183.

embarked on journeys of digital transformation across government, private sector, and academia so as to better understand challenges and opportunities.

THE DIGITAL AIR FORCE

Hon. Gina Ortiz Jones, Under Secretary of the Air Force, described the Secretary of the Air Force's priority to ensure that the United States is best postured to compete with its near-peer and peer competitors in the new digital environment and, ultimately, win the fight. Sharing her perspective on digital transformation, Hon. Ortiz Jones emphasized the value of leveraging expertise and experiences external to the DAF. Noting how quickly technology has evolved over the past two decades, she said that the expectation to be able to connect, process data, and share information has become the norm. Therefore, digital transformation within the DAF is key to enabling the nation to compete for talent, meet the threat, and be good stewards of the American people's trust and resources.

Reflecting on her time as an intelligence officer supporting close air support operations, Hon. Ortiz Jones underscored how quickly information should move between a collector and a shooter, for example, as well as the need for tools to ensure that the Air Force is "doing the right things and doing things right." Digital transformation, she continued, should be geared toward achieving these objectives.

As part of the U.S. Africa Command (AFRICOM), Hon. Ortiz Jones was responsible for incorporating sociocultural analysis into an overall understanding of the challenges and opportunities of security engagement activities on the continent. This experience made clear the value of pulling in the right data layers (some of which may not initially be readily accessible or comprehensible) to understand how U.S. words and actions are received by other countries with different cultures and belief systems. Thus, digital transformation is critical to helping the United States recognize its blind spots and ensure that it is communicating and achieving its intended goals. The objective of digital transformation is not only to make decisions faster but also to make decisions better, with a refined understanding of risk (including risk that could be introduced via the supply chain) and how that risk could be mitigated.

Hon. Ortiz Jones described a recent report on China's efforts to fuse military and civilian capabilities, an approach that will shape how it constructs and implements its own digital transformation. The report emphasized applying a whole-of-government approach to achieve the following six national digital transformation goals: (1) infuse the national defense industrial base with the civilian technology and industrial base, (2) integrate and leverage science and technology innovations across military and civilian sectors, (3) cultivate talent and blend military and civilian expertise and knowledge, (4) look to build military requirements into civilian infrastructure and leverage civilian construction for military purposes, (5) leverage civilian service and logistics capabilities for military purposes in order to prosper, and (6) expand and deepen the national defense mobilization system to include all relevant aspects of the society and economy for use in competition and war.

Hon. Ortiz Jones explained that Secretary Kendall will set priorities for the United States based both on leveraging current capabilities and assessing those capabilities for a fight with a peer across the ocean. The Air Force has a legacy of developing and delivering high-end warfighting technology, and ongoing assessment will motivate how vigorously digital transformation is pursued. Incorporating partners and allies into sense-making capabilities will be crucial to the success of digital transformation, she continued, and building relationships and the digital infrastructure to share data is fundamental to U.S. national strategy. One particularly important goal is to shorten the kill chain; however, because so much of the information about how systems operate and communicate is classified, it is difficult to engage partners in this effort. It is important to ensure rapid and appropriate authorization to share this information as well as to ensure that partners have access to information that will allow them to defend themselves from attack. An alternate solution, although more challenging to achieve, would be to build a pathway for data from a highly classified system to flow down to a network so that U.S. partners are part of the system, would automatically get the data, and would make their own decisions about what to do with the data. She reiterated the need to embrace the strengths of allies and partners, as well as interoperable capabilities, for strategic competition.

Hon. Ortiz Jones noted that, currently, too many systems rely on airmen and guardians to transfer information manually or verbally, creating a lengthy decision-making process. The Advanced Battle Management System (ABMS) could play an important role in allowing secure processing at all classification levels—connecting sensors and critical nodes in a spectrum of communication environments, managing all data, building an application (using artificial intelligence [AI] and machine learning [ML] to process data), and integrating sensors and effects (kinetic and non-kinetic) to produce desired outcomes. Reducing dependence on the human-in-the-loop speeds up the kill chain and reduces the chance of human error that could cause catastrophic loss. To achieve this vision for the future, she explained that the DAF needs airmen and guardians who understand the value of these systems and can cooperate within these networks, transforming them when necessary. It is important for the DAF to consider strategies to retain and continually challenge these airmen and guardians; it cannot risk losing these digital natives over their frustration with antiquated processes and procedures. The DAF has to recruit a diverse, inclusive, and talented team and allow flexibility in career development. She mentioned the DAF's world-class training programs (e.g., Digital University) and added that senior leaders are responsible for incentivizing professional development and personal improvement for airmen and guardians.

Hon. Ortiz Jones remarked that industry will help lead the government's digital transformation. She advocated for the Department of Defense (DoD) to remove barriers to entry for both small and large industry enterprises so as to best tap into the nation's talent pool. The defense and technical industry has built itself around DoD's requirements, but moving forward, it is important that DoD becomes more inclusive. While the digital portfolio is constructed, she continued, industry and academic partners should be provided with a degree of predictability and stability so that they can invest appropriately and reduce their own risk and uncertainty. She emphasized that, as the nation's digital economy continues to grow, the United States cannot afford to lose competitors in the defense sector.

To integrate the digital transformation timeline, partners, and processes at the department level, the J6 will engage closely with the joint partners on the joint all-domain command and control (JADC2) effort. Governance structures will also need to be adapted as the Space Force continues to strengthen: now that the two forces are operating as one team, she asserted that decision-making processes should be structured accordingly. In closing, Hon. Ortiz Jones solicited feedback from the Air Force Studies Board about any missed opportunities to recruit and retain airmen and guardians; risks, challenges, and opportunities that should be considered when assessing capabilities and generating timelines; and better ways to communicate with appropriators in Congress the message that although the digital transformation will be expensive and challenging, it is necessary to become a more resilient digital force that can confront the threat.

Mr. Alden Munson, senior fellow and member, Board of Regents, Potomac Institute for Policy Studies, said that it could be a disservice to the nation if digitization efforts move beyond DoD's ability to defend those efforts—a vulnerable infrastructure still exists. He asked if the suppliers of the infrastructure on which digitization will occur would be expected to address this security challenge. Hon. Ortiz Jones recognized Mr. Munson's concern and agreed that critical infrastructure should be survivable. She emphasized the importance of the ability to protect communications nodes and to identify and act upon potential threats quickly. Lt. Gen. Hamel noted that transformations are not destinations; they are "journeys" with an ever-changing set of dynamics.

DIGITAL TRANSFORMATION

Gen. David W. Allvin, Vice Chief of Staff, U.S. Air Force, expressed his excitement about the future state of digital transformation when data-driven decisions could be made at much greater speed but also noted his frustration with the amount of time it is taking to achieve this vision. He referenced Chief of Staff Gen. Charles Q. Brown Jr.—"We must Accelerate Change or Lose (ACOL), and the ACOL paper is the result of my detailed assessment."[4] Gen. Allvin emphasized that accelerating digital transformation is the

---

[4] See CSAF-22-Strategic-Approach-Accelerate-Change-or-Lose-31-Aug-2020.pdf, airforcemag.com, p. 3.

key to maintaining—or regaining—the edge that the United States has been losing in competition. He underscored the importance of security from the start of any digital transformation endeavor, especially the integration of a zero-trust architecture.

While Gen. Allvin commended the joint force for its efforts to limit loss of life and enhance lifesaving during the recent Afghanistan retrograde, he wondered how much of that effort had to be performed without the proper tools—tools that could have enabled a more seamless understanding and awareness of the situation, streamlined and accelerated responses, and increased efficiency. Without a digital infrastructure that allows data sharing that enables machine learning (ML) and artificial intelligence (AI) to make better decisions at the speed of relevance, the United States could be at an operational disadvantage with respect to its strategic competitors. ABMS is expected to address this need for operational speed, he continued, but fully integrated data analytics are also needed to enhance investment decisions in a relevant time frame so that decisions are not solely based on past experiences.

Gen. Allvin posited that additional digital processes would add value to the force; for example, robotic processes and automation could perform manual tasks, giving airmen more time and space to use their cognitive skills. A digitally transformed Air Force that relies on data-driven insights also enhances decision making related to human capital—for example, better understanding areas of risk and better allocation of resources and talent to maintain airmen's resiliency. His primary objective is to achieve the future state of digital transformation as quickly as possible; the first step is ensuring that this new *culture* is fully integrated in the people and processes of the Air Force, where speed is rewarded over deliberation.

Ms. Westphal suggested that because decision making is and will remain a human endeavor, accelerated decision-making requires practice *before* the future state of digitization is realized. She asked how the Air Force is practicing accelerated decision making with the technology and tools it currently has. Gen. Allvin remarked that practicing accelerated decision making and achieving the state of digitization are transformations that could happen in parallel. The culture has to change to accept more risk, but if more data are available, people will be more likely to accept risk. The bureaucracy presents a challenge in that its level of risk aversion and its comfort with slower decision making could cause the nation to lose the fight, he continued.

Lt. Gen. Ted Bowlds (USAF, ret.), chief executive officer, IAI North America, pointed out that overloading a decision maker with too much data could also be problematic. Gen. Allvin proposed thinking carefully about this issue and developing a structured information hierarchy for the types and quantities of data that would be most useful for decision making. This is especially important for time-bound decisions, he asserted, because as the future unfolds, decisions will need to be made faster.

Gen. David D. ("DT") Thompson, Vice Chief of Space Operations, U.S. Space Force, described the symbiotic relationship of the Air Force and Space Force: (1) the Space Force's digital transformation efforts are built on the infrastructure and support apparatus provided by the Air Force; (2) the Space Force has an opportunity to be a "pathfinder" and implement its successful efforts in the larger, more diverse Air Force; and (3) the Air Force and Space Force have to be tightly integrated for efforts such as ABMS and JADC2 to be effective.

Gen. Thompson provided an overview of the Space Force's functions: space operations; development and fielding of space systems; intelligence associated with developing, fielding, and operating space systems; and cyberspace operations. Gen. Thompson thinks the Space Force seeks digital transformation not because digital is the reality of the future but because digital is the reality of today. However, the Space Force, which he described as a "digital dinosaur," is neither state of the world nor state of the art in its current capabilities. If the Space Force does not transform quickly and become a leader, he continued, it could become irrelevant and obsolete, which could have grave consequences for the nation. He reiterated that because the Space Force is small and digitally focused, it has the opportunity to experiment in areas that may be too difficult or too risky for larger, more complex services.

Gen. Thompson remarked that in order to demonstrate space superiority and protect the nation's interests in space; to deter aggressive acts from others; and to ensure freedom of action for the space forces, the space systems, and the forces in the air, on the ground, and at sea, the Space Force has to dominate the digital domain. Space capabilities revolve around information and data being provided to the rest of the joint force and to national decision makers. To operate effectively, he asserted that the Space Force has to drive an innovative mindset into the culture and be interconnected (i.e., sharing data and information as well as analysis and capabilities). This interconnection would enable fluid, fluent, and confident operations in the digital domain. To build this digital service, Gen. Thompson is pursuing the following initiatives:

1. *Digital Workforce*. Every member of the Space Force needs a foundational level of knowledge in networks, data, data structures, interfaces for exchange of data, and cybersecurity, for instance. Much of this knowledge can be obtained through the DAF's Digital University. Additionally, a "Supra Coders" course provides 6 weeks of training in advanced coding techniques that can be used to improve processes, products, and tools. Some of the individuals who have completed this training will join combat development teams who work with operators to try to understand their challenges and improve their effectiveness. The third tier of training available is for those who strive to be "cyber ninjas," with expertise in cyberspace operations, network operations, and network defense. Guardians will be expected to pursue advanced degrees, research, and certificates in cybersecurity and cyber operations to ensure that the workforce has the digital fluency to meet future challenges.
2. *Digital Engineering*. Acquisition processes have to be built on model-based digital engineering platforms, with the addition of long-term maintenance and sustainability plans for the life cycle of the system.
3. *Digital Headquarters*. The ability to sense, understand, and provide the right information in context in a timely fashion to decision makers will allow for quicker responses. Because action unfolds rapidly in space, some responses will be automated and automatic.
4. *Digital Operations*. Underlying agile processes make it possible to achieve this rapid, innovative culture.

Emphasizing the importance of cybersecurity, Dr. Marv Langston (USN, ret.), independent consultant, asked how the DAF plans to address the issue that the adversary can access information through the operational defense industrial base infrastructure. Gen. Thompson expressed his frustration and confusion at how this exfiltration of data has occurred for years. He emphasized that if data are on an unclassified network, one should assume that those data are exposed and available to an adversary. Better approaches are needed to protect these data. One solution is using a higher classification level. But, not an extreme classification level—an approach that has been problematic in the past. The attack surface could also be reduced by building requirements to adequately protect the data into contracts with vendors, and limiting the amount of data available at the subcontractor, subvendor, and vendor levels. Gen. Allvin added that a zero-trust architecture is key to addressing this issue. The old information protection mentality was to remove data suspected to have been compromised from the networks. But this mentality slows down the Air Force and cedes space to the enemy. This path must be altered to achieve accelerated decision making. In addition, Dr. Langston sees a lack of productivity related to classified information and processes—not protecting what needs to be protected the most! This negates the whole thrust to be agile in the digital world. Gen. Allvin commented that it is crucial to make decisions about cybersecurity in the context of strategic risks—the risk of exfiltration, the risk of *not* making a decision, and the risk of overclassification.

Ms. Westphal asked if the Space Force's digitization efforts will be different from those of the Air Force. Gen. Thompson reiterated that the Air Force has provided an excellent digital education platform. So, the Air Force will train the Space Force's cyberspace operators. It is expected that some of the approaches to digital transformation between the Air Force and the Space Force could and should be different as long as the operational effectiveness and ability to integrate and interoperate are not compromised. Gen. Allvin commented that while efforts could diverge in the operational sense, an enterprise approach will still exist. There are fundamental decision-making levels that require a certain amount of data fusion, aggregation, and rights. A unified forward movement is needed for these enterprise decisions.

Lt. Gen. Hamel asked Gen. Allvin and Gen. Thompson how this workshop series could be most helpful for the respective services. Gen. Allvin sought insights on the synchronization and sequence of digital transformation efforts and lessons from industry about strategies to evolve culture rapidly. Which business apparatus allows the fastest forward movement would also be useful. Gen. Thompson emphasized his desire to make the right investments, in the right order, at the right rime, based on the right information, and he solicited workshop participants' feedback on those challenges. He also requested feedback on whether the vision for the digital service makes sense and if there are potential opportunities or pitfalls.

WHY DIGITAL TRANSFORMATION? A PANEL PRESENTATION

Lt. Gen. Bradley "Salty" Saltzman, Deputy Chief for Operations, Space Force, offered his perspective of the digital transformation, based on Gen. John Raymond's intent in the Space Force's *Vision for a Digital Service*.[5] Lt. Gen. Saltzman stressed that, given the lean nature of the Space Force, leveraging technology is a necessity to be effective and agile (e.g., reducing manpower through automation or making better and more rapid decisions with AI, ML, and software decision aids).

He explained that the Space Force views digital transformation in terms of decision speed, resource allocation, and acquisition enhancement, all in support of operations. The four initiatives described by Gen. Thompson are key to achieving this transformation, he continued. First, a *digital workforce* has the expertise to evaluate available technologies. The Space Force guardians will have digital fluency, with the ability to understand and use the appropriate digital vocabulary to select technologies that will support operational outcomes. Thus, there is strong motivation to provide education and training for these guardians. Second, an emphasis on *digital engineering* allows the Space Force to fail more quickly. For example, the use of digital twins enables faster, less expensive testing. Digital engineering could enhance the acquisition process by resolving unknowns and helping to mature technology, selecting the right systems and subsystems, and doing rapid integration, all in a cost-effective manner. Third, the *digital headquarters* is responsible for identifying the gaps in the Space Force's ability to meet the mission set and shifting resources to maintain readiness or to maintain an effective scale and timeline for force modernization. Decision support software powered by AI and ML (e.g., data collected in a dashboard format) could enable key leaders to make informed decisions for resourcing. Fourth, *digital operations* (i.e., a composite of digital workforce, engineering, and headquarters) is the realization that the space domain is essentially a virtual domain—the interactions in the space domain are primarily enabled by software and radio frequency energy. Lt. Gen. Saltzman said that it is critical to create a virtual environment in which operators can train on their tactics against a thinking adversary, improve their tradecraft, and be prepared to face peer competitors. Leveraging emerging virtual operational test and training infrastructure requires a digital shift in how exercises and advanced training are conducted.

Brig. Gen. Robert Lyman, Assistant Deputy Chief of Staff for Cyber Effects, Headquarters Air Force (HAF) A2/6, remarked that technology changes the nature of warfare, and command and control is underpinned by digital capabilities that provide decision support. Digital capabilities are also critical for solving problems related to intelligence, surveillance, and reconnaissance (ISR). He described digital transformation as the opportunity to combat engineer the landscape on which we fight in the cyber domain; in other words, digital transformation is about maintaining or regaining competitive advantage against adversaries. Focusing on the threat creates an opportunity to prioritize investments for digital transformation. If the Air Force does not prioritize investments in digital transformation, he continued, it is accepting a substantial amount of risk. He emphasized that a culture shift is needed to eliminate the "tribalism" of the Air Force, to embrace expertise, and to invest in building the right team of senior-level warfighters.

---

[5] SF/CTIO, 2021, *U.S. Space Force Vision for a Digital Service,* https://media.defense.gov/2021/May/06/2002635623/-1/-1/1/USSF%20VISION%20FOR%20A%20DIGITAL%20SERVICE%202021%20(2).PDF.

Brig. Gen. Lyman described several transformative efforts emerging from the A2/6. For example, a Program Action Directive (PAD) could transform communication squadrons into cyber squadrons by standing up mission defense teams that would defend the cyber terrain associated with various weapons systems. However, in the past 2 years, this effort has not survived the Program Objective Memorandum, and the A2/6 is now working on making that PAD more affordable. Another A2/6 initiative is an expeditionary communications PAD associated with combat communication, engineering, and installation squadrons. The objective of this initiative is to organize, train, and equip more expeditionary communicators so as to be able to support the agile combat employment that will empower forces in the Pacific and in Europe to move quickly between locations and continue to operate. There are also ongoing efforts related to the electromagnetic spectrum (EMS) superiority strategy, the A2/6's Air Force ISR cloud strategy, and high-frequency network modernization to improve communication and capabilities in the Arctic.

Mr. Edwin Oshiba, Senior Executive Service, Director of Resource Integration, Deputy Chief of Staff for Logistics, Engineering, and Force Protection, HAF A4, explained that digital transformation is essential to support logistics for the men, women, and machines at war. Because resources will always be limited, he continued, it is essential to know what technology is available, where it is located, and where it needs to be moved. Furthermore, it is crucial to understand the implications of these decisions: for every action there is a reaction, and that cycle moves quickly while under kinetic and non-kinetic attack. Technology provides global visibility, enables knowledge-sharing, clarifies complex relationships from seemingly unrelated data, predicts (versus reacts), and presents the opportunity to experiment before building (via digital engineering), which speeds up the cycle of testing, failing, and improving.

Mr. Oshiba asserted that technology is not the barrier to digital transformation—technology is readily available and accessible from industry. The challenge is the culture change needed to leverage that technology and to convince people to experiment and accept failure. Although funding and policy for transformative efforts can sometimes prove difficult, resources can typically be found and policy can be changed. He reiterated that the DAF will lose the fight if it does not accelerate change.

Mr. Oshiba highlighted two white papers that address the problem of conducting logistics under attack: (1) "Operational Business of Basing Logistics" describes the role of digital transformation in striking a balance between combat effectiveness and resource efficiency.[6] From the business perspective, it is important to understand root causes and reduce the growth in sustaining requirements (e.g., integrating sustainability into weapons system design, perhaps utilizing digital engineering, or by leveraging what already exists). Enterprise suite management is only possible with visibility, and enterprise materiel support could be improved by aligning and synchronizing diverse supply chains. In addition to reducing the reliance on single sources of supply and adding resilience into the supply chain, it is important to expand repair networks by leveraging available capabilities and capacities from the depots to the backshops. Most importantly, he continued, the DAF has to capitalize on data, and apply data analytics and industry best practices to make the best decisions at a rapid pace. (2) "Persistent Logistics" describes the value of the following actions from an operational perspective:[7]

- *Posture for interstate competition* by expanding sustainment partnerships with allies to access interoperable supplies, parts, commodities, and repair capabilities; presenting forces in a way that supports distributive adaptive operations; delivering agile energy sources; and instituting passive defense measures.
- *Use sensing for shared understanding* by modernizing IT systems and integrating those systems with allies and partners, delivering situational awareness by fusing disparate data sets, and leveraging AI and ML to help increase the speed of decision making.

---

[6] The "Operational Business of Basing & Logistics" White Paper is CUI.

[7] The "Persistent Logistics" White Paper is CUI; however, there is a publicly releasable version released as a Mitchell Institute Forum paper at https://mitchellaerospacepower.org/air-force-persistent-logistics-sustaining-combat-power-during-21st-century-competition-and-conflict/.

- *Respond to warfighter needs at the speed of relevance* by providing resilient distribution options while under attack, leveraging autonomous systems to minimize personnel footprint, and rapidly repairing. If the posture and sensing are done correctly, response could be reduced.

In closing, Mr. Oshiba reiterated that the foundation for all of these efforts is data. He advocated for treating data as a valuable commodity; rewarding innovation; valuing outcome over activity; prioritizing diversity, equity, and inclusion in problem-solving; and creating a culture that is comfortable with change, accepting of mistakes, trustworthy, and empowered to make decisions at the lowest levels.

Open Discussion

Workshop One chair Gen. James (Mike) Holmes (USAF, ret.), senior advisor, The Roosevelt Group, asked how a digital strategy could enable virtual training aids. Lt. Gen. Saltzman described an analysis that revealed that operators do not have the tools to reach the next level of advanced training; for example, the simulators in use are simply emulators of the consoles to interact with the weapons systems, and there is no connection to a thinking adversary trying to deny mission effects. If there were an augmented reality of the space domain and available systems where operators could take actions and a thinking adversary could try to deny the missions the operators were trying to accomplish, this could better prepare operators to maintain a mission set in a contested environment and help validate tactics in a new way. If high-fidelity digital twins are integrated into the augmented reality, meaningful conclusions could be drawn. Lt. Gen. Saltzman envisioned a day in which operators wear three-dimensional virtual reality goggles while competing in an emulator as an "adversary" tries to block tactics, and then creating a demand signal for the acquisition community to enhance the weapons system.

Ms. Westphal inquired about frameworks to identify steps forward in the digital transformation. Mr. Oshiba emphasized the value of "soft skills," such as the development of culture and partnerships. For example, the Air Force has an Australian exchange officer embedded, which helps to understand the issues of allies and partners. He also described Air Force internships with Delta Tech Ops, Amazon, and General Electric—all of which have dealt with logistical sustainment problems—that have allowed the Air Force to learn and adapt relevant lessons.

Lt. Gen. Hamel asked how DAF leaders could articulate the data accessibility and computational capabilities they need to do their jobs. Lt. Gen. Saltzman remarked that operators and the acquisition community sometimes have a difficult time describing their needs to industry. The creation of a DevSecOps environment, in which software experts are invited to work collaboratively with operators, has been a successful approach. Having all of the communities work together in a common environment to solve a problem is much more effective than defining requirements in isolation and then passing them on to another group. Brig. Gen. Lyman added that the Air Force is still trying to create and *scale* the innovation ecosystem needed to achieve this vision (e.g., the federated cloud capability to make data available and the DevSecOps platform that allows tool developers to do quick work alongside the operations community). Lt. Gen. Saltzman explained that universal access to data is a foundation of this new approach; data and policy stovepipes prevent full exploitation of available technology. Mr. Oshiba noted that in terms of the requirements process, the Air Force should discuss its desired capability with industry and let industry help derive the answer (instead of the Air Force trying to provide the answer). Gen. Holmes commented that an important aspect of this cultural change is using the digital transformation to create an effective narrative that will draw funding for efforts that use data to solve problems. Mr. Munson added that several sensitive issues may arise in the attempt to change culture. For example, military services are built around the potential to fight and die as well as the associated chain of command considerations. Because there is no analogue to this mentality in industry (i.e., the communities have different value and trade-off priorities), he continued, effective communication between the two communities can be difficult. Mr. Munson and Gen. Holmes suggested the creation of a new model for interaction between operators and industry.

DIGITAL TRANSFORMATION PLANS AND PROGRAMS: A PANEL PRESENTATION

Col. Jeff Mrazik, Deputy Chief of the ABMS Cross-Functional Team, Air Force Futures, HAF A5, explained that ABMS is central to operationalizing the digital transformation that will enable future warfighting. ABMS combines advances in infrastructure and software with the evolution in policy and training to connect the combined force, with an objective for ubiquitous discovery, access, understanding, transporting, and use of real-time data across service, domain, and national classification boundaries. To achieve digital transformation, he continued, an effective planner begins at the top of the organization, involving partners and supporting the joint warfighting strategy and concepts. HAF A5 works closely with the Joint Staff J6 via the JADC2 efforts. Progress is occurring quickly and in parallel to the writing of joint documentation.

The JADC2 reference architecture helps to ensure coherence among the services, especially in their approaches to acquisition, programming, and the creation of the future joint force. Col. Mrazik described a concerted effort to prevent services from entering "stovepipes of excellence." He noted that transformation requires prioritization and sequencing, for which a campaign plan is being developed. This campaign plan details eight required warfighting capabilities: data sharing, advanced communications, advanced sensing, distributed decision making, integrated planning, accelerated decision making, and commanding and controlling the convergence of effects, all of which are underpinned by human capital development. The data-sharing tenet of the campaign plan has resulted in a data-sharing capability development plan for ABMS as well as a capability development memorandum, both of which are motivated by the Chief of Staff of the Air Force's commitment to "accelerate change or lose." The ABMS Cross-Functional Team is closely partnered with the Rapid Capabilities Office (RCO) for component acquisition; with DoD to host a series of data summits; and with the Defense Advanced Research Projects Agency to ensure coherence with the Air Force's strategy.

Col. Mrazik explained that the first step of digital transformation is the creation of the underlying digital infrastructure. The RCO is developing some of this digital architecture and working closely with the Office of the Chief Information Officer, the Air Force Chief Data Office, A2/6, and across the rest of Air Force Futures to ensure coherence. The first phase of operation is to connect the force in a way that is inherently resilient to major attack. Modernized technology (e.g., AI, ML, digital translation) also enables the acceleration of processes—to generate more efficiency, for example, by optimizing the role of the human in processes and letting the machine take over tasks for which the human does not add value. By better connecting sensors and data sources, he continued, it would be possible to provide higher-quality data faster to decision makers; this decision making could be accelerated even further with machine-introduced courses of action and machine-enabled co-development. In closing, Col. Mrazik remarked that what is most challenging about the digital transformation is the number of moving parts involved in the search for winning approaches. Gen. Holmes pointed out that the security framework should also underpin the components of the campaign plan that Col. Mrazik described, and Mr. Munson underscored the need to think about the cyber implications of integration techniques and to make these challenges clear to those producing the infrastructure.

Col. Sean Kern, Chief of the Cyberspace Superiority Panel, HAF A8, echoed the notion presented by previous panelists that "fast beats slow." Referencing Gen. Charles Brown's vision for the future of the Air Force, he explained that information advantage leads to decision advantage, which leads to operational advantage. Deb Westphal commented that while these relations are possible, they are not guaranteed. Information advantage can still be lost if decision makers have not prepared and trained themselves to make critical decisions. She cautioned about relying too much on a technical silver bullet without also preparing the human decision maker via exercises.

One strength that the United States has over its adversaries is its relationships with its allies and partners. Given that this joint approach to warfighting is essential, the challenge, then, is in adding and removing partners at the speed the mission requires to deliver the required outcomes, Col. Kern emphasized that the Air Force's transformation to faster operations thus demands rapid technological change; a change in the character of war; initiation of a joint warfighting concept; and expanded maneuver, which requires aggregating and disaggregating at mission-relevant speed to achieve the desired effects in a denied, destructed, intermittent, and low-bandwidth environment. An understanding of the balance of edge computing and core computing capabilities is also needed for planning and programming. If the Air Force can close thousands of kill chains in hundreds of hours, he continued, it could consider itself successful.

Col. Kern commented that the Air Force needs to increase its speed in agile combat employment—the ability to sense, infer, and act locally; tag relevant data; and transport those data to the core to learn globally. Inferring locally but only tagging what is relevant reduces the amount of data that need to be transported, which benefits the decision maker who will interact with those data. However, the practice of tagging relevant data is not yet part of the Air Force's strategy. It is also critical to plan and continue to program for software factory capabilities. Because the limits of hardware have been reached and the competitive advantage will come from software, software factories have begun to emerge. Reiterating the perspective of the Defense Innovation Board, Col. Kern said that the Air Force does not have a technology problem; it has a technology *adoption* problem. Because much of the needed technology already exists in the commercial sector, he continued, a new culture should be built in the Air Force, and policies that prevent leveraging leading-edge capabilities should be reviewed.

Col. Kern explained that Air Force Futures includes design elements based on the operational problems that best suit a deep dive (e.g., logistics under attack, critical infrastructure defense, long-range kill-chain, agile combat employment); the A9 conducts analysis against the design; the A8 facilitates discussion about how to resource that design; and the design is eventually included in the 30-year resource allocation plan. It is difficult to find the right balance between planning in the current platform-centric approach and planning for the transition to a network-centric approach. One way to enable that shift is to engage in more crosscutting dialogue—for example, discussing cybersecurity and defense of cyber operations in the context of securing and assuring the ABMS military Internet of Things. He described two efforts that have surfaced in the planning choices[8] for the 30-year resource allocation plan for future force design. The first is the "critical path," which includes Cloud One, a hybrid multi-cloud capability at the enterprise level, and the DAF's "data fabric," which is intended to federate six known data platforms to democratize data. He reiterated that data have to be treated as a strategic asset and aggregated to generate insights for decision making. The critical path also includes Platform One, an agile software development construct. The second effort for which a wedge has been inserted in the resource allocation plan relates to zero trust. In a zero-trust environment, the user, device, and operational context are always "untrusted until trusted" for each individual transaction within a session. The Air Force believes that this is the only way to adequately secure the military Internet of Things and the people connected to it. The Non-Classified Internet Protocol Router Network, the Secret Internet Protocol Router Network, and the Joint Worldwide Intelligence Communications System would essentially be collapsed in a zero-trust environment, he continued, and, based on the nature of the mission, users could be added and removed from the environment at will.

Mr. Rowayne "Wayne" Schatz, Senior Executive Service, Director for Studies, Analyses, and Assessments, HAF A9, explained that the Air Force is trying to create an organization that can deploy forward with connectivity to a centralized ABMS, that when disconnected retains the talent and capability to fight under commander's intent with the tools available at the wing level. The doctrine, training, and experiments needed to realize that vision are under way. Gen. Holmes asked if doctrine will support digital modernization, and Mr. Schatz replied that doctrine promotes the adoption of the information technology and the data strategy to operations. Gen. Holmes noted that the Air Force believes that the threat drives the need to disaggregate forces, which drives the complexity and the difficulty in the modernization strategy (i.e., deciding how to command and control, support, and sustain that disaggregated approach).

Mr. Schatz mentioned that part of the Air Force's data journey includes identifying key use cases to drive experimentation, to learn about the value of data science, and to deliver products that help change internal processes and improve performance. He explained that the Air Force stood up its digital initiative

---

[8] A planning choice is a "wedge" in the resource allocation plan for some amount of resourcing associated with whatever capability that the Air Force is trying to prepare for in the future force design.

4 years ago, which included a "readiness pathfinder" led by the A3. Over a period of 2 years, 20 different data sources from across the Air Force were moved to a secure environment—essentially the first secure data cloud approved for use in the Air Force—and the A3 helped the Major Commands and Air Combat Command to become more comfortable using live data dashboards for monthly readiness reviews. This enabled those at the squadron level to have the same view of data as those at the chief-of-staff level. He described this effort as an accelerator for the data journey: the Air Force now has an enterprise-level platform, the Vault (hosted by Cloud One and provisioned by the tools in Platform One), into which all data feed.

Mr. Schatz expressed his belief that the Air Force has reached the inflection point at which it will begin to benefit from data. For example, with the conduct of deep dives for the A8 and the weapons systems sustainment portfolio, it is possible to review data over 10- and 15-year periods and begin to connect mission-capable rates and aircraft availability to funding. Data from planning, programming, budgeting, and execution systems can also be used to connect planning and programming to actual expenditures, which is crucial for the business aspect of organizing, training, and equipping the Air Force. Not only do these data allow for better business management, he continued, but they also benefit operations. He anticipated that it could be 2 years before the connective features of ABMS are fully realized; in the meantime, a data architecture and a cloud environment are being constructed that will link several main air operations centers with high-bandwidth communications to create a resilient, connected ecosystem, which will change the state of air warfare. In closing, Mr. Schatz emphasized the role of human capital management in the Air Force's digital transformation: despite all of the hype around AI and ML, it is important to remember that technology functions when smart data scientists and operations research analysts help convert data into useful applications for leaders to make decisions.

Open Discussion

Mr. Martin Akerman, Chief Data Strategist, Office of the Chief Data Officer, DAF, noted that to create data pipelines, funding should be allocated for the data provider even though the data user benefits. The current model, he continued, presents a disincentive to improve data. Col. Kern said that the Air Force is considering a tiered structure to manage and prioritize resourcing. For example, Tier 1 would be centrally managed and centrally funded (e.g., a Cloud One enterprise, with benefit to all airmen); and Tier 2 would centrally manage the foundational services, but the customer would pay to play, which would require additional compute and store capabilities. Mr. Akerman suggested consulting with industry about approaches to costing and cost recovery.

Lt. Gen. Hamel inquired about the use cases that are being developed for communities of interest and responsibility. Col. Mrazik mentioned that the A5 is working on end-to-end kill chain analysis, alongside the A8, A9, A2/6, and the Air Warfare Center, as well as with the LeMay Center on disconnected disaggregation. Mr. Schatz added that the A9 is trying to develop a strategy to prioritize data efforts; for example, projects that bring new data sources to the enterprise portfolio would be funded before those that utilize already available data. Such a strategy would promote obtaining data that provide insight as well as expanding enterprise capability.

Gen. Holmes asked how the Air Force is managing the technology it fields now alongside the technology it will field in the future. Col. Kern described the challenge of trying to meet the needs of Congress, the Office of Management and Budget, and the Office of the Secretary of Defense, while still having tradespace to make a transformative, strategic redirection for the Air Force. He noted that approximately $12 billion to $15 billion per year is being spent on IT-related costs; however, the DAF chief information officer (CIO) only has access to 10 percent of that budget. With that little centralized control, the CIO will not be able to make a strategic impact on the digital capabilities of the DAF. Different funding models are being considered so that the CIO could prioritize and deliver a reliable enterprise service. Lt. Gen. Hamel asked how much funding is being allocated for common user infrastructure and services as well as who is responsible for advocating for this funding. Col. Kern asserted that the DAF CIO should be the primary advocate for strategic prioritization of 21st century digital infrastructure, but she does not have the resources to do so. He said that the DAF first has to establish the right policies to better manage the spending of limited resources. A potential approach would be to identify offsets that have saved the organization money (e.g., closing on-premise data centers) and reprogram those funds into the portfolio to articulate priorities moving forward. He depicted the tension between doing trend analysis and earmarking funds for centralization versus the need for commanders to have flexibility in execution to accommodate shifting operational priorities.

DOD DIGITAL MODERNIZATION STRATEGY

Mr. John Sherman, Acting DoD CIO, defined the four key pillars of DoD's modernization strategy: (1) cloud; (2) cybersecurity; (3) AI; and (4) command, control, and communications. Introduced in 2019, this "unifying strategy" continues to drive modernization across DoD. The Joint AI Center was also launched in 2019, followed by the establishment of the chief data officer position. Under the current administration, new priorities have emerged that emphasize preparation for near-peer competition and joint all-domain warfighting. He described JADC2 as the unifying operational vision for digital modernization: it will transfer data and insight across coalition boundaries from a disconnected environment to the point of decision and help to access the enemy's decision cycle.

Mr. Sherman explained that DoD's early cybersecurity efforts focused on hygiene and compliance as a first step on the path to zero trust—a defense strategy that assumes that the enemy is already inside the network. To gain advantage over potential attackers, DoD could defend its network by segregating the data in a more granular way than in the past, using sensors across the network, and moving from signature-based analysis to behavioral-based analysis. DoD will look to the DAF, which has made progress in identity, credential, and access management (ICAM), to share lessons learned from its initial implementation of zero trust. He mentioned that DoD has begun to move to a multi-cloud environment—the Joint Warfighting Cloud Capability—to best support JADC2 and noted that the Air Force has also been a leader in enterprise cloud efforts.

Mr. Sherman described DoD's AI and Data Accelerator Initiative (a partnership with the Joint Staff), in which data teams and AI teams will be sent to Combatant Commands to help unlock the power of AI and data. A related initiative is the Global Information Dominance Experiments, which offer a future vision for the Combatant Command. He emphasized that data and software development are essential for the success of JADC2 and AI, respectively, and it is critical that security is "baked in" to software development activities to enable continuous authority to operate. He added that the EMS is essential to prepare to fight in future contested environments, as is the operation of 5G networks. His team works closely with Research and Engineering, Acquisition and Sustainment, and the services, as well as the Federal Communications Commission and the Department of Commerce, on efforts to ensure that U.S. telecommunications dominate Chinese endeavors in this realm.

Mr. Jeff Jones, Senior Executive Service, Vice Director, Command, Control, Communications, and Computers, Joint Staff/J6, outlined his portfolio, which includes cyberspace operations, warfighting communications, and JADC2, as well as serving as the voice for the Combatant Commands. JADC2 is a framework that defines how DoD senses, makes sense, and acts across all domains with partners in support of the future warfighter. His team has spent the past several months developing the foundational documents required for DoD to move forward in conjunction with all of the services on JADC2, and the implementation plan to remedy gaps across DoD to enable JADC2 is awaiting approval. There is a sense of urgency across DoD to enable joint operations—the events unfolding in Afghanistan serve as a prime use case.

Mr. Jones explained that the J6's cross-functional team has a direct line to the Joint Requirements Oversight Council to validate joint warfighting requirements and a direct line to the Deputy Secretary of Defense to make funding recommendations. The Air Force's involvement in the cross-functional team has been valuable, he continued, and involvement from the other services will also be critical because the Joint Staff only creates the framework for what the services build to enable joint operations. The Joint Staff is, however, leading an effort to create minimum viable products (MVPs); it would like to leverage Platform One for some of those MVPs, pending funding decisions, to determine how best to create a secure, interoperable environment for the Combatant Commanders to share, store, and process data so as to make better decisions at a faster pace. The Joint Staff would also like to do small test cases for ICAM, data, zero trust, DevSecOps, and transport. He asserted that zero trust and ICAM are foundational for JADC2: without the ability to authenticate and provide a level of trust for a person or a weapons system, challenges will arise throughout the process. Questions remain as to whether zero trust could be federated and whether there is enough bandwidth on classified networks to do AI and data exchanges for transport at speed. Another MVP opportunity is the Mission Partner Environment (MPE), which enables the fast and reliable exchange of information among coalition partners—a critical aspect of a JADC2 environment. In closing, he reiterated that DoD's data challenges are significant (i.e., accessing real-time data in a contested environment from numerous systems and data feeds), and timely, reliable data are key to achieving globally integrated operations.

Open Discussion

Gen. Holmes asked if DoD's primary challenges result from an inability to do globally integrated operations (i.e., the chairman cannot see everything that is occurring) or an inability to do *centrally directed* globally integrated operations (i.e., the chairman is unable to pass intent down to commanders to make decisions). Mr. Jones explained that the challenge is achieving real-time command and control in a data-centric environment. For example, if it is not possible to make sense because there is no sensing, it will be difficult to act. There is a tremendous amount of data feeds, but the feeds and systems do not speak the same language, and there are no application programming interfaces across the board to enable full collation of those data to drive operations. He suggested that executing data policies and holding people accountable for adhering to those policies would lead to authoritative and accessible data feeds. A participant wondered how to incentivize radical data transparency with suppliers, services, and Combatant Commands. Mr. Jones replied that the intention is to address and resolve gaps across DoD by identifying systems and organizations that do not provide data transparency and creating a requirement for future systems.

Gen. Holmes questioned whether there are other use cases that demonstrate the need to modernize. Mr. Sherman described capability testing that is part of Bold Quest 21, which will hopefully lead to realizing the vision for MPE. Furthermore, the Marine Corps and the Department of the Navy are conducting exercises to better understand potential edge capabilities. However, there is much more work to be done in terms of use cases. For example, he envisioned aircraft flying in a global positioning system-degraded environment using purely alternative forms of positioning, navigation, and timing "to put steel on target" in a real-world scenario and in a highly electronic warfare-contested environment. Mr. Munson asked if there is any interest in making use cases the vehicle to drive implementation and validation of digital transformation progress. Mr. Sherman referenced the governance in place to understand how a mission would apply a capability, but he championed the potential for more use cases. Mr. Jones added that operational use cases are driving the JADC2 reference architecture, which will define how everything across DoD will connect.

Gen. Holmes asked if there is consideration at the Joint Staff and CIO levels for counter data warfare, and Mr. Jones and Mr. Sherman acknowledged ongoing efforts in this area. Lt. Gen. Hamel inquired about the structure of the JADC2 cross-functional team, and Mr. Jones stated that although the J6 is the cross-functional team chair, the effort extends across DoD—the services play a key role in achieving joint operations. In addition to validating requirements and providing funding recommendations, the cross-functional team addresses five lines of effort: (1) data; (2) human enterprise (training and doctrine requirements to build a future force that can leverage capabilities for command and control); (3) technical enterprise (building transport and operating in a disconnected environment); (4) nuclear command, control, and communications; and (5) MPE.

In response to a participant's question about human capital, Mr. Sherman remarked that DoD is in the process of updating its cyber workforce strategy to achieve a whole-of-nation approach for cybersecurity. Goals include increasing diversity; changing approaches to recruitment, retention, and reskilling; targeting high-demand, low density skillsets (e.g., data scientists); and reviewing security clearance processes. He emphasized the urgent need to think differently about talent management, especially as potential staff may be more attracted by employment opportunities in industry.

Ms. Westphal asked the panelists to look *ahead* 10 years and reflect on DoD's priorities for transformation. Mr. Jones responded that data are the driver for the success of all DoD efforts, and Mr. Sherman added that cybersecurity is equally critical. Mr. Sherman shared his vision to transform the environment with zero trust so that the adversaries become perplexed by their inability to access the DoD network and affect Americans' and allies' power on the battlefield. He affirmed that protecting data is a key part of achieving security: if the United States does not protect its information advantage, it would regret that decision 10 years from now.

2

Workshop One, Part Two

OPENING REMARKS

Workshop series co-chair Lt. Gen. Michael Hamel (USAF, ret.), independent consultant, welcomed participants to the second day of the workshop series. Workshop One chair Gen. James (Mike) Holmes (USAF, ret.), senior advisor, The Roosevelt Group, recapped the previous day's discussion on Air Force strategy and needs in preparation for the forthcoming panel presentations from the capability providers and data contributors pursuing those challenges. Workshop series co-chair Ms. Deborah Westphal, chairman of the board, Toffler Associates, encouraged participants to share their insights as to whether the Department of the Air Force (DAF) is on the right path toward digital transformation. Mr. Edward Drolet, deputy director, Chief of Staff of the Air Force Strategic Studies Group, noted that the restrictions of the COVID-19 pandemic motivated some of the DAF's digital transformation progress, and he emphasized the value of learning lessons during a crisis. In light of recent operations in Afghanistan, he expressed his hope that access to information for commanders to make decisions would continue to increase.

Gen. Holmes shared an anecdote about Air Combat Command's (ACC's) responsibility to coordinate rescue operations after a hurricane several years ago. He explained that because no effective Air Force tool was available for this task, airmen created a common app for rescue operations within hours using a chat app and Google maps. Airmen are compelled to operate outside of the Department of Defense Information Networks (DoDIN) and use their own coding knowledge to create one-off tools because DoDIN does not meet the airmen's needs. He suggested that the DAF leverage existing technologies and tools that make it easier to share information instead of taking several years to build its own capabilities. However, he cautioned that the Space Force, given its increased efforts to provide coding education, could have challenges with version control; the likelihood of vulnerabilities increases as modifications are continually made to software. In response to Gen. Holmes's concern about version control, Dr. Paul Nielsen (USAF, ret.), director and chief executive officer, Software Engineering Institute, Carnegie Mellon University, said that the commercial world has faced and overcome this challenge.[1]

Reflecting on the previous day's discussion, Ms. Westphal questioned the DAF's 30-year budgeting outlook, given how difficult it is to predict the future state. Gen. Holmes suggested focusing programming on a 5- to 7-year time frame instead so as to achieve better results. Dr. Marv Langston (USN, ret.), independent consultant, added that by 2027, there could be 12,000 low-earth orbit Starlink satellites floating around the earth, and denied, disrupted, intermittent, and limited bandwidth problems will be unlikely for those outside of the Department of Defense (DoD) system. Dr. Nielsen explained that the DAF's hurdle is not simply a technical problem that can be solved with better infrastructure and faster decision making. Instead, there is a human element, for which practice and exercise are critical. He emphasized that the improvement process for the DAF will be incremental.

LEADERSHIP FOR TRANSFORMATION

Mr. Anthony Reardon, Senior Executive Service, Administrative Assistant to the Secretary of the Air Force, explained that the DAF lacks a cogent strategy for digital transformation—without a unity of effort, disparate solutions arise among the several Air Force chiefs. Another challenge is resource management. He underscored the need for the DAF to become more competitive with industry, by hiring individuals who have experience with transformation on a broad scale.

Mr. Reardon described Disney World as a model of the development of integrated systems. Over the course of only 1 year and $1 billion, the theme parks successfully united their data and operations. Despite the fact that 4 of the theme parks were each separated by a decade and each built on a different IT backbone, Disney World integrated 7 theme parks, 27 resorts, 100 attractions, and 150 restaurants, along with its reservation system. The DAF struggles to implement a similar transition on a larger scale—for example, the DAF is located in several countries and has a multitude of systems, some of which are 50 years old. He emphasized that because the DAF's budgeting cycle is too short to build an integrated plan for the future, people find their own near-term solutions that are not interoperable. For example, while everyone supports the development of a program that interfaces with the Mission Partner Environment, no one wants to work toward the standards that were established by the program.

Mr. Rich Lombardi, Chief Management Officer, Office of the Under Secretary of the Air Force, reiterated that the first step in any transformation is the development of a coherent strategy. Although many across the Air Force are doing exceptional work, individual units remain unintegrated in stovepipes and have to stitch activities together to complete missions. He observed that although people claim to support an enterprise system, they remain reluctant to collaborate. Once a strategy is developed, he continued, a governance process will be needed to synchronize efforts among people, processes, and technology. Furthermore, achieving an enterprise system is not possible without enterprise-level funding, and there is a balance needed so that this enterprise-level funding is protected and functional areas retain flexibility. Another problem is that everyone wants to develop their own case management systems, yet there is no need for 20 different case management systems on the air staff, especially given that most likely seek the same data and none are fully funded. Instead, because the requirements are likely 90 percent similar, he suggested pooling the funding—his team is building one such unified case management system as a pilot. Pilots are also under way with the AI community to build a concept of operations (CONOPS). The ultimate goal is to eliminate many manual tasks so that airmen have more time to do their jobs. A service catalogue of capabilities is also being developed, which could be used by functional leaders to better determine gaps. Mr. Lombardi's team has partnered with a program executive office (PEO) for business systems at Maxwell-Gunter Annex Air Force Base to begin that effort. Although progress continues to be made in siloes, the objective to move toward an enterprise perspective remains. In closing, he remarked that it is

---

[1] Commercial software companies have developed and adopted automated version control and collaboration tools that address this problem. DoD contractors and organic coders need to adopt these tools.

critical to ensure that the innovative work of the airmen impacts the overarching desired capabilities of the DAF.

Open Discussion

Lt. Gen. Hamel wondered if there is consensus across the DAF on the need for a digital strategy and, if so, how it would be created. He also asked how to harmonize roles, responsibilities, resources, and governance across the DAF. Mr. Reardon acknowledged that while most understand the need for a cohesive and coherent strategy, many do not understand the specific purposes of programming—there is no strategy that unites different components and assigns responsibility for each. The most significant barrier, however, is the translation into a resource requirement. Part of the challenge, Mr. Lombardi added, is that "digital" has many definitions. The chief software officer, chief architect, chief technology officer, chief data officer, and chief information officer play essential roles, but it is important that all of their initiatives connect. He explained that the current model of governance is not set up to govern a department of two services; a new model of governance is needed in which only optimal innovations based on enterprise goals and mission needs are funded.

Recognizing the vastness of the future digital environment of operations, Ms. Westphal asked if a CONOPS and doctrine are driving the DAF's strategy. Although he was not aware of any CONOPS driving the strategy, Mr. Lombardi acknowledged the urgent need to understand the facets of "digital" to determine how to develop the strategy. Ms. Westphal added that a misplaced emphasis on what the DAF will *purchase* still exists. Gen. Holmes noted that the A5 has been tasked to develop an overall vision of the future environment and the threat, including the CONOPS that will drive requirements and platforms. However, he wondered whether the "underlying digital backbone" is receiving adequate attention. Mr. Reardon explained that there are many steps that need to taken *before* the joint all-domain command and control (JADC2) environment that is being constructed could function effectively. Capabilities are being built that may not integrate seamlessly into JADC2 or future constructs, simply because money is available. He asserted that a strategy for incrementally building capabilities would be more beneficial.

Dr. Julie Ryan, chief executive officer, Wyndrose Technical Group, discouraged "digitization for digitization's sake." Instead, processes could be reengineered and adapted to technologies to accomplish goals, and become more efficient and effective. When processes are reengineered, they have to be reengineered with consideration for modern threats. A critical area that has been systematically ignored by program developers thus far is security—confidentiality, availability, integrity, protection, detection, and correction. "Bolting on" instead of "baking in" security is ineffective, she continued. Mr. Reardon commented on the value of zero-trust architectures and noted that the DAF is working to integrate security from the beginning. Mr. Lombardi remarked that when people become enamored with technology, they lose sight of the difficult work required for process engineering and try to modify the technology to fit existing inefficient processes. He suggested reviewing processes and determining which technology could help achieve the goals instead of allowing the technology to drive the solution. Mr. Reardon added that outcomes have to be the focus when reengineering processes. Dr. Annie Green, data governance specialist, George Mason University, said that it is impossible to reengineer something that has not been engineered. And if something has not been engineered, she continued, it cannot be managed. She emphasized the need to focus not only on digital technology but also on digital representation. When the components of an enterprise are represented in digital form and better understood, they can be used for both strategy and operation. Another element missing from the current framework is the levels of abstraction in the enterprise in terms of strategic, tactical, operational, and cognitive decision making, as well as the intelligence. Instead of repeating what has been done in the past, she highlighted the value of understanding steps forward as current operations are maintained and improvements are being built for the future. Mr. Martin Akerman, Chief Data Strategist, Office of the Chief Data Officer, DAF, agreed with Dr. Green about the need to better use the knowledge layer as well as the data fabric that drives it. He described Air Force leadership as well positioned to change the culture and target the risk appetite of the DAF in the movement to a new model of decision making. Dr. Green added that digital transformation also requires consideration for paradigm changes, and she suggested focusing on the integration of knowledge management in the flow of digital transformation.

Mr. Alden Munson, senior fellow and member, Board of Regents, Potomac Institute for Policy Studies, observed that the DAF tends to select commercial products that are the best *approximation* to its requirements and modifies them to better fit its needs. He advocated for another step in the process: after selecting the commercial product that has the best approximate fit, go back to the requirements and the architecture, and consider whether the *requirements* need to be modified. He emphasized that the standard "requirements, to design, to implementation approach" is ineffective; flexibility is needed based on the availability of commercial products. Dr. Ryan added that it is not feasible to avoid commercial products; furthermore, because many products are rushed to market, it is critical that contracts demand proven security before product delivery. She proposed maintaining products in a sandbox to avoid downstream liability with other parts of the architecture.

Gen. Holmes perceived the desired outcome of the DAF strategy to be collecting available data and using them to sense better, to make decisions better, to command and control better, and to support headquarters better; he wondered whether there are indicators to monitor those outcomes. Mr. Jay Santee (USAF, ret.), vice president, Strategic Space Operations, Defense Systems Group, The Aerospace Corporation, observed that process improvement should be based on empowering individuals to make faster and better data-driven decisions. He explained that requirements are driven by the decisions we want to make, the information we want available, and the person we want in charge of making that decision. Thus, a mechanism to pass requirements *to developers* to improve processes is needed. He asked about the DAF's broader plan for process-driven, data-driven decision making by empowered individuals at a proper level of authority. Mr. Lombardi commented that over the past year, the DAF has begun to empower decision makers at different levels, but the DAF does not yet have a solid understanding of the connective threads of processes. In closing, Mr. Lombardi noted that the DAF is aware of its blind spots and the need to eliminate stovepipes, as well as the need to focus on how technology will integrate with current and future plans before acquiring, but it first needs to develop a coherent strategy to achieve digital transformation.

ORGANIZATION AND TECHNOLOGY FOR TRANSFORMATION

Ms. Lauren Knausenberger, Chief Information Officer, DAF, explained that consistent agility could lead to consistent advantage—a feature that the DAF currently lacks. She described four pillars to enable seamless JADC2 across the enterprise:

1. Creating a digital foundation, including reliance on a 21st century network, availability of cloud-based services, use of a DevSecOps platform, development of a zero-trust framework, integration of cybersecurity that protects against ever-changing threats and reduces overall threat surface, and creation of a data fabric.
2. Focusing on the user experience for warfighter effect by understanding what tools and data the warfighters need to be more effective in their missions, what barriers exist, how to measure and improve performance of tools with automation, and where to insert IT-driven capabilities.
3. Enabling digital talent, with initiatives such as Digital University,[2] retention incentives, and diversity and inclusion efforts. Digital University provides a path to upskill and/or reskill the entire existing force, maintain technical edge by equipping airmen with digital skills, and recruit talented individuals that can help move the DAF forward with its digital transformation.
4. Attacking manual process, outdated policy, and redundant IT. In Operation Flamethrower, for example, airmen advise which systems should be eliminated and which should be sustained, with the goal to open tradespace and better spend funds.

---

[2] The website for Digital University is https://digitalu.af.mil, accessed November 23, 2021.

On the journey of digital transformation, Ms. Knausenberger commented that first, digitally savvy airmen and guardians could help adapt technology and find new ways to conduct missions. Second, the right apps would enhance the fight of the future—for example, a future in which the majority of weapons systems are integrated software platforms. Third, digitization would be enabled by an artificial intelligence (AI)-ready technology stack at scale (i.e., AI, machine learning [ML], sensors/Internet of Things, data fabric, cloud/edge computing, and connectivity). With the addition of zero trust, the use of more reliable commercial lines could be a low-risk way to improve connectivity. She summarized the coordination of these DAF efforts as follows: airmen and guardians and their missions are at the core of the DAF. Enterprise IT delivers the data that are needed to operate in a contested battlespace. Data then feed into advanced applications, which require usable data (e.g., via the Visible, Accessible, Understandable, Linked and Trustworthy [VAULT] data platform; Core Data Service; Unified Data Library), and those data require a reliable network. Enterprise IT (i.e., the digital foundation, with services such as Cloud One[3] and Cloud-Hosted Enterprise Services) capabilities support the warfighter and the mission. The data fabric is an essential part of how all of these steps connect.

Ms. Knausenberger explained that all of the DAF's public-facing websites are on Cloud One. Cloud One's recent statistics include 19 million monthly log-ins, and more than 600,000 prevented attacks in August 2021. The next objective is to move more of the secret enterprise into the cloud. Platform One, which allows the DAF to develop, deploy, operate, and sustain software in a secure and agile manner, can deploy code 49 times per day to a warfighter in locations permitted by the infrastructure. The goal is to increase code deployment to thousands of times per day in the future. Iron Bank, the Air Force's container repository, has more than 700 products and services that can be used securely across any environment.

She emphasized that zero trust offers security, simplicity, and accessibility, and enables the Advanced Battle Management System and JADC2. Zero trust allows a transition from an environment of sophisticated cyber threats, diminishing warfare advantages, and constrained technology to an environment that imposes a cost to the adversary, offers the freedom to operate, and provides a cyber-enabled warfare advantage. Identity, credential, and access management and critical data tagging are foundational to zero trust (see Figure 2.1). While newer software is already built for a zero-trust environment, older software has to be brought into the future. With the underlying data fabric and zero-trust architecture, she expressed her hope to advance to one Secret Internet Protocol Router Network (SIPRNet) for warfighting and then ultimately to one collapsed multi-level classification environment, where it would be possible to collaborate across the joint community and with allies and to release software updates in real time.

Ms. Knausenberger described the Joint Warfighting Cloud Capability, which is an enterprise-wide multi-vendor cloud solution that could be available for use globally in June 2022. This capability could increase the speed of moving data to the tactical edge. However, she emphasized that the DAF has had more than a decade of underinvestment and has much work to do to move into the 21st century of digitization. Although she asserted that the focus should be on investment in modern infrastructure for digital transformation instead of in the sustainment of aging infrastructure, it is difficult to abandon existing technology without up-front investments for new technology.

Ms. Eileen Vidrine, Chief Data Officer, DAF, explained that her team works closely with the chief information officer's team to move products forward and develop a common architecture across the DAF. The priorities of the chief data office (CDO) include operationalizing the seven strategic goals of the DoD data strategy: visible, accessible, understandable, linked, trustworthy, secure, and interoperable.

---

[3] Cloud One is a multi-cloud environment that hosts the Air Force's enterprise general purpose applications.

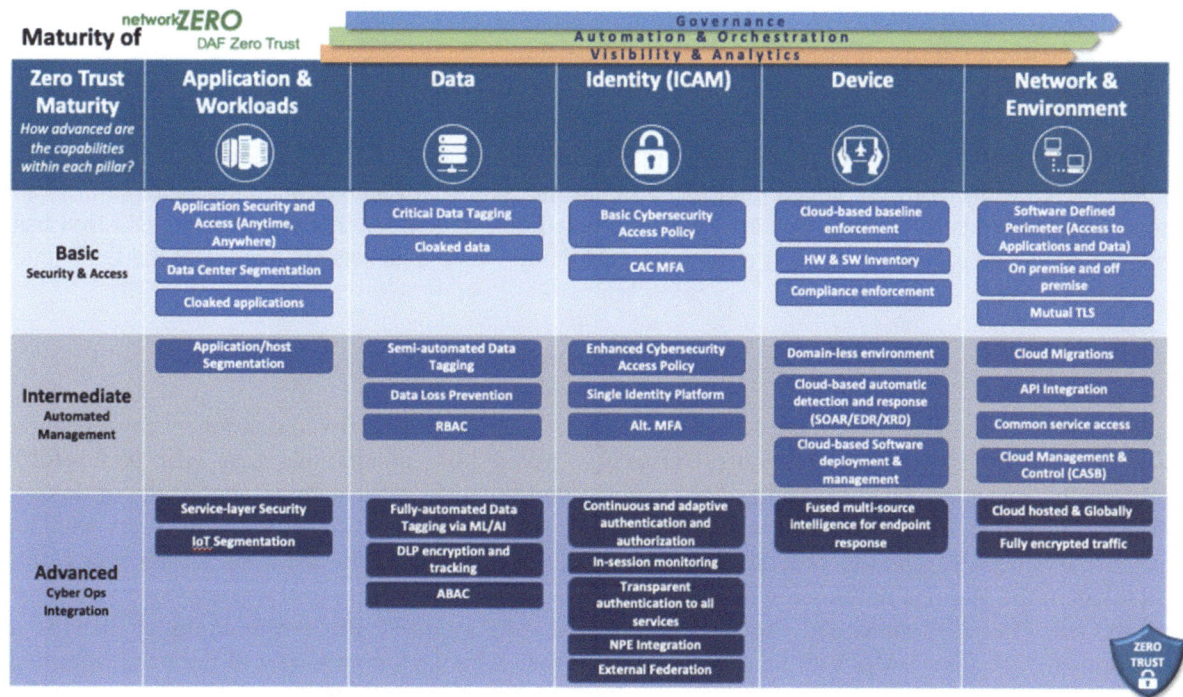

FIGURE 2.1 Maturity of the zero-trust network. SOURCE: Lauren Knausenberger, presentation to the workshop, September 2, 2021.

Ms. Vidrine noted that the first step to achieving this vision and improving efficiency is the democratization of data. The DAF is currently piloting a data catalogue that will make data more visible and accessible by federating to the DoD data catalogue. It is essential that data are part of the digital foundation in order to use ML and AI at the speed of mission, she continued. A strong data governance foundation and an enterprise perspective of data are also critical. Under the Federal Data Strategy Action Plan, the DAF published its Data Maturity Assessment Model, which has also been embraced at the DoD level. Another priority for the CDO is building data acumen at all levels, beginning with the creation of a pipeline of talent into the DAF. For example, the Air Force Academy now offers data science majors and minors to cadets, and the CDO partnered with the Air Force Institute of Technology to pilot a data science graduate certificate program. Other approaches to empower airmen and guardians at all levels include collaborative activities such as datathons. She also described a small data laboratory based out of Andrews Air Force Base, where any airman or guardian can enter a problem set and, if it has enterprise relevance, run a use case. The final piece of the DoD data strategy relates to interoperable and secure data, through the development of trusted partnerships and the eventual convergence of data platforms. She stressed that interoperability is the cornerstone of all CDO efforts and added that "vendor lock" has to be reduced or prevented for this strategy to succeed.

Because the CDO is part of the 2023 Program Objective Memorandum, it can make deliberate decisions about investments in data at an enterprise level moving forward. Ms. Vidrine detailed the progress that has been made on the VAULT data platform, the goal for which is to provide self-service analytics. Within only 100 days of conception, the data platform reached Impact Level 4; with agile development, additional capabilities are released every few weeks. One initiative of the data platform is "bring your own tool"; in other words, to meet a mission need in the field, it is possible to fast-track an emerging technology into the platform safely and securely through a partnership with the acquisition community and the security team.

Today, VAULT has reached Impact Level 6 with a cross-domain solution using "Infrastructure-as-Code," which makes it possible to onboard airmen within hours.[4]

In closing, Ms. Vidrine described the DAF data fabric, the common architecture for department-level data. VAULT and other capabilities will be deployed on this data fabric, offering a truly interoperable solution. It maximizes return on investment, breaks down siloes, and automates data pipelines quickly to support the mission, with the added goal of reducing the number of standalone data feeds and creating automated data feeds for critical data sets. She explained that to achieve this vision, the CDO first has to identify which data sets are used most often in the DAF and which data sets are needed at the DoD level.

Open Discussion

Dr. Rama Chellappa, Bloomberg Distinguished Professor of electrical and computer engineering and biomedical engineering, Johns Hopkins University, asked how annotations that will be useful for downstream tasks are created as well as how experts are trained to work with an abundance of data. Ms. Vidrine replied that the CDO has a team of data scientists, data architects, and data engineers who work alongside functional experts to generate solutions, and she emphasized the value of having access to the right talent at the moment the mission need arises.

Lt. Gen. Hamel commended the CDO's progress and inquired about remaining challenges and aspirations for the future. Ms. Vidrine accentuated that the technology component of the transformation is less difficult than the change management aspect. More "change champions" and "chief data evangelists" who invest their resources and staff to work on difficult problems are needed to accelerate change. She expressed her hope that people will stop thinking about how the Air Force operates today and start thinking about how the Air Force should be operating tomorrow by investing in the future. It is crucial that investments in legacy systems are eliminated, she continued, because such investments are too costly and do not accelerate change. She added that if the Air Force wants to retain its newest airmen, who are digital natives, it should embrace modern capabilities. Ms. Knausenberger explained that the Air Force has to select one of the following three paths: (1) change the organizational structure by aligning authority, funding, and competency and empowering a leader who is held accountable; (2) continue with the current coalition; or (3) fund a path forward. Although the Major Commands (MAJCOMs) recognize the value of having access to data and are eager to invest, the resources are not available (e.g., this year, the Air Force faced a $30 billion top-line reduction). Mandating enterprise solutions has not proven effective in the past, primarily because people do not realize how much up-front funding is needed to ensure that an enterprise service is ready for the fight. She surmised that most agree with the vision to transform and are ready to eliminate stovepipes, but an investment to enable this progress has not been committed. She emphasized that if a substantial investment to kick-start innovation is made now, a foundation could emerge, and billions of dollars would then be saved each year as expensive stove-piped secret networks that are open to many security threats are gradually eliminated. The likely most effective approach for transformation, she continued, is to target the Air Force's organizational structure and authorities and improve the timing associated with funding. In response to a question from Lt. Gen. Hamel about whether money is being spent appropriately, Ms. Knausenberger said that money is not being spent on the right initiatives, not because people are being irresponsible but because people do not have the foundational enterprise systems to support

---

[4] See https://cloudify.co/blog/infrastructure-as-code-is-it-really-enough-for-devops/:

An Infrastructure-as-Code (IaC) architecture is the management of networks, virtual machines, load balancers, and connection topology in a descriptive model. It uses the same versioning as a DevOps team uses for a source code. Like a key that only opens a single door, an IaC model generates the same environment every time it is applied. It is essential to the DevOps process and is used simultaneously with continuous delivery.

An example of how enterprises can use IaC is for software development. Programmers use IaC to create and launch sandbox applications. At the same time, QA professionals can run tests with perfect copies of product environments to test for errors. And then, when it's time for deployment, you can push both infrastructure and code to production in one swift stroke.

current needs. She added that the Army and Navy are outspending the Air Force. Lt. Gen. Hamel wondered how much time it would take to redirect funds or create new investment streams to affect the desired transition, and Ms. Knausenberger remarked that real progress could be made in 1 to 2 years, as the chief information office has already identified billions of dollars in savings that could be realized by shutting down a few entities.

LEARNING FOR TRANSFORMATION: A PANEL PRESENTATION

Brig. Gen. Shawn Campbell, Deputy Human Capital Officer, Chief of Space Operations, noted that people have varied interpretations of what it means to be the "first truly digital service." For guardians, a digital service incorporates the use of available digital capabilities and harnesses the power of data using digital platforms.

He described the development of the human capital strategy for guardians, which extends beyond simply generating and engaging talent. The first objective of the strategy is to connect in a collaborative, digitized environment, using a single platform for communication that is also connected to data sources for decision making. Guardians would be able to access this platform from any device while maintaining an appropriate level of security. The second objective of the strategy is to lead "digital enablement" by establishing a "digital cadre." For example, when the Space Force has its first group of Supra Coders this year, a new set of skills will be available. The Space Force also plans to optimize its data infrastructure, because data will win or lose the next war. Brig. Gen. Campbell explained that it is crucial to be able to conduct data assessment in the human capital space—data on each guardian could be used to make decisions about gap analysis and to better align guardians and their skillsets with particular mission needs. The Space Force also aims to "supercharge" the way it automates processes, in particular fielding a talent operations platform that would digitize the talent management life cycle from recruitment through retirement.

A participant asked Brig. Gen. Campbell about undergraduate education for officer candidates. He replied that it is important for equitable talent to be distributed across both the Air Force and the Space Force. The U.S. Air Force Academy (USAFA) ensures that all cadets are exposed to space-related curriculum, which will help cadets to better determine whether they would like to pursue a Space Force specialty code. The Reserve Officers' Training Corps (ROTC) is another area in which space programs could be incorporated. In Summer 2022, the Azimuth Program will expose cadets to space-related topics, and Officer Training School (OTS) recruits will be given an iPad prior to arrival to begin working on space mission sets. Gen. Holmes commended Brig. Gen. Campbell for this effort, emphasizing that the officer talent pool should not be limited to those who have chosen a career path at age 17.

Lt. Gen. Bill Liquori, Chief Strategy and Resourcing Officer, Space Force, noted that capability development processes are also shifting into the digital realm. Currently, DoD relies on capability development documents (CDDs) to generate requirements. These documents are ~100 pages and contain much repetition, owing to the standard template. As CDDs are reviewed at various levels, additional documents are created with commentary, which means that a final requirements document may not be generated for another 2 years. By this time, the threat has likely evolved and a different need has emerged. He advocated for a more streamlined process for capability development.

The requirements team and the Chief Technology Innovation Office team have begun to address this problem with the vision to create a "digital backbone" that would host a series of tools to generate "digital requirements packages." In other words, Lt. Gen. Liquori continued, individuals would have access to multiple tools to build "artifacts" (i.e., sections of a digital requirements package). For example, a mission-area requirements package would have annexes for individual systems instead of requirements packages for each individual system.

Lt. Gen. Liquori explained that, ultimately, the goal is for the model-based systems engineering environment to move to this digital backbone so that during force design, the needed architectures and key performance parameters become apparent. This information could then be passed to the requirements team, creating an opportunity to eliminate much of the repetitive content in CDDs. People could coordinate digitally in real time as this digital requirements package is being generated. Furthermore, with Space Systems Command on this digital backbone, insight about the future could be evaluated much sooner. He added that when Systems Command procures a system from industry, a digital twin will accompany it. This digital twin could replace a model with an actual digital twin, creating a time-saving cycle—force design, to requirements, to acquisition, and back. Another objective is for the Joint Requirements Oversight Council to have access to this digital backbone so as to provide ongoing oversight and maintain focus on strategic-level warfighting needs.

Lt. Gen. Hamel asked Lt. Gen. Liquori how to make better use of commercial and allied capabilities in force structures. He also wondered about the roles within the requirements process of those who will be expected to develop, acquire, field, and support capabilities. Lt. Gen. Liquori noted that international and commercial contributions occur during both force design and acquisition. In the force design stage, purely commercial, purely government-developed, and hybrid solutions are analyzed before a recommendation is made. With the creation of a digital backbone, the requirements team would have visibility into this ongoing work. Mr. Munson pointed out that (1) a commercial solution that matches some of the requirements will not be an exact match, and (2) commercial components from another set of approximate requirements cannot be modified without destroying the underlying economic model that supports the use of commercial products. He suggested adding a "go-back" step in the requirements process: once the commercial components become part of the reality, it is important to consider modifying the architecture and requirements, instead of leaving this problem for acquisition to address. Lt. Gen. Liquori said that there is no plan to mandate the use of commercial products for particular functions in a digital requirements packages. He noted that evaluation of commercial product availability occurs during the force design phase; in a situation in which a commercial product is identified as the best option, he would consider making adjustments to the requirements.

Ms. Gwendolyn DeFilippi, Assistant Deputy Chief of Staff, Manpower, Personnel and Services (Headquarters Air Force [HAF] A1), remarked that her team has been working to reduce the Air Force's 118 disparate personnel management platforms to 5 to 6 interoperable platforms. In some cases, the adoption of commercial-off-the-shelf products is most effective; in other cases, customization is required. To address this challenge, her team partnered with an agile company to design a platform that supports the Air Force's desired business changes. The primary objective of this new platform is to ensure that data interact and are accessible, which will reduce the instances of redundant or erroneous data input. She explained that plans for an integrated pay and personnel system are also under consideration. She emphasized the value of change management; it is the Air Force's responsibility to communicate its needs to IT developers instead of expecting them to anticipate those needs and potentially create a process that will not work. She underscored the importance of both working with the community to think about ways to use technology to adapt an agile mindset and committing to iterate and improve incrementally (instead of setting full requirements).

Ms. DeFilippi described a significant barrier to developing digital talent: there is no specific functional authority that helps define requirements. Her approach to the digital talent development strategy is to have (1) executives with enough digital awareness to create environments that will facilitate a digital workforce, (2) mid-level staff with enough digital knowledge to navigate the digital space, and (3) a cadre of digital experts. She asserted that the Air Force will continue to struggle with a coherent digital strategy until it formally designates a lead for digital and cyber in HAF A1. Airmen will also continue to struggle until legacy IT platforms are retired—airmen need more modern technology that they can navigate.

Brig. Gen. Melissa Cunningham, Director, Cyberspace Operations, Deputy Chief of Staff, Intelligence, Surveillance, Reconnaissance, and Cyber Effects Operations, HAF A2/6, noted that in addition to the digital skills that are valued in the Air Force, storytelling and an understanding of programming and budget are key attributes. She reiterated that the new airmen arriving to the Air Force are digital natives, and the talent pool is exceptional. However, because the competition for this talent is significant, the services have to think about rebranding in a way that motivates people to join the organization. Another challenge is managing the talent that is already in the pipeline, which is currently done assignment-by-assignment. Retention is an issue for the civilian workforce as well. She emphasized that it is crucial to create a culture in which civilians know that they are valued members of the workforce—in other words, train them so well that everyone wants to hire them but simultaneously treat them so well that they have no interest in leaving the organization.

Lt. Gen. Hamel asked about both the motivations and the frustrations that respectively attract and deter mid-level Air Force officers. Brig. Gen. Cunningham said that the most significant frustration for mid-level officers is identifying a career development path. Another challenge is when the spouses of military members have a career path with significantly higher earnings. It is critical to promote stability and convince family members of the value of the officer's next assignment, she continued, because the most significant motivator for mid-level officers is the mission and the ability to defend the nation and maintain the trust of the American people.

EXECUTING TRANSFORMATION: A PANEL PRESENTATION

Lt. Gen. Tim Haugh, Commander, 16th Air Force (16 AF), explained that 16 AF operates and defends networks and supports Cyber Command to present offensive capabilities and operations in the information environment. He mentioned several areas in which his unit is succeeding. From an operational perspective, unity of effort is increasing inside of the enterprise based on the capabilities ACC has provided to work with data. A substantial investment has been made in a data platform that enables data aggregation across the network for more coherent defense. This creates consistency among the airmen that are defending the edge of the network, the airmen operating in the cyber protection teams, the mission defense teams, and the cybersecurity service providers at the weapons system level. Furthermore, 16 AF has created a network operations center and a security operations center in the 688 Cyberspace Wing—the Non-Classified Internet Protocol Router Network (NIPRNet), the SIPRNet, the Joint Worldwide Intelligence Communications System, and some Special Access Programs are aggregated inside of the 688 Cyberspace Wing, which also leads to more cohesive defense and operation of networks. The Air Force is also experiencing success with its cloud strategy: Cloud One and Platform One have increased attack surface and the ability to leverage data. Now that this foundation exists, he suggested that it begin to extend up networks and levels of classification.

Lt. Gen. Haugh also discussed areas in need of improvement from an operational perspective, including developing a better understanding of the threat and how it applies to the technical debt that the Air Force has created. Many of the Air Force's weapons systems were built in a different world with a different threat—the adversary can now collect data on the United States every day as well as leverage commercial data to target the defense industrial base. He emphasized the need to *think* like a digital Air Force, creating and defending capabilities without allowing the adversary to gain advantage. To better confront the threat, he proposed securing weapons systems and ensuring that compute power is available at the edge to be resilient. He advocated for the development of key performance parameters for every new weapons system so as to avoid acquiring more technical debt and risk, both in cybersecurity and cryptography.

Gen. Holmes asked how mission defense teams operate at the wing level and coordinate with 16 AF. Lt. Gen. Haugh explained that the mission defense teams emerged as a strategy to buy down technical risk by dedicating a cyber-defensive team to the operational wing. Although the intent was to replicate this vision throughout the Air Force, resources are too constrained, and the initiative is now very targeted. He noted that there may be opportunities to use this construct for weapons systems, bringing the data back to more central locations where having a mission defense team is not feasible.

Col. Heather Blackwell, Director of Cyberspace and Info Dominance, ACC/A6, discussed the importance of instituting a data standard—for all data, not just cyber data—so that data can be collected on the data platform that Lt. Gen. Haugh described and used to inform decision making. She also noted the value of the Air Force's cloud strategy and championed efforts to create a template to enable smart and secure migration to the cloud. Understanding risk is critical: decisions and initiatives need to be informed by existing cyber threats in order for the United States to remain competitive against the adversary. With unity of effort behind these ideas, she continued, the Air Force could become truly digital.

Col. Blackwell expressed her support for mission defense teams as a strategy for weapons system security, and she continues to push that effort forward. This approach helps to identify vulnerabilities not only in the weapons system but also in the components of the weapons system. She cautioned that adversaries can disrupt capabilities in air power in other ways beyond Internet protocol attacks. In closing, she underscored that culture change—investing in and educating people—is a significant part of digital transformation. As the push for digital transformation continues, it is crucial to focus on how to become more competitive against peer adversaries instead of focusing only on how to save costs.

Mr. Steven Wert, PEO Digital, Air Force Life Cycle Management Center, explained that the Air Force is making significant changes in how it acquires software—for example, with the emergence of software factories. Reflecting on the Air Force's current acquisition processes, he noted that because industry partners use applications and models that the government typically does not own, paper reports are produced. In order for the government to conduct analysis, this information then has to be entered into models manually. Industry's networks are not connected to the government's networks, and the government uses outdated tools (e.g., Microsoft PowerPoint, Word, and Excel spreadsheets) instead of relying on automation for assistance. Mr. Wert stressed that using applications that do not communicate and air-gapping networks as a security strategy (rather than using identification- and authentication-based access) will not equip the force to win a 21st century conflict.

Mr. Wert compared the success of agile DevOps for software to the potential of digital transformation for more hardware-intensive systems, all of which are operated with software. He explained that digital execution for hardware begins with having access to data, source code, and tools. The Air Force's working relationship with its industry partners would need to change fundamentally to enable this transformation. He noted that agile DevOps changed the Air Force's approach to requirements—a recognition of the important "requirements" among users and operators initiated new methods for contracting, testing, and funding; digital acquisition will have similar impact and will require a whole-of-Air Force transformation.

Currently, requirements development and programming begin several years prior to funding; requirements are fully defined before contracting and must be fully met before a weapons system is delivered for operational acceptance. This method delays the fielding of capabilities, and immediately after the system is delivered, it is modified and the process continues. He explained that digital acquisition, which requires a different way of thinking about programs, could radically change this process. He advocated for running thousands of iterations using digital models to discover what requirements could or should be instead of fully defining requirements up front. This would generate a better understanding of the cost implications of design traits as well as allow end users and government engineers to have a voice in the design process. He emphasized that the Air Force is "behind the curve" because its funding and execution process is too slow, and he reiterated the value of having a continuous focus on the next design rather than on the production and sustainment of the current design.

Mr. Wert mentioned that his directorate has been successful with modern software practices: it relies on the defense industrial base more as a service, has changed its relationship with industry, and has experience implementing open architectures. Remaining challenges for the Air Force more broadly include addressing workforce issues, maintaining business relationships, and embracing change at scale. There is also a need to expand the size and skillsets of the government's technical workforce to enable hands-on modeling, simulation, and analysis, he continued. An ongoing related effort focuses on strengthening partnerships with industry and federally funded research and development centers, as well as collaborating with university affiliated research centers. He emphasized that the magnitude of the change required for digital transformation is perhaps larger than what was required for agile DevOps, because it demands modifications to requirements, budgeting, testing, contracting, and logistic support processes. In closing, he stressed that acquisition strategy approval requires understanding how agile software, open systems, and digital engineering will be implemented.

Open Discussion

Mr. Santee resonated with Mr. Wert's commentary on the urgent need for agile solutions to everchanging requirements with integration into an open architecture. In order for the Air Force to achieve a different outcome, he continued, it is essential to change the current approach to requirements, resourcing (i.e., budgeting and execution), and acquisition and to create a data-driven environment. He asked Mr. Wert to share lessons learned that may apply to the DAF's transformation journey. Mr. Wert reiterated that agile DevOps resulted in large-scale changes—digital engineering can have a similar effect. He emphasized that each PEO should have the authority to drive change, as was the case for agile software development.

Dr. Ryan explained the concept of the digital twin, in which data from the operational twin feed back into the digital model to increase understanding of how operational parameters are affecting the performance of the operational twin. Once problems are addressed in the digital model, it is possible to roll out upgrades. However, the notion that an adversary could modify the data so that the data being transferred over the thread to the digital twin are not representational of the operational twin is very dangerous; she cautioned the Air Force to be mindful of how this could ultimately cause the operational twin to become vulnerable to attack or to fail.

Mr. Munson wondered how the relationship with the defense industrial base is evolving. Mr. Wert responded that although the progress has been slow, it has been beneficial to have a service acquisition authority to challenge industry on its business models and intellectual property strategies. Strong leadership will also be key in the Air Force's transition to digital engineering.

Lt. Gen. Hamel asked Lt. Gen. Haugh whether he has command authority over mission teams and if he can advocate for capabilities. Lt. Gen. Haugh replied that in its defense of the Air Force's networks, 16 AF has authority to direct a change in the configuration of a network, add defensive layers, or remove someone from a network, based off of the threat or guidance from the Joint Force Headquarters DoDIN Commander. Changes to mitigate network threats are executed through Operation Cartwheel: a unity of effort among airmen that aligns defensive activities—starting at the network edge down to the individual elements at a base level—that are configuring the network to operate and then layers defenses with the mission defense teams and cyber protection teams. In addition to delivering networks and network defense for the Air Force and the Space Force, 16 AF also conducts offensive and defensive cyber space operations and operations in the information environment in support of multiple Combatant Commands. Lt. Gen. Hamel wondered if provisioning is still the responsibility of the respective MAJCOMs and the Space Force, in terms of their mission systems or their base-level capabilities. Lt. Gen. Haugh responded that, from the overall network perspective, ACC is the lead for provisioning; 16 AF is involved in the operational readiness reviews before the capabilities reach the network to ensure that they are executed in accordance with the guidance of the chief information office and Cyber Command. Although gaps remain in configuration control, as well as in roles and responsibilities, 16 AF is working tirelessly to ensure resiliency. Col. Blackwell added that ACC works closely with the operators to understand their priorities for cyber weapons systems and then advocates for funding lines. ACC also ensures that the MAJCOMs understand the overall constructs of the big data platform and of command and control.

In response to a question from a participant about Air Force culture, Col. Blackwell said that culture changes begin at the Cyber Schoolhouse, where officers and enlisted are taught not only about devices but also about how to be operational problem solvers who can conduct briefings and debriefings and embrace critical feedback. The Cyber Schoolhouse now offers modular lessons so that recruits, who already have digital talent, are learning at the speed of cyber. Testing is another area that would benefit from culture change; Col. Blackwell advocated for using the test environment and sandboxes to test capabilities in a rigorous model before integrating them on the operational network. She asserted that agile solutions and a better articulation of risk in funding and threat vectors are also key to demonstrating the consequences of *not* investing.

Mr. Munson inquired about the contrast between a democratized service of digital natives with access to data and connectivity, and the traditional chain of command structure of the Air Force. Col. Blackwell explained that even though the data are available, service members are still expected to comply with the orders they are given and work within their purview. She expressed confidence in this new realm of data transparency, owing to clear commander's intent and accountability for those who abuse authority or data access. Lt. Gen. Haugh added that he has not experienced any issues with airmen engaging inappropriately with the data. Mr. Wert noted that lieutenants and captains are now able to implement and execute change, in part owing to their increased coding abilities. Given the value that these individuals have to companies beyond the Air Force, he emphasized the importance of considering retention strategies for this talent—if they do not see a career path that includes innovative work, they will leave the Air Force.

Ms. Westphal asked about the possible role of chaos engineering[5] in the digital transformation. Dr. Nielsen responded that Netflix created a tool a decade ago, Chaos Monkey, to ensure that its system was resilient: by randomly turning off parts of the system's software, the tool tested how well the system could work around issues in its applications and services. This practice of looking for both vulnerabilities and resiliency by testing for random failures in major systems is one that the DAF should consider, he continued. Such tools are constantly evolving to keep pace with the changing environment, and they are either free or very inexpensive to use under a license (i.e., the Air Force could lease them without needing to maintain them). Mr. Wert explained that in its experiments with chaos engineering, Kessel Run[6] discovered a sense of resilience and revealed a way to do maintenance without taking down a system. Dr. Nielsen added that Amazon, Netflix, and Google are constantly (and successfully) implementing system changes while operating.

Gen. Holmes asked Dr. Nielsen to talk about digital modernization in the context of software factories. Nielsen replied that the modern way to build software is via a "software factory," which creates an environment of productive programmers by automating routine tasks such as configuration control, version control, and nightly security testing. This technology approach was developed in the commercial world, and the military-based software factories currently in existence were initially conducted as experiments, with Kessel Run as the first. DoD considered how to scale up from these experiments and learned that it is important to let each software factory specialize in particular systems; standardization has the potential to freeze technology in place, which is undesirable given how quickly software engineering technology changes.

Gen. Holmes pointed out that it is difficult to find money for updating the Air Force's legacy systems within a construct built to assign money to programs that primarily focus on hardware. He wondered how to balance resources so as to have a dedicated, predictable stream to recruit and retain talent without having those people waiting between projects and searching for jobs with other organizations. He said that more incentives are needed to motivate people to have careers in the Air Force and share their expertise to help DoD compete with China. Dr. Nielsen noted that it is motivational for people to see their work making a real-world difference (in contrast to the more traditional acquisition system, in which even after years of work, a product might never be developed).

WORKSHOP ONE CLOSING REMARKS

Lt. Gen. Hamel invited planning committee members and workshop participants to share their observations and takeaways from the first workshop of the series. Gen. Holmes observed that the infrastructure required to support digital modernization, as well as the related bandwidth and technologies, had not been discussed. Lt. Gen. Hamel added that balancing the maintenance of legacy systems with investment in the future is a long-standing problem for the Air Force. Gen. Holmes noted that people often choose only to blame Congress for its denial of funding requests; however, the Air Force has to overcome its tendency to buy more things and focus on making things work. Lt. Gen. Hamel pointed out that industry has similar issues, but Gen. Holmes emphasized that industry charges its customers. Recalling Mr.

---

[5] Chaos engineering is the discipline of testing the resiliency of a system.
[6] U.S. Air Force, 2021, "Kessel Run Delivers Chaos Engineering Practices to Black Pearl," Press Release, https://kesselrun.af.mil/news/CHAOS-Engineering.html.

Reardon's and Mr. Lombardi's presentations, Gen. Holmes reiterated that the Air Force is not currently organized to direct and implement a major transformation: doctrinal and organizational changes are needed to successfully leverage the abundant data available and the tools to connect them.

Ms. Westphal shared key takeaways from the first two days of the workshop series—most importantly, the Air Force has a lot of collaboration without a unity of effort. She observed that there is a high usage of data without representation of how those data could be used; the Air Force cannot increase speed or efficiency if data are being layered onto an old structure of operations. It is also important to identify and analyze risk, both today and for the future. She advocated for chaos engineering as one step toward modernization, because achieving resiliency in an everchanging world is key. She cautioned against creating large programs with significant funding that do not achieve intended outcomes, and she recognized that people (i.e., developing a culture of practice and exercise) are an important component of the DAF's digital transformation.

Lt. Gen. Hamel remarked that the existing rigid ecosystem and processes of the Air Force are misaligned with the nature of digital technology and its evolution; resource allocation, skillsets, and acquisition all have to be approached differently. Dr. Nielsen added that the requirements engineering process perfected over the past 30 years has hurt the Air Force: it takes 5 to 6 years for a capability to emerge, and by that time the technology and the threat have both changed, rendering the capability outdated. He said that it is important to design more adaptable systems that evolve, just as commercial software companies do. Gen. Holmes agreed with Dr. Nielsen that the Air Force has an opportunity as it begins to acquire new things in new ways to change the process; instead of trying to fit software systems into the old model, it is time to create a requirements process that both works for software-intensive systems and casts back to other systems. Dr. Langston noted that the tools for software-intensive acquisition are already available, but the budgeting process cannot be fixed without congressional assistance. He suggested building budgets that would allow the chief information office and the CDO to leverage funds as seed money to add to other people's resources, which would create a unity of effort across the enterprise. Dr. Green said that "competent" (instead of "capable") people should work on requirements. Ms. Westphal added that definitions of words like "requirements" vary across the enterprise, which makes it difficult to achieve change. Gen. Holmes pointed out that although the requirements process currently is driven by congressional oversight and fairness in the contracting system, it should be driven by the need to compete with China.

Dr. Chellappa commented that "digital transformation" is also a general term with several interpretations. He added that if the DAF continues to forgo relationships with the nation's best companies and top talent, the United States will be at a disadvantage to China. Mr. Munson noted that China operates differently than the United States because it has a state-run capitalist system. The United States does not have industrial policy or industrial planning; U.S. industry operates primarily on one of two business models, and neither is well matched to the way the government operates. Although the nation's best companies could help the DAF, their business incentives keep them from doing so. He explained that the Air Force has yet to determine how to create an entirely new structure and culture to support data, despite the common belief that data will win the next war, and he reiterated that the notion of a horizontal data architecture will challenge the traditional notion of commander's control. Col. Douglas DeMaio, 187th Fighter Wing Commander, Alabama Air National Guard, pointed out that the same concerns surfaced when the concept of multi-domain emerged, and doctrine clarified how airmen would act as well as how to move forward with mission orders alongside the vision to accelerate change or lose. He suggested that the same approach be taken with digitization—define and issue direction in doctrine, and balance top-down and bottom-up approaches that set the pace for the Air Force.

Lt. Gen. Ted Bowlds (USAF, ret.), chief executive officer, IAI North America, expressed concern about the Air Force's disparate activities and lack of strategy and governance. Current contracting requirements hinder the Air Force's ability to work with talented individuals from industry. He cautioned that the tools to manage data (e.g., AI) do not seem to be moving forward in parallel to the increasing generation of data, even though these tools are needed to help focus the data for the decision maker. He emphasized the need for the Air Force to plan for continued operations in a disconnected environment.

Mr. Santee observed a philosophical culture clash between the younger and the more seasoned members of the Air Force in terms of their commitment to digitization and transparency. Without a unity of effort, he continued, it will not be possible to achieve a digital transformation. For example, if the Air Force believes that information is going to win the next war, why would it purchase another platform? Instead, he suggested that the Air Force find, pool, share, and link data in the cloud, and reallocate limited resources. He advocated for embracing the digital talents and contributions of the younger generation and empowering them to make decisions. He raised a question about the relationship between radical data transparency and security and also wondered if this new level of transparency might change the relationship with Congress for the better with increased information access. He added that force structure will also experience changes as a result of the digital transformation; for example, the Space Force plans to have far fewer people than the other services but still accomplish the same tasks by utilizing data and applications for automation.

Ms. Westphal referenced a 2011 Center for a New American Security lecture about why generals in WWII were more successful than those in Korea, Vietnam, Iraq, and Afghanistan. In WWII, if generals did not achieve within 90 days, they were relieved and moved to a different task where they could be more successful. Now, leaders remain in positions even when they are not successful, and so the motivation to achieve and transform is lacking. Gen. Holmes clarified that most WWII generals were warfighters. He noted that the centrally directed culture of today's Air Force is problematic because processes are driven by accountability and oversight instead of by reward for producing results beyond the norm, stifling individual initiative. Ms. Westphal pointed out that the culture of decision making has to change; new architectures and technologies alone will not solve this problem. Lt. Gen. Hamel added that leadership and collaboration are important components of the success of digital transformation. He described the need for a common conviction about what is essential for the future of the Air Force.

Mr. Drolet acknowledged Mr. Lombardi's concern about the variation in the definitions of "digital" but added that sometimes progress is stalled by an overemphasis on the need to define concepts. The Air Force has to be agile, but technology is not the barrier: the current bureaucracy, culture, policies, and processes tend to slow progress. He noted that the Air Force has much farther to go to achieve unity of effort, and he suggested an increased focus on the importance of its people in the digital transformation.

Lt. Gen. Hamel reiterated that despite several innovative efforts, the Air Force remains uncertain about how best to attack the problem of its organizing principles. It is difficult for an organization as large as the Air Force to think from an enterprise perspective, especially without the dedication of more resources, commitment, and talent to this challenge. He emphasized that organizations across the world confront similar problems as the digital revolution continues.

Dr. Green noticed a limited discussion of digital representation during the first workshop. She stressed the importance of understanding that democratization means having a common language and common understanding. It is also necessary to consider how to separate digital talent from processes and procedures, and determine what tasks can be automated and what tasks can be augmented to best leverage intellectual capital. She explained that bright young people often leave the Air Force because they do not know where they fit in—they are not shown the "big picture"—and it is crucial to create pathways for the development of new skills and how they will align with the organization.

3

Workshop Two, Part One

OPENING REMARKS

Workshop series co-chair Lt. Gen. Michael Hamel (USAF, ret.), independent consultant, highlighted key topics shared by Department of the Air Force (DAF) leadership during Workshop One. He recalled Gen. David Allvin's focus on the imperative to accelerate to establish a stronger posture against emerging global threats, as well as Gen. David Thompson's description of the Space Force's position as a digital force and its dependence on the Air Force for information capabilities. He noted Gen. Allvin's interest in understanding specifically how information will improve decision making and how transformation efforts could be best sequenced to enable rapid acceleration, and Gen. Thompson's request for feedback on whether the DAF is on the right track with its digital strategy.

Workshop Two chair Dr. Pamela Drew, former executive vice president and president of information systems, Exelis, welcomed participants to the second workshop in the series, which would reveal experiences with and best practices for digital transformations from the perspectives of information systems experts and managers in industry, academia, and other government agencies. She posited that the DAF could bring to bear these lessons learned in its journey of digital transformation.

WHY DIGITIZE?
A PANEL PRESENTATION

Mr. Robert Tross, principal, Deloitte Digital, explained that digitization should prioritize the customer with human-centered design and elevate the human experience. Digitization that embraces an agile mindset leads to rapid change and faster decision making. Because "culture eats strategy for breakfast," he suggested that organizations who are beginning a transformation journey adopt the Scaled Agile Framework®

(SAFe®)[1]—a delivery model that removes tribal thinking, aligns teams, helps move to fast programmatic decision making, and fosters stronger organizations. With this decentralization of trust, the hierarchy shifts and decisions can be made at a lower level. He remarked that data are the "fuel" for organizations that embrace artificial intelligence (AI) for data-driven decision making and asserted that digitization is no longer optional. Millennials and tech savvy individuals *expect* digital platforms that enable self-service; with AI, machines can complete manual tasks, and highly skilled individuals can focus on more impactful work.

Mr. Tross described the three pillars of realizing a digital vision: (1) embrace iterative, fast, lean, high-touch, value-added, point-of-contact delivery; (2) perform demonstrations, vet technologies, and utilize software to collect real-time feedback so that customers receive useful products; and (3) strategize by focusing on outcomes instead of outputs (i.e., focus on what you want *to achieve* to meet a user need, not what you want *to build*). Having witnessed slow, bureaucratic decision-making processes in the federal government, he advocated for changing the approach to problem solving: instead of asking "*what* technology are we going to use," ask "*how* am I going to solve this problem with X technology." This shift from "what" to "how" enables acceleration and, ultimately, true transformation.

Mr. Tross shared three recent examples of successful transformation led by Deloitte Digital. First, the company delivered 17 applications in only 18 months, each of which solves a particular problem. Second, the company digitized a U.S. Department of Agriculture nationwide food distribution system for the Indian Tribal Organizations (ITOs) by putting the system online and moving it to the cloud. Because the ITOs were comfortable with technology and engaged in this process, Deloitte Digital also delivered an iPad app based on customer feedback to better meet user needs. Third, the company began working with the Space Force and Cisco ~10 months ago, using Salesforce to power a digital transformation for commercial satellite usage and consumption. He highlighted this final example as a solid use case for customer relationship management, because this project requires managing relationships with both providers and distributors, and ensuring that the digital transformation aligns with Gen. John Raymond's intent.

In closing, Mr. Tross described several ongoing challenges and lessons learned in digital transformation:

- Eliminate siloes, such as the barrier between IT and business, to avoid the derailment of programs.
- Create an organic feedback loop that involves real users; simulated users are not a substitute for real users.
- Instead of changing for the sake of change, go "all-in" on agile: begin with the outcome in mind, and create roadmaps and time frames to hold people accountable.
- Have a supportive, agile contracting structure that is fixed-outcome and capacity-based instead of fixed-price.
- Embrace minimum viable products that can be placed in the hands of users quickly instead of striving for perfection.
- Hire a team that is comfortable with transformation, because digitization will feel chaotic to those new to the concept.
- Use platforms that support rapid change to experiment, fail fast, and adapt.

Ms. Danielle Ullner, partner and managing director, Boston Consulting Group (BCG) Digital Ventures, explained that her organization works with other institutions to invent, launch, and scale game-changing digital products and platforms as part of broader digital transformation efforts. She echoed Mr. Tross's mantra to fail often, fail fast, and then pivot to something else.

The right multidisciplinary team makes it possible to transform at warp speed: in 7 years, BCG Digital Ventures has built more than 160 digital solutions.

---

[1] The website for SAFe is https://www.scaledagileframework.com/, accessed November 23, 2021.

She emphasized that digital transformation is no longer a choice for organizations. However, only ~30 percent of organizations achieve successful digital transformations because digital transformations are difficult to execute; delivering such fundamental change at scale in large, sometimes global, complex organizations is challenging, especially when there are short-term pressures and leaders may have to put their careers on the line. The cost of failure is high—large IT write-downs, poor user experiences, missed growth and productivity opportunities, and loss of time. She suggested six steps for organizations, which could increase the success rate of digital transformation to ~80 percent:

1. An integrated strategy with clear transformation goals;
2. Leadership commitment from the chief executive officer through middle management;
3. Deployment of high-caliber talent, including a balance of change managers and product managers focused on the end user;
4. An agile governance mindset that drives broader adoption;
5. Effective monitoring of progress toward defined outcomes; and
6. Business-led modular technology and data platform.

Ms. Ullner stressed the need for leadership to avoid "analysis paralysis," which can destroy an activity before it can be scaled from pilot to funded program. These six key success factors are imperative to develop a "bionic organization"—in other words, instead of making one-off, standalone digital improvements, intentionally combining the human element with the technological capabilities to ensure that organizations can thrive in the face of change and uncertainty, drive breakthrough innovation, and solve significant problems (see Figure 3.1).

FIGURE 3.1 The components of a successful bionic organization. SOURCE: Danielle Ullner, presentation to the workshop, September 8, 2021. Courtesy of Boston Consulting Group (BCG).

Ms. Ullner shared a case study on transforming a multinational utility with everyday innovation at speed and scale. Although this is a real-world industry example, she emphasized its relevance to the DAF. For example, the utility operates in a complex stakeholder environment, has constant resource issues, and is eager to gain competitive advantage. The utility's specific challenges included an inability to meet customer expectations for seamless digital experiences, the threat of digital-first utilities leveraging technology to change industry rules, a new generation of workers expecting increased efficiency through technology, fragmented and data-poor planning efforts leading to poor capital investments, and new regulations forcing cuts to operating budgets. The utility had a bold vision to reinvent its business through digital transformation with optimized maintenance (e.g., better use of data and predictive analytics to maintain and repair equipment), dynamic grid operations, on-demand deployment of the field force, and seamless customer experience. A new chief information and digital officer worked to develop a trusted relationship between the utility's business and technology communities, and employees were invested in delivering results in real time. As a result, the organization as a whole became more empowered. BCG Digital Ventures developed a program for this utility that was anchored to five principles: (1) start small but think big, (2) learn by building, (3) deliver impact at speed, (4) build capabilities just-in-time, and (5) change from the inside out. BCG Digital Ventures also helped the utility to create outcome-focused digital roadmaps with a portfolio of products that reimagined "business as usual" processes. She added that any transformation process is most effective when it is stage-gated and milestone-based, and when ineffective initiatives are promptly eliminated. With BCG Digital Ventures' assistance, the utility launched four new products in less than 18 months, supporting teams with enabling talent development, governance, and technology platforms. During the next phase of the project, BCG Digital Ventures and the utility strengthened the operating system to scale capabilities and support successive waves of digital products. More than 40 new digital hires were made; staff have been exposed to digital processes, agile mindset, and quick decision making; and products are delivering value.

Ms. M. Nadia Vincent, digital transformation and innovation executive advisor, Digital Transformation Leaders, observed that because many organizations begin to digitize either in direct response to a regulation change or to regain advantage against their competitors, the transition likely reveals additional organizational problems. To avoid this outcome, it is critical to create a strategy for digital transformation *prior to* implementation. She presented a model that could help leaders strategize their vision for digital transformation—the Digital Wheel of Wealth (see Figure 3.2) reveals the many opportunities of the digital age as well as the six characteristics of digital intelligence:

1. *Broken time, distance, volume, and physical barriers.* Time is the most precious asset to manage; once time is optimized, it is possible to define and achieve more outcomes. There is less distinction between the physical world and the virtual world. Digital transformation enables easier collaboration across distances, and computers have become so powerful that organizations are increasing investments in storage.
2. *New efficiency.* Digitization increases productivity, accessibility (specifically with AI and mobility), measurability (when tasks are delegated to computers), visualization, understandability, and assistance in achieving goals.
3. *Limitless possibilities.* Progress comes in the form of creations from imagination, innovation of new processes, and improvement of existing processes.
4. *Leadership.* Because computers are still guided by humans, visionary leaders who are dreamers, protectors, innovators, and rainmakers are needed to inspire people at every level of an organization and to enable action.
5. *Growth and expansion.* Changing people's mindsets and creating new habits requires investment in people. Expansion of organizations, communities, businesses, and societies begins with individual human growth.
6. *New relationships.* New technologies allow for greater connectivity. The man/machine relationship, in particular, is the most challenging. Instead of replacing humans, machines could

collaborate with human intelligence to produce and achieve at a higher level.

Ms. Vincent explained that before creating a digital strategy, organizations should consider the following questions: What opportunities can you foresee for your organization if barriers are broken? What digital efficiencies could benefit your organization? What are possibilities you can imagine for the future of your organization? Who are the leaders that will inspire the organization at various levels? What are possible future growth and expansion opportunities for your people and your organization? What benefits could emerge from improving relationships in your organization? Once these questions are answered, and potential opportunities and capabilities are recognized, it is possible to define a strategy for digital transformation. She emphasized that data need to be given special attention within this strategy, because an organization cannot survive without data.

In closing, Ms. Vincent suggested the development of guidelines and processes for people to adopt the transformation and make investments in the right leadership team. Because innovation should be an ongoing process, she advocated for organizations to create innovation business units.

Dr. David Bray, executive director, GeoTech Commission, Atlantic Council, and former chief information officer, Federal Communications Commission (FCC), explained that digital transformation is 20 percent technology and 80 percent "hearts and minds."

He described his experience leading a bipartisan commission to review all research and development efforts in the intelligence community in 2011. As the fourth person to attempt this effort in only 3 months, he emphasized that the barrier to success was not one of technical execution; instead, it was the difficulty of managing the expectations of Congress, the troops, and contractors during this "disruption." Thus, it is critical for organizations to have leaders who are aware that transformations ask people do things with which they may be unfamiliar or uncomfortable.

FIGURE 3.2 The Digital Wheel of Wealth. SOURCE: M. Nadia Vincent, presentation to the workshop, September 8, 2021. Courtesy of Digital Transformation Leaders, digitaltransformationleaders.com.

In a similar experience, Dr. Bray arrived at the FCC as the ninth chief information officer in 9 years. Upon arrival, he considered an important question: What is the level of acceptance for change in the organization? Many government organizations have "change fatigue"; when that is the case and people are reluctant to change, he continued, it is important to consider new strategies. He noted that the Air Force often relies on doctrine to codify people's actions, but he wondered whether the current doctrine rewards and incentivizes the desired behaviors. Without that component, people will not change and digital transformation will not be successful.

Dr. Bray explained that the first step in digital transformation is to understand the "why," by identifying the problem that needs to be solved. Bray emphasized that the "why" for Congress (e.g., to be more effective with available resources) may differ from the "why" for commanders and airmen (e.g., to become nimbler and more adaptive in future environments), as well as from the "why" for contractors. He pointed out that the incumbent contractor workforce is often the most resistant to change. It can be difficult to break long-standing relationships with contractors; however, in a digital transformation, often different and fewer contractors are needed.

Dr. Bray advocated for the government to embrace private sector partners on its journey to innovation, and encouraged the Department of Defense (DoD) to use the combination of cooperation and competitiveness that exists within the services to provide incentives so that change also comes from the bottom up. This approach is more effective than creating an isolated "innovation office" at the top, because digital transformation involves everyone in the organization. He suggested adopting the "melted iceberg approach," where people share their approach to a challenge, others provide feedback and recommendations, ideas are spotlighted, and a competitive rivalry within the service is created to move ideas forward. He emphasized that digital transformation is enabled by a shift in mindset, in which everyone is considered to be a valuable part of the broader effort. Allowing people in an organization to voice their concerns is another way to shift people from being "problem holders" to "problem solvers."

Dr. Bray underscored that a successful transformation starts with low-hanging quick wins, with bigger, bolder actions emerging 1 year into the transformation. He cautioned that even at this point, 10–15 percent of people likely will still resist or even sabotage efforts, and those people may ultimately need to be reassigned or released. An important part of leadership during a digital transformation is helping people navigate the loss of "the old way of doing things"; it is critical to consider how to blend new thinking with old thinking, providing opportunities for collaboration and for programmatic units to highlight their accomplishments. He emphasized that successful digital transformation results from changing programmatic processes as much as from changing technology; there is no separation between IT and mission, as IT is part of the mission. In closing, he suggested assembling a diversity of perspectives both inside and outside of an organization to try to manage any friction that could hinder a transformation.

Open Discussion

Dr. Drew described several themes that emerged throughout this session of the workshop. While senior executives in industry understand the need for government to be more efficient and will find ways in the long term to support the government, not everyone in an organization will share that perspective. She also reiterated that although technology is important, it is not the foundation for digital transformation. Instead, digital transformation is enabled by breaking down barriers, reimagining processes, and reinventing approaches. Because the people carrying out existing processes might resist these changes, it is crucial that they are part of the solutions. She added that eliminating funding barriers across components and departments of the Air Force is particularly difficult. Gen. James (Mike) Holmes (USAF, ret.), senior advisor, The Roosevelt Group, observed that although Air Force leadership has a transformation strategy, it does not have funding to recruit the right talent to conduct agile operations in support of that strategy. This cycle persists in part because the Air Force continues to buy "stuff" instead of focusing on investing in its network for operations.

Reflecting on the value of "quick wins" to build momentum for transformation, Col. Scott McKeever, director, Chief of Staff of the Air Force Strategic Studies Group, asked about methodologies for project selection. Ms. Ullner described four criteria for choosing the first program of a transformation: (1) high value and impact; (2) a low level of implementation difficulty (i.e., select a project with known, minimal technological and operational risk that can be readily addressed); (3) few dependencies, so as to reduce delays that could hinder success; and (4) a middle-management-level champion. Dr. Bray added that early projects should also demonstrate cost savings (e.g., moving the cost from an operation and maintenance expense to a capital expense). It would also be beneficial if an early project could demonstrate a new model for security. Ms. Vincent suggested using design-thinking to create value in different phases of a project. Mr. Tross noted that sustainability should be a consideration, even in the "quick wins" phase. For example, to determine which projects to do first, his team built rationalization scorecards based on complexity level and potential benefits (i.e., how many users a process has, how many customers it affects, etc.). This exercise instills organizational rigor, and could be used to measure success and to determine a course for future projects.

Lt. Gen. Hamel observed that large, complex organizations such as the Air Force have numerous internal processes, stakeholders, and customers to prioritize and engage. Dr. Bray suggested thinking about this challenge from the perspective of a venture capitalist. He asserted that a transformation effort should not come from a single office; it requires a communications strategy that is accessible to all stakeholders, which describes the why and how of the transformation as well as identifies appropriate behaviors. Mr. Tross added that SAFe enables the collaboration of mission and IT—and once that unity is achieved, it becomes possible to prioritize and engage. Furthermore, SAFe enables the management of a few programs around a few technologies, which is more scalable and digestible than managing a portfolio of many disparate technologies.

Lt. Gen. Hamel described a unique challenge for the Air Force: commercial elements have to be purpose-built and designed to operate across multiple operating domains. He wondered how to avoid a fixation on "stuff" but have a trustworthy infrastructure purpose-built to support missions. Dr. Bray responded with the following transportation ecosystem analogy: the transformation effort would have one team focused on "roads" and the safety features of those roads, and another team focused on assembling the features of the "car" that will drive on those roads (i.e., the application). The car should have the assurance that it can safely drive on those roads. Translating that analogy to the digital transformation, such an approach ensures that each time there is a new effort, there is no need to start from scratch: the security is baked in, no matter who hosts the platform.

LESSONS FROM OTHERS "LIKE THE AIR FORCE": PANEL ONE

Mr. Rahul Welde, executive vice president of digital transformation, Unilever, explained that Unilever is one of the world's largest consumer goods companies, and it is driven by a mission to make sustainable living commonplace. Unilever has a presence in more than 190 countries, and more than 2.5 billion people use its products (400 brands) every day.

He observed a commonality between the Air Force and Unilever—both are a force for good that serve the needs of people. Although digital transformation in industry is different from that in other sectors, he continued, shared core principles exist: no matter the sector, opportunities and challenges arise related to the substantial impact that technology can have on people's lives. He noted that the recovery effort from the COVID-19 pandemic has been led by new technologies, just as the recovery effort from the 1929 Great Depression was led by new industries as part of the Industrial Revolution.

Mr. Welde remarked that digital transformation is a broad term with varied meanings. Unilever understands digital transformation as the intersection of technology, consumer behavior, and a large customer supply chain-organizational interface. Digital transformation is thus about end-to-end business and how to impact that spectrum through tools, technologies, and capabilities. He described four "thinks" to consider for digital transformation within any organization:

1. When people, processes, and technology work in balance and in tandem, there is exponential impact on transformation.
2. It is important to harness the power of data and insights about consumer needs. Unilever's Foundry, People Data Centres, and internal studios (where it shares information about products with consumers) are unique, new capabilities that have emerged to deal with the enormous amount of available data. Technology enables real-time data processing and decision making, which has implications for the fundamental capabilities of any organization. Agility is needed to meet the challenges of the supply chain and evolving consumer practices: speed (with precision) is the new currency.
3. Partnerships are essential for innovation. Because technology is developed by universities and large companies, it is important to welcome more and more partners into the ecosystem to mine insights and better serve consumers.
4. Culture change can be achieved through empowerment (i.e., invert the hierarchy so that the front line can make decisions, which better serves consumers), collaboration, and experimentation (i.e., move quickly from ideas to viable products to scale). Leadership can establish a "learning culture" that harnesses skills and talent by recruiting, motivating, and retaining the right people.

Mr. Dale Tutt, vice president, Aerospace and Defense Industry Strategy, Siemens Digital Industries Software, explained that the cost of aircraft programs increases by a factor of 10 every 30 years. At the same time, defense programs have been on an increasing trajectory over the past 80 years in terms of how long it takes to move a program into operational capability. This unsustainable path creates a sense of urgency for transformation. He referenced the automotive industry, which has reduced its manufacturing processes (from program start to roll out) to only 2 to 3 years, as a model of achieving transformational results with digitization. He asserted that to survive disruption and thrive in the digital era, companies need to become digital enterprises—this requires taking a holistic approach that looks beyond digital tools as solutions and both changes processes and manages change.

Mr. Tutt provided an overview of Siemens' digital journey. Its "Xcelerator" portfolio is the catalyst for the digital enterprise and is intended to scale for programs of any size. Three keys to gaining competitive advantage in this environment are the use of a comprehensive digital twin; the use of personalized, adaptable, modern solutions; and operation in a flexible, open ecosystem. A comprehensive digital twin includes the digital twin product (virtual product), digital twin production (virtual production line), and digital twin performance (real production, real product) (see Figure 3.3). He emphasized that leveraging this capability to simulate manufacturing facilities before developing them is critical to avoid potentially wasting tens of millions of dollars. Performance data can be driven back into the digital twin of the product to optimize models, and insights from performance can be used for continuous improvement on this and future products. Thus, the use of a digital twin reduces costs and schedules as well as builds momentum.

He explained that integrated solutions (e.g., model-based systems engineering, product design and engineering, verification management, integrated program planning and execution, supplier collaboration and management, intelligent manufacturing, and product support and management) accelerate programs by connecting different tools and workflows, and automating some of those workflows, to provide seamless transitions in the movement from one solution to another. These solutions are organized around five functional areas, which have varying roles throughout the product development life cycle for any program: conceptual design, product design, verification and certification, production, and deployment and sustainment. Horizontal solutions in these functional areas and vertical interconnections create a "fabric," which makes it possible to pull verification planning, manufacturing concepts, and sustainment design forward to drive the initial design and drive program efficiencies. The concept of a digital thread for defense elevates this process by decreasing the amount of time it takes to cycle through a complete acquisition program and improving the collaboration between industry and the Air Force via better information sharing and more aligned activities. A phase in which industry is working on the program could lead to faster delivery of the capability, he continued. The objectives of this process are not only to speed up acquisition

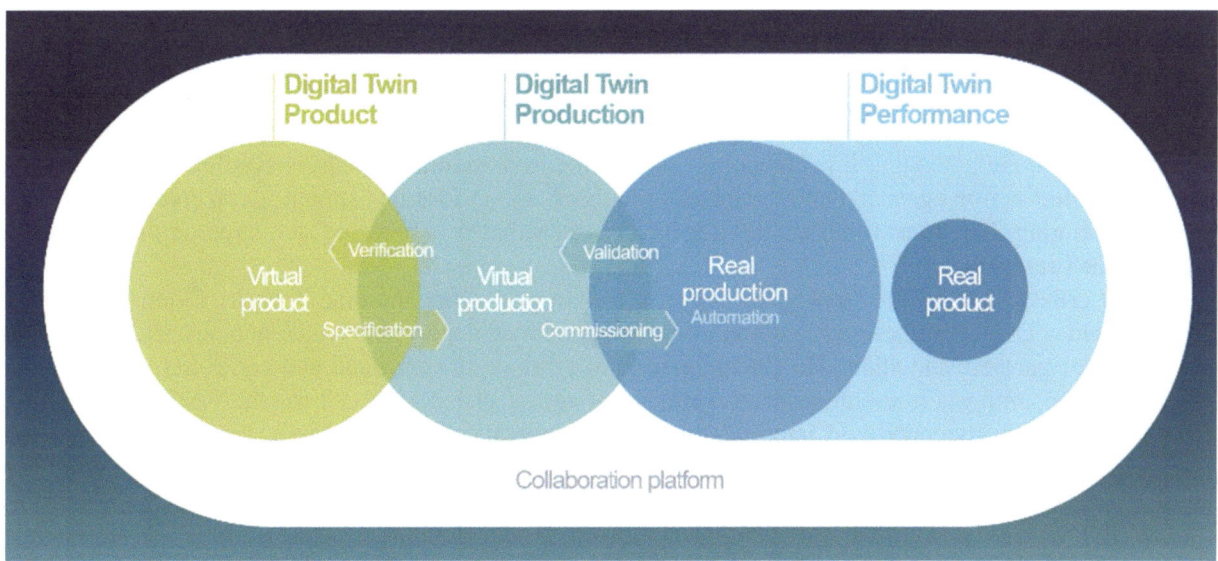

FIGURE 3.3 Comprehensive digital twin. SOURCE: Dale Tutt, presentation to the workshop, September 8, 2021.

and product delivery but also to increase operational availability and sustain effectively throughout the life cycle of a product.

Mr. Tutt shared an example of a startup company, Bye Aerospace, that has fully adopted digital—its digital enterprise provides seamless transition between design and analysis. It uses digital tools and makes connections to increase speed, thus evaluating more concepts and enhancing collaboration. With its investment in digital tools, Bye Aerospace has experienced a 60 percent reduction in engineering hours as it develops new programs. Because it is always difficult to hire the right number of people with the right expertise, this ability to move faster with fewer people is imperative, he asserted. Another company, Pilatus, has embraced digital transformation for new product development. By adopting digital tools and going faster with fewer people, it took Pilatus less than 5 years to move from program introduction to delivery of a new jet. He explained that digital transformation could also be useful for legacy programs; for example, the A-10 program transitioned from legacy, paper-based technical data and manuals to a product life cycle management-centric environment for model-based definition, configuration management, contract data management, service engineering, and wire harness design. This investment in digitization created a better understanding of the product and led to increased availability and reduced depot flow times.

Mr. Tutt offered another example of how a digital mindset can change an organization's processes. The U.S. Navy has created digital twin models of four shipyards, and simulation is used to ensure that maintenance operations are as effective as possible now and in the future. The complex B-21 program is also making progress, using digital solutions for risk reduction. He mentioned that the first e-series aircraft, the eT-7A, embraced model-based engineering and was able to move from concept to first flight within only 3 years. A 75 percent increase in first pass quality and 80 percent fewer assembly hours were also achieved. These examples demonstrate that digital manufacturing reduces costs and increases sustainment.

In closing, Mr. Tutt underscored that digital transformation has the potential to accelerate new programs and capabilities with its focus on faster program acquisition and execution. Digital transformation can be achieved with a flexible, open ecosystem to bring technology to bear faster; improved collaboration across the value chain; and a holistic approach that considers the full life cycle early in the program as well as the roles of the people, tools, and processes.

Mr. Charles Rybeck, co-founder, Digital Mobilizations, Inc., emphasized that although Gen. Charles Brown committed the Air Force to accelerate change or lose, many misinterpreted this mandate as doing more of what is already being done but faster and with a different name. Instead, he continued, digital transformation should be tangible, measurable, consequential, and different from "business as usual." He asserted that the DAF has only just begun to define and respond to this challenge in ways comparable to those who have succeeded in other parts of the U.S. government, among great power competitors, and in private industry. He noted that it is difficult to sustain focused attention on any multidimensional subject; and creating an "action agenda" that prioritizes, sequences, and guides investment for an enterprise is even more challenging. However, other enterprises have proven that it is possible to overcome this barrier to digital transformation.

He described the Air Force and Space Force in the context of the National Security Enterprise (NSE), which includes DoD, the intelligence community, all associated departments and agencies, and public and private sector partners and allies. He championed joint all-domain command and control (JADC2) as the first step in becoming a true enterprise. Several years ago, a vision emerged for the NSE's information environment to be integrated and interoperable with its operational environment; however, this did not initiate an enterprise-level digital transformation. By private industry standards, he continued, the NSE has underprioritized the need to transform enterprise-level decision making and accountabilities.

Mr. Rybeck defined digital transformation as follows: fundamentally changing the NSE's effectiveness in prosecuting its mission to ensure strategic surprise—in other words, anticipating and overmatching potential adversaries' capabilities and eliminating new threats. Strategic surprise is unlocked by integrating and interoperating the NSE's information environment with its operational environment and seizing two opportunities: (1) leapfrogging competitors' capabilities (i.e., modeling and projecting competitors' future capabilities, taking into account their potential use of emerging but not yet operational technologies, and leapfrogging to win against these advanced capabilities instead of just overwhelming their current capabilities); and (2) mobilizing the entire enterprise's ecosystem (including all of its human and machine assets by realigning mission partner authorities and optimizing accountabilities, drawing on each ecosystem partner's unique capabilities to maximize the overall effectiveness and efficiency of the ecosystem). He explained that to operationalize these critical success factors, prioritized criteria are needed to predict strategic surprise effectiveness as well as maturity grids to quantify the different levels of performance capability for these criteria (i.e., decision-support benchmarks).

Despite the fact that DoD and Air Force leadership have discussed an enterprise-level digital transformation for several years, Mr. Rybeck underscored that the objectives have not been achieved. He pointed out that private sector leaders (e.g., Amazon, Apple, Google, Microsoft, Facebook) have successfully implemented platform-era technologies to merge their information environments with their operational environments. The successful enterprise visions of private sector leaders required developing both new technologies and data prioritization techniques. However, he emphasized that technologies are never a substitute for enterprise-level, proprietary strategic surprise visions. Thus, he continued, if the DAF continues to assume that supporting only one-off innovative projects will advance the mission without changing how and when investments are made in programs of record, the enterprise mission model will not evolve.

Mr. Rybeck shared three case studies that demonstrate why JADC2 has emerged as the potential "forcing function" for digital transformation, what enterprise-level decisions need to be made, and who needs to take what actions. First, he explained that the Pentagon's Office of Net Assessment (ONA), founded in 1973, understood the need to aggregate expertise and to scope work appropriate to a challenge (i.e., "tie the ribbon properly"). However, China has been more proficient than the United States in operationalizing ONA's insights about digital transformation.[2] China achieved strategic surprise on classified and unclassified fronts and announced multiple reorganizations of its own national security

---

[2] C. Rybeck, L. Cornwell, and P. Sagan, 2017, "Digital Dimension Disruption: A National Security Enterprise Response," *PRISM* 7(2), https://cco.ndu.edu/PRISM-7-2/Article/1401866/a-national-security-enterprise-response-digital-dimension-disruption/; C. Rybeck, L. Cornwell, and P. Sagan, 2018, "America's Superpowers: How the U.S. Should Respond to China's Informatization Strategy," War on the Rocks, https://warontherocks.com/2018/09/applying-americas-superpowers-how-the-u-s-should-respond-to-chinas-informatization-strategy/.

enterprise. China leapfrogged the United States and its competitors with technology inspired by or stolen from the United States, and China used "informatization" as the basis for a national reorientation and a national mobilization. Therefore, he stressed that China serves as both a threat and a model to the United States.

Second, he remarked that Walmart rescoped its entire business, using the Internet to transform its relationship with its suppliers. Walmart reimagined and mobilized its ecosystems, developed interoperable collaboration software and systems to attract suppliers, and eventually became the largest retailer in the world. Walmart pioneered the use of internal cross-functional teams and ecosystem-level teams to develop ecosystem-level solutions, and it changed its business model by sharing end-consumer, point-of-sales demand data with supplier partners.

Third, the intelligence community's Information Technology Enterprise Initiative moved the intelligence community to the cloud (using a commercial cloud services contract to make Amazon Web Services available to the entire community); however, the initiative was misunderstood and unable to gain traction. Mr. Rybeck pointed out that this example demonstrates the limitations of "tying the ribbon" too narrowly or of not having the authority to tie it at all.

He summarized that each case utilized benchmarking to design and build competitive barriers to entry, was iterative, emphasized surpassing the competition instead of striving for perfection, and began with a disruptive enterprise vision. He underscored that the most important success factor in digital transformation is "tying the ribbon properly": the right decision scope creates the conditions for digital transformation to provide enterprise-level value. He suggested that the DAF leadership select a portfolio of transformational initiatives that are achievable within acceptable risk-return parameters.

Mr. Rybeck observed that the success factors for a broader decision scope almost always contradict the success factors used by functional siloes. Bottom-up, non-integrated, functional, siloed initiatives negatively impact the performance of other elements of an enterprise. He stated that JADC2 is necessary but not sufficient; the DAF needs mechanisms to operationalize its objective. In closing, he advocated for the DAF to use fifth generation decision support to align, orchestrate, and instrument digital transformation solutions by tying the ribbon properly, doing what is necessary to use those decision support benchmarks, and chartering a rigorous and expedited net assessment of enterprise-level digital transformation. This net assessment, he continued, should include comprehensive benchmarking to illuminate a path for the enterprise to prioritize, sequence, and invest, with the purpose of leveraging the Advanced Battle Management System and JADC2 to ensure strategic surprise success against competitors and adversaries.

Open Discussion

A participant inquired about cross-sector partnerships and how to establish a baseline level of understanding. Mr. Welde explained that establishing a baseline and the returns on investment is a collaborative activity; the partners co-create a brief that describes the task at hand. Alignment is feasible when partners are involved upfront in the *process* of innovation.

Another participant asked which users the Air Force should be targeting in its digital transformation. Mr. Rybeck noted that focusing only on the end user (e.g., the fighter pilot) is too limited; it is also critical to focus on the adversary's use of new capabilities in the physical and cyber realms. He added that it is important to consider man-machine collaboration instead of thinking only about individual human beings as end users. Mr. Rybeck and Dr. Drew suggested that it is not a matter of identifying all of the *actual* end users but rather locating the actionable decision makers at a proper scope that can increase efficiency related to digital transformation.

In response to a participant's question about how to balance an enterprise approach with a "quick wins" approach, Mr. Rybeck said that the two approaches could be combined. He emphasized that although quick wins are instructive and help illuminate the right path, incremental progress is not transformational; if too much credit is given to people in an organization for making small changes to existing processes, there is no motivation to make large-scale changes. He noted that the Air Force and Space Force currently have a low tolerance for failure, and the initiatives presented all claim success. He advocated for more honest conversation, frank assessment, and lessons learned as a "quick win."

Dr. Annie Green, data governance specialist, George Mason University, asked Mr. Rybeck how levels of abstraction (e.g., processes, products, and analytics) are delineated and integrated to accommodate scope, goals, and objectives in JADC2. He noted that JADC2 has the advantage of being focused on next-generation capabilities. Next, leaders need to consider how the Joint Requirements Oversight Council could operationalize the construct. The simple approach, he continued, is to compare the packages of capabilities to those of the adversaries in a classified environment to confirm whether the United States is leapfrogging their capabilities.

Lt. Gen. Hamel asked the panelists about their experiences of achieving digital transformation in the business sector with both bottom-up (i.e., innovation, digital infrastructure, data, people, process) and top-down (i.e., vision and strategy) approaches. Mr. Welde said that although digital transformation starts with the top-down vision and strategy, the bottom-up approach plays an equally important role, as digital transformation cannot be executed in a vacuum. He stressed that a grand vision for transformation is useless without clearly articulated milestones and measurable objectives, and he described the biggest challenge as achieving end-to-end integration across an organization. Mr. Tutt echoed Mr. Welde's observations and reiterated that the top-down strategy is needed to guide the organization but the bottom-up perspective provides the buy-in that is critical to success. He emphasized that all members of the organization need to feel comfortable that their jobs are secure, that their jobs could improve or become easier, and that they will be empowered to solve problems creatively.

Dr. Drew supported the notion that change management is critical to the success of any digital transformation, and she invited the panelists to share related lessons learned. Mr. Rybeck noted that once people understand how different "business as usual" is from digital transformation, it is possible to apply standards to measure whether the right team is in place and the right conversations are occurring. In a transformative environment, he continued, people should be evaluated based on their contributions to the enterprise vision, and it is important for champions to provide top-cover for people doing innovative work. Mr. Welde observed that successful leadership and execution of a digital transformation requires a specific type of expertise. In any transformational effort, people want to see results quickly, but it is important for change leaders to calibrate decisions carefully: not too fast so as to leave the organization behind, but not too slow so that the competition moves ahead. Leadership is also responsible for ensuring that individual initiatives are moving in unison toward the "big picture." He emphasized that change management is foundational to transformation. Mr. Tutt explained that the success of a change is the product of the acceptance and the quality of the change. A change champion expresses and communicates a vision continuously, with an achievable objective and quick wins.

Mr. Alden Munson, senior fellow and member, Board of Regents, Potomac Institute for Policy Studies, asked whether industry experiences could realistically be applied to government institutions. Dr. Drew acknowledged that the basic tenets of process improvement and efficiency apply to both domains. Mr. Tutt added that there are several similarities between the domains. For example, in both industry and government, people are continually changing roles, and arriving and departing, over the course of a long-term initiative; managing that change appropriately is critical. The notion of "profitability" in industry is also applicable to DoD, which deals with taxpayers and ever-shrinking defense budgets that affect national security.

Dr. Rama Chellappa, Bloomberg Distinguished Professor of electrical and computer engineering and biomedical engineering, Johns Hopkins University, wondered if people have misinterpreted digitization as government surveillance. Mr. Welde suggested that this concern about digitization could be reduced if leaders addressed safety and security, thus removing any perceived threats, and communicated the principled uses for data analytics.

LESSONS FROM OTHERS "LIKE THE AIR FORCE": PANEL TWO

Dr. Jay Walsh, interim vice president for economic development and innovation in the University of Illinois system, described his time as vice president for research at Northwestern University, where he supported efforts analogous to those found in industry: he oversaw 2,000 "small businesses" (run by faculty), each of which wrote its own "business plan" (i.e., proposals), ran its own operations, cultivated a strategic vision, created "revenue" (i.e., grants), and developed a "product" (i.e., new knowledge and graduates). To facilitate this amount of research, the university needed to be agile, provide a service for its "customers" (i.e., the researchers) that was available 24/7, and enable self-service. Because each researcher ran a slightly different "business," each needed slightly different services. During Dr. Walsh's 12-year tenure, the university enabled more research by significantly increasing its IT infrastructure with the purchase of one new system each year.

He described a major initiative in Northwestern University's healthcare system to create an electronic data warehouse. About 20 years ago, the notion of connecting genomic data to healthcare data was nascent, and healthcare data were not readily accessible to researchers because the hospital owned those data. It was particularly challenging to develop a system that allowed the university's researchers to access clinical data that had been generated in collaboration with physicians. Approximately 14 years ago, an agreement was reached that allowed the university to move the data from the electronic healthcare system into a research system. That system now contains data from 17 million patients, and each night the system moves ~3 billion data elements from the healthcare systems into the electronic data warehouse from ~140 sources. He explained that significant synchronization enables this process each night. The electronic data warehouse now serves as a comprehensive repository containing all of the clinical and research data associated with the university's medical school—an effort that was driven by the researchers. Although the hospital was initially not very interested in this activity, its perspective has changed because the incoming data include operations and financial data. As a result, this database is valuable for patient care, healthcare operations, and medical education: the hospital can provide better care for patients, and the medical school can advance research and train the next generation of clinicians. He designated this case study as applicable to the DAF because if the Air Force, Space Force, and other organizations combine their data, they could analyze the relationship among those data and determine how to operate better and achieve the mission.

Dr. Walsh emphasized the value of researchers having access to data but noted that the regulatory environment presents challenges. Data security was built into the electronic data warehouse from the beginning to protect identities, although this was difficult because the 2,000 "companies" (faculty members) worked independently. Governance and policies were needed to address these challenges, which are similar to those faced by the Air Force and Space Force. Building this system at the university also included creating a system of support *people* to help researchers access and operate the system so as to be able to collect and analyze data—an action that contributed to the success of this transformation.

Another major initiative related to moving large quantities of data. Whereas healthcare data are largely confined geographically in hospitals and do not have to be moved long distances, Dr. Walsh remarked that other types of data, such as astronomy data, are much more difficult to move. Yet large quantities of data have to be moved around the planet in order for astronomers to compute and analyze those data. The AI stack has at its foundation computing and devices that collect data; once the data are on a computer, it is possible to do machine learning (ML) and decision support to eventually reach a level of autonomy. Academic researchers have built a network of fibers across the globe to enable this work, which will accelerate the innovation and advanced global communications of the Internet. He clarified that these are mostly private fibers used for the explicit purpose of academic research (the use of commercial fiber was too expensive). Academia drove the development of these fiber-based systems and related components because they could not do their jobs without them. Companies are primarily directing advances in computing, although research laboratories and universities are also driving new ways of computing, new devices, and new mechanisms to gather and move data.

In closing, Dr. Walsh explained that a university, with its varied faculties and laboratories, is a decentralized system that needs centralized services to operate. This situation parallels that of industry and uses a similarly consumer-centric, program-driven approach. If any part of the ecosystem (e.g., computers, algorithms, models, devices, human support) were missing, the ecosystem would not be functional.

Ms. Margaret Palmieri, Special Assistant to the Vice Chief of Naval Operations, U.S. Navy, said that the Navy's journey of digital transformation began in 2016, although the Navy warfare community has been on a mission to connect weapons sensors and shooters since 2000. She considered cultural issues to be the primary barrier to realizing this goal, as well as organizational challenges such as budgeting processes.

She explained that the Navy has four distinct communities: surface warfare, submarine warfare, aviation warfare, and information warfare. The Navy recognized the need to transition into a more multi-domain, cross-domain service, which could be enabled by digital transformation. A taskforce including representatives from across the Navy—systems commands, program offices, engineers, requirements officers, and members of the research and development community—was stood up in 2016. Recognizing this as a cross-functional problem, as opposed to one only for the requirements or acquisition community, a Digital Warfare Office (DWO) materialized, which included detailees from the engineering community. DWO aligned its efforts with the operational concept Distributed Maritime Operations. Other organizations were benchmarked and consulting literature on successful digital transformation was reviewed, revealing opportunities both to improve warfighting systems with better networking and integration and to improve readiness with better use of data. DWO thus stood up two lines of effort: (1) using data and analytics to better support decision making to increase the readiness of aircraft, ships, and submarines; and (2) creating an architecture and a data approach for warfare to connect weapons sensors and shooters. DWO used a "bimodal approach" to garner quick wins, generate buy-in, and learn through pilot projects—five readiness pilots and five warfighting pilots were created, and a blueprint for a future architecture was developed. This architecture was envisioned to be more agile than the vertically integrated, tightly coupled, single-purpose systems in existence and to allow the implementation of needed software approaches (e.g., containerization). After a few years, when decisions needed to be made about the architecture, Ms. Palmieri credited her team for their assistance, noting that the best leadership has expertise in change management and is technically savvy. She also described the Navy's creation of Project Overmatch in 2019 to address the warfare effort and its development of the Perform-to-Plan process ("Get Real, Get Better"), where data and analytics are used to identify readiness challenges.

Ms. Palmieri detailed some of the successes of the Navy's early efforts in digital transformation. She and her team were able to identify the barriers to connecting weapons sensors and shooters: culture, processes, and organization were the problem, not technology. There was also a realization that a senior-level leader who understood and was willing to remove those barriers was needed. Another success was that the transformation with structured with a mission focus: all initiatives had an associated mission outcome. In addition to developing the architecture and trying to integrate systems, the team worked toward having these systems speak the same language, which made it possible to create standard definitions for the requirements process. She emphasized that even though transformation work is highly mission focused, it also needs to be highly collaborative.

She noted that the transformation effort was initially too focused on systems engineering (i.e., trying to pursue the "perfect" architecture) and not focused enough on software. An important lesson learned was to balance the architecture for current and future systems with the agility of add-ons for immediate implementation. She added that the team was able to gain more momentum, moving from pilot to scale, when it could reduce risk by providing the needed talent to other mission leaders for their projects. A new unmanned system cross-functional team works to minimize the handoffs among requirements, acquisition, experimentation, and the fleet, aligning everyone on the same team, with a 4-star leader to help remove barriers.

In closing, Ms. Palmieri shared key takeaways for successful digital transformation: define the outcome and work backward, find cross-functional collaborative leaders with technical fluency, have consistency in goals to overcome turnover in military leadership, balance centralized approaches with more decentralized approaches, expect to be surprised during the journey, harness the talent of digital natives, make learning and risk-taking acceptable, and determine who is going to eliminate barriers and translate mission to technology. Dr. Drew emphasized how many of these lessons learned apply directly to the Air Force.

Dr. Jan Neumann, executive director of machine learning, Comcast, said that despite the differences between industry and the military, several principles and lessons learned apply. He explained that the Applied AI and Discovery Group that he leads at Comcast has a mission to "delight [its] customers by connecting them to the moments that matter." The group's approach is to eliminate intermediaries and connect directly with the customers, and it is responsible for voice control from the remote, content discovery (i.e., recommending the right show at the right time), media analytics, digital home (e.g., smart cameras, door sensors, temperature sensors), and customer experience and customer service (i.e., proactively solving billing and repair issues). Underlying all of these services are platforms for experimentation, data, and AI and ML. He emphasized that customer feedback is essential to understanding product efficacy—digital transformation makes it possible to connect directly with customers to get feedback more regularly and use automation to accelerate speed to value. He noted that it is challenging to translate complex problems into programs rapidly. However, ML can be used to create a nested feedback loop to learn faster and provide solutions more quickly. For example, natural language processing can be used to translate natural speech into words with higher accuracy than humans.

Dr. Neumann shared a use case about the digital transformation of Comcast's customer service. Comcast built AI- and ML-driven assistance for its customer service agents so that data from all agents across geographic locations could be aggregated for collective learning and for quicker problem solving. In some cases, with the use of predictive algorithms, customers will no longer need to interact with an agent at all (e.g., if a customer enters Comcast's app to troubleshoot a slowdown in an Internet connection, the interface will be adjusted based on that specific context). This makes it possible both for the customer to address the problem more quickly, and for Comcast to learn whether its predictions are accurate and if changes are needed. Comcast is also working to be more proactive: it has the ability to monitor for issues and send a repair truck before a customer is aware of a problem. These services are enabled by the Xfinity Assistant, which can be accessed via Facebook Messenger, general apps, the television, the website, or an Apple watch. If customers type a problem into the Assistant, ML algorithms are used to understand what type of problem exists and offer the best troubleshooting solution, only escalating to a human agent when needed. This reduces time and streamlines the customer experience. It also offers a way to measure outcomes and improve, with continual iteration of the models. He explained that the feedback loops are used to optimize decision making, detect anomalies, and customize entertainment based on what customers need and what is known about them: faster feedback cycles create better, more personalized customer experiences (see Figure 3.4).

Dr. Neumann described several lessons learned during Comcast's journey to improve customer experiences. It is important to focus on the fundamentals in order to make sense of the data by using the digital hierarchy of needs. First, information is logged and collected from applications. The next step is to build an infrastructure that can move and store the data. It is at this stage that issues of security, privacy, and access become critical, as the data are now ready to be explored and transformed. The next step is to provide accurate labels to ensure that the systems can learn, and then use simple ML or optimization algorithms (or, if necessary and if enabled by the data, AI and reinforcement learning) to find solutions. Another important lesson learned is the importance of creating loosely coupled yet highly aligned teams focused on *products* (not projects) that improve customer experience. It is critical to establish the right incentives as well as to develop appropriate metrics as indicators for the desired outcomes. He suggested that the best aligned incentives emerge in teams that are responsible for both costs and benefits. He emphasized the value of experimentation and using data for decision making, as well as building platforms that make it easier to test hypotheses and to iterate faster. Software and data science are creative acts with high variability, which makes estimation difficult. He advocated for less time spent planning and more time working through a priority list.

He noted that Comcast developed a Center of Excellence to establish best practices. Self-service data and compute platforms codified these best practices to make it easier for everyone to access the data and compute needed to solve their problems. Data scientists and ML researchers from the Center of Excellence

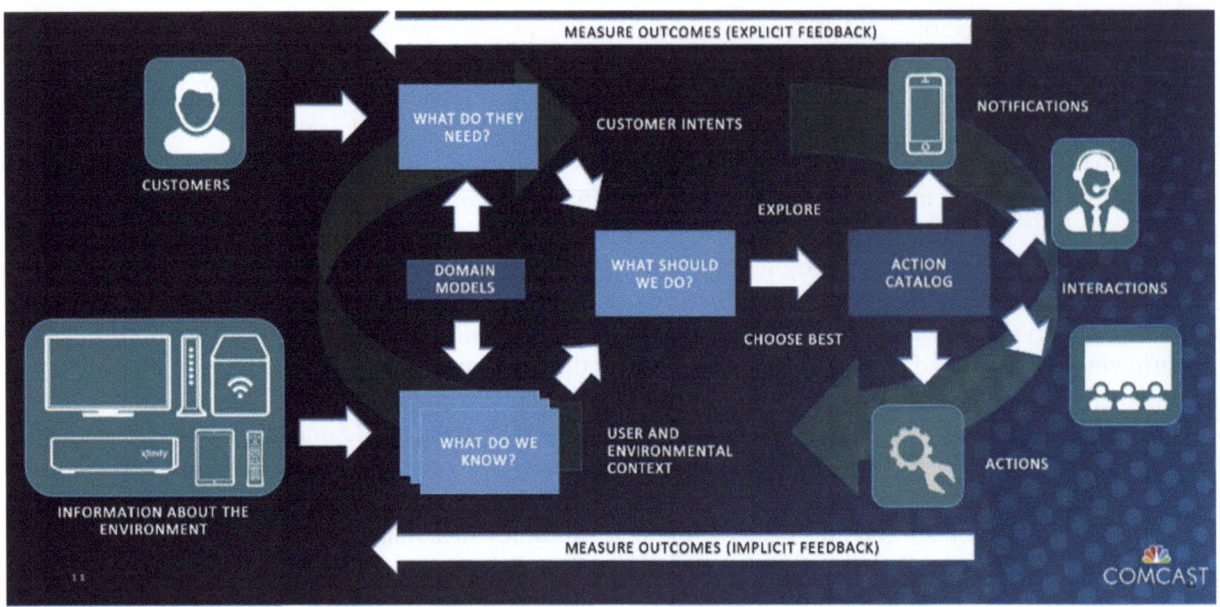

FIGURE 3.4 The Comcast feedback loop for entertainment. SOURCE: Jan Neumann, presentation to the workshop, September 8, 2021. Courtesy of Comcast Corporation.

were embedded with the product and business teams to better combine technical and domain knowledge. Change management is crucial for transformation, he continued, because new approaches can be viewed as threatening to teams. He suggested that organizations implement the ADKAR (Awareness, Desire, Knowledge, Ability, Reinforcement) model for change management. Retaining the human-in-the-loop also helps with the adoption of a transformation, with a focus on "assistance" over "automation," because the human experience is key to solving problems where data do not tell the whole story. Last, he advocated for beginning the process using the rules of existing code as baselines, setting up data pipelines and storage, and then improving upon them using ML.

Open Discussion

Dr. Drew observed several common themes throughout the presentations in this session: experimentation, change management, faster learning, and AI. She wondered which lessons learned from the development of DWO could be most valuable for the Air Force. Lt. Gen. Hamel noted that each service has a unique, long-standing organizational structure and culture. For example, the Navy has well-established warfare communities among surface, subsurface, aviation, and information operations, and the Air Force has more platform- and mission-oriented alignments with Air Combat Command, Mobility Command, and Special Operations. The Air Force tends to be organized around functions more than communities, and he hypothesized that this influences how well initiatives work in one service versus another. Gen. Holmes mentioned that the functions in the Air Force model are united in that all expect centralized control and decentralized execution through an operations center. Because a key aspect of digital modernization is recreating that command-and-control process, he suggested that the Air Force focus on unification at the command-and-control level instead of within the communities. Lt. Gen. Hamel posited that the Air Force has an advantage over some of the other services in that it has an experimentation center that crosscuts every mission area. Gen. Holmes added that while the Navy has a long tradition of tailoring individual ships, the Air Force often applies more standardization across a platform. The Navy seems to be more willing to experiment, he continued, perhaps because a ship captain has more independence than his Air Force counterpart.

Lt. Gen. Hamel asked what resources (i.e., talent and dollars) are needed to achieve the transformations described by the panelists. Ms. Palmieri replied that it depends on whether an organization's execution model is decentralized or centralized. For example, even though the Navy created DWO, the digital transformation was mandated by the Chief of Naval Operations (which is equivalent to commander's intent in the Air Force), so many individual commands stood up their own efforts with decentralized resourcing. DWO pursued a new funding line to obtain the right expertise in data analytics and network design to integrate the communities. Individual commands were also encouraged to contribute to DWO's pilots. However, gaining the support of the authorizers does not necessarily translate to increased budgets; she proposed clearly articulating what will be produced and how the funding is directly linked to achieving a specific outcome. Dr. Walsh described securing talent and money as a challenge for every organization. In academia, it is important to identify the mission, determine how a digital transformation will help achieve the mission, and communicate clearly to the administration and the board of trustees how their resources will enable the mission. Dr. Neumann added that the difficulty of securing funds correlates to the amount of money needed. Detailed business development is expected for large investments. He explained that it is crucial to calculate and identify potential payoff versus risk when seeking investment; in industry, if a company does not change, it will be left behind its competitors (e.g., Netflix, Roku).

Mr. Munson wondered about the security of Northwestern's data warehouse. Dr. Walsh responded that it is connected to the Internet, but a more secure system with fewer connections would not be as useful for researchers. The data warehouse is located behind a robust firewall, and the university stood up an organization to ensure that everyone follows the rules for access and device registration. Mr. Munson questioned the applicability of this use case to the Air Force; he expressed concern that an advanced persistent threat could breach that level of security. Dr. Walsh reiterated that the data are well protected and that there is a team working on defenses; however, he emphasized that anything electronic could always be vulnerable. Dr. Drew pointed out that when disparate data sources are brought together in any enterprise and used in unanticipated ways, unexpected capabilities emerge. Thus, classified entities may be created, which is an important security issue for the Air Force to consider.

4

Workshop Two, Part Two

OPENING REMARKS

Workshop series co-chair Lt. Gen. Michael Hamel (USAF, ret.), independent consultant, welcomed participants to the second day of the second workshop in the series. He explained that the forthcoming panel presentations would highlight the essential dynamics for transformation from an organizational standpoint. Achieving such dynamics makes it possible for transformation efforts to gain traction and for the transformation mindset to become the new normal way of conducting business.

OUT-OF-THE-BOX LEARNING: PANEL ONE

Mr. Gerald J. Caron III, Chief Information Officer, Office of the Assistant Inspector General for Information Technology, Office of the Inspector General, Department of Health and Human Services, explained that zero trust offers a different approach to cybersecurity. Although many people talk about zero trust, they may not really understand what it requires and thus may not be achieving that level of security. He added that many vendors *contribute* to zero trust, but no single vendor *does* zero trust. As a result, vendors are beginning to form partnerships to enable zero-trust architectures.

Mr. Caron compared legacy networks, most of which are architected as flat networks, to Tootsie Roll Pops, with a "hard outer shell with a soft, gooey center"—once adversaries find an opening in the perimeter security, they can leverage vulnerabilities and gain full access. Many efforts have been made to prevent such breaches, but, referencing Frederick the Great, he said that "he who defends everything defends nothing." He asserted that trying to protect all systems, applications, and data equally leads to a situation in which some are overprotected, others are underprotected, and overall network functionality is constrained. Instead, the optimal approach to cybersecurity is to determine where protections are needed based on the sensitivity and associated risk of individual components. Because zero trust assumes that all users and devices pose a threat, it protects against both outsider and insider threats, if done correctly.

Mr. Caron emphasized that zero trust revolves around the need to protect data. He shared the five core principles of zero trust: (1) know the users and devices, (2) design systems assuming that they are all compromised, (3) use dynamic access controls, (4) constantly evaluate risk, and (5) invest in defenses based on the classification levels of the data. He underscored that zero trust is not a tool; it is an architecture. In order to protect data, it is critical to understand what and where they are. Data need to be properly categorized in terms of threat vectors and the related level of risk based on sensitivity (i.e., not all data are equally important). It is also critical to know where the data are going and how they are being accessed. Because some system owners do not understand their data flows (i.e., how data are moving from Point A to Point B), he suggested creating a baseline that highlights what is normal, and, even more importantly, when activity is abnormal and action needs to be taken.

Network segmentation, with its use of firewalls and perimeters to group like applications together, is a common approach to security; however, zero trust is a much more granular approach to segmentation in which *applications and databases* may be segmented (i.e., microsegmentation of data). He explained that the groupings are based on function, not physical location, and protections are tailored to the data's sensitivity and mission criticality. Many other factors are critical for zero trust, such as different levels of risk related to identity (e.g., an on-site, cleared government employee has less risk than a vendor partner with a lower-level clearance). Zero trust considers the user's role and location, the state of the device, and the type of data or services being accessed. He stressed that seeking security compliance is insufficient: security *effectiveness* is key.

Mr. Caron noted that zero trust also offers dynamic access control. Instead of providing authentication only once at the start of a user's session, zero-trust authentication is ongoing and allows only the right access to the right data at the right time by authenticating each time new data are accessed and each time a change in risk is triggered (see Figure 4.1). To better describe dynamic access control, he provided an analogy to a movie theater experience: instead of scanning a ticket in the lobby and allowing patrons to enter as many individual movie screenings as desired, the ticket would be scanned directly at the entrance to each movie screening, and ushers would check tickets again inside so that people only view the one movie for which they paid.

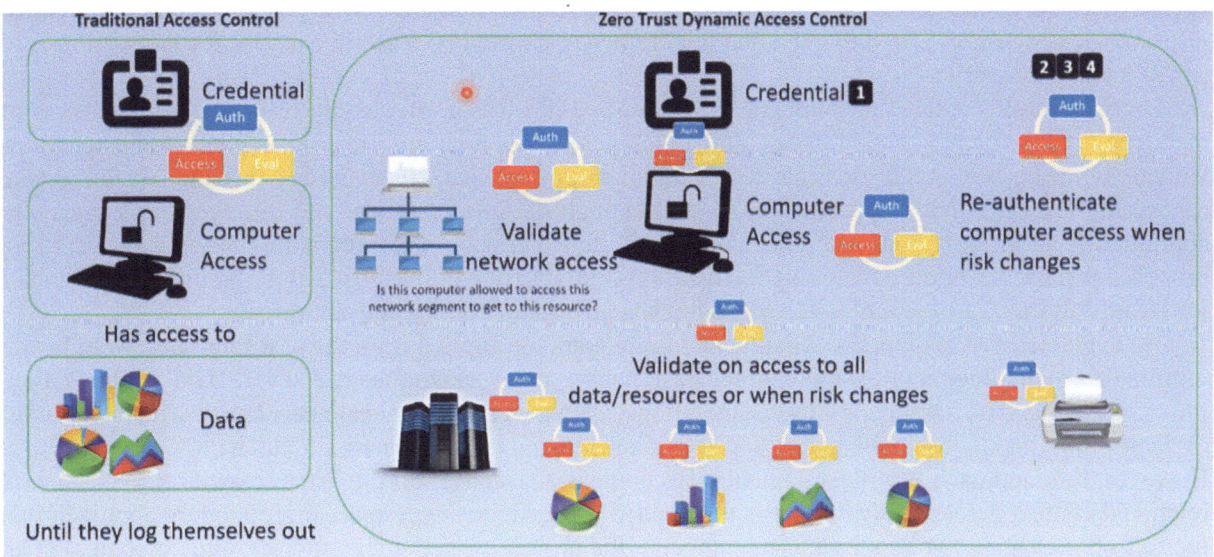

FIGURE 4.1 Dynamic access control in a zero-trust architecture. SOURCE: Gerald Caron, presentation to the workshop, September 9, 2021.

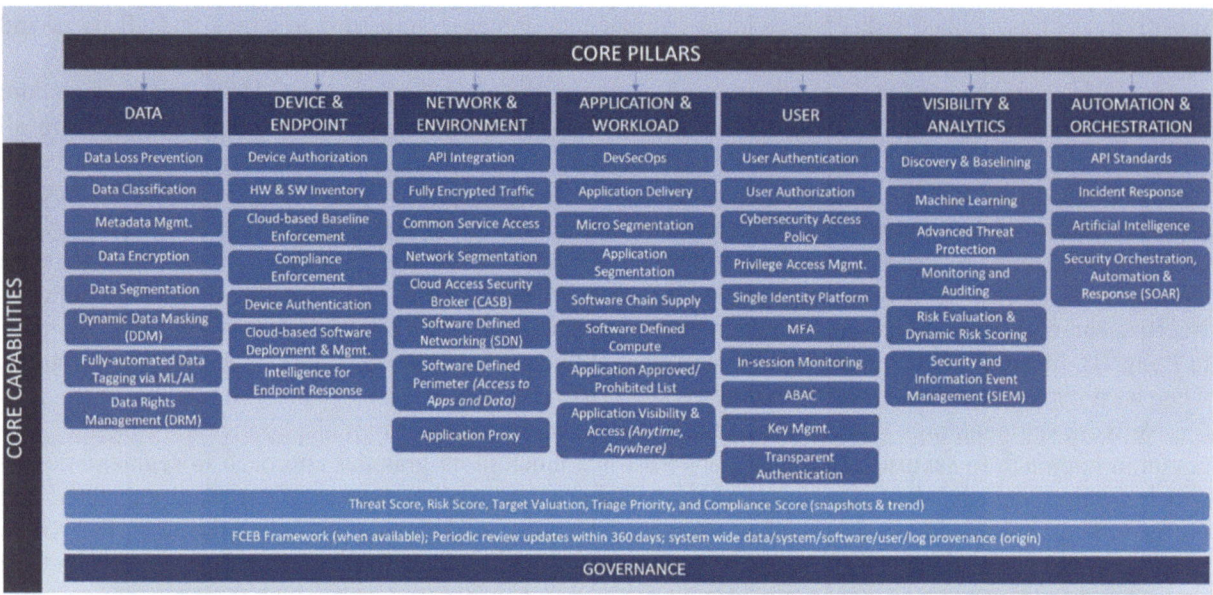

FIGURE 4.2 Zero-trust capabilities model. SOURCE: Gerald Caron, presentation to the workshop, September 9, 2021.

Zero trust also assesses the state of each device attempting to access the network to ensure that the client does not introduce additional risk to the environment. Continuous monitoring is a key aspect of zero trust; real-time data collected during this monitoring can be linked with known threats and data/system sensitivity to drive cyber protections. Mr. Caron highlighted the most significant advantage with zero trust: it is an integration effort (as opposed to the stovepiped approach of the past) that connects factors to determine a dynamic risk score (based on risk tolerance and the methodology to classify the data that need to be protected) and determine appropriate protective action. In closing, he shared a zero-trust capabilities framework, which helps to conduct an inventory of all capabilities and illuminates where gaps exist (see Figure 4.2). Workshop Two chair Dr. Pamela Drew, former executive vice president and president of information systems, Exelis, remarked that this framework would be a useful exercise for the Air Force to assess its data infrastructure.

Dr. Christopher Chute, Bloomberg Distinguished Professor of Health Informatics; professor of medicine, public health, and nursing; and chief health research information officer, Johns Hopkins University, discussed digital medical records and data governance. He suggested that the Air Force take advantage of digitization's opportunities to enable analysis, interpretation, and discovery as a means to continuously improve the infrastructure, processes, and methods of its operations moving forward. He proposed that the Air Force develop an organization similar to that of the Office of the National Coordinator for Health Information Technology to facilitate data governance across the enterprise.

He explained that lessons about data governance could be applied from the past four decades of health information technology. For example, in the past, healthcare organizations had severe data fragmentation, few standards, and no interoperability specifications. Data governance in healthcare began with the creation of large entity relationship diagrams for relational structures to normalize data within an enterprise. However, this approach was unsustainable. He emphasized that a large master schema of all data in a relational context across the Air Force is not needed. Instead, he suggested a more modern approach that focuses on managing the important elements (e.g., the processes, activities, statuses, and outcomes) in an object framework.

Dr. Chute articulated that healthcare data are expected to be FAIR: findable, accessible, interoperable, and reusable. Interoperable data are comparable (to draw conclusions) and consistent (i.e., people throughout the organization use the same processes). He emphasized that interoperable objects require a dynamic infrastructure that will continuously improve and add new dimensions and components. The comparability and consistency allow for a "graceful evolution" of these objects, which can be related to other objects for inference and analysis.

He described two dimensions of having governance around an object or element: (1) syntactic (i.e., how to structure objects and elements, and having significant associated metadata to interpret and make sense of them) and (2) semantic (a formalized and reproducible way of managing vocabulary, names, tags, and identifiers so that they can be reconciled). Healthcare organizations seek to identify "off-the-shelf" ontological frameworks and schema, which increases interpretability across the broader healthcare community. However, not knowing fully what kind of data the Air Force has to organize and integrate, he was unsure whether it would practical for the Air Force to consider externalized standard resources. He emphasized that however the approach is structured in the Air Force, a *coordinated, centralized* data governance activity with decision-making authority is essential.

Dr. Chute explained that once (1) there is a catalogue of elements, functions, activities, outcomes, and statuses that are relevant to the Air Force enterprise; (2) a syntactic structure has been defined for each object; and (3) the elements of those syntactic layers have been populated with significant data types that are reproducible, the next step is to consider how the objects are connected (i.e., graph relationships, semantic relationships). If left ungoverned, however, this process can consume an entire organization with diminishing returns. Thus, he said that part of the data governance process is making rational decisions about the level of granularity needed to prioritize activities. He described the "sweet spot" as identifying enough data governance to enable the enterprise to sustain, manage, and scale the desired level of inquiry and discovery—enterprise-level digitization cannot happen with any efficiency without careful attention to data governance.

Mr. Michael Pack, founder and director of the Center for Advanced Transportation Technology Laboratory (CATT Lab), University of Maryland, discussed lessons learned while working with public safety and transportation officials to digitize and make sense of their data. Founded in 2002, the CATT Lab is comprised of more than 75 data scientists, software developers, designers, program managers, and IT and network engineers, as well as students and affiliated researchers, who build and deploy data analytics tools to manage, integrate, and archive these large data sets.

Mr. Pack explained that the transportation industry has many disparate systems; each department has deployed their own data sets and data collection technologies for their own individual use cases (e.g., travelers might see a light pole with several different sensors from several different agencies all collecting the exact same information). In addition to traffic data, there are weather data from ground-based weather stations, computer dispatch data from first responders, crowdsourced data from Waze usage, data from media reports, data from maintenance vehicles, data from traffic cameras, and data from cell phones. Yet, he emphasized that no one has a complete picture of what is occurring on the roadways, and there is a lack of situational awareness. Furthermore, data collected by individual departments for specific purposes are often used only in real time and then discarded instead of being archived for later use in planning decisions and after-action review. To eliminate this waste, the CATT Lab was asked to fuse these data to make them more readily accessible and usable by all of the different departments of transportation. Doing so would cut down on digital waste and excess spending. He underscored that data are only worth archiving if they are easily understandable for, usable by, and accessible to managers, decision makers, users, and applications. Because most users are not data experts or computer scientists, the CATT Lab builds compelling visual analytics tools (i.e., user interfaces) that simplify data access and increase buy-in for data sharing.

The CATT Lab has now built more than 50 data analytics platforms used by ~14,000 people in the United States. Mr. Pack provided an overview of a multi-agency common operational view of the roadways, which was created by fusing disparate data. This system is operational nationwide, with billions of data points and measurements collected in real time that are archived indefinitely. For example, when a crash occurs, it is possible to collect data on the locations of the first responders, on the number of lanes blocked, and from radio systems in the area. There are also videos being captured of the scene from the ground (e.g., dashcams) and from the sky. Cellular telephones and connected vehicles also provide a substantial amount of data to the CATT Lab's efforts (e.g., people using weather apps or map apps on their phones are contributing to the data samples). He emphasized that the data being collected from vehicles (e.g., using indications of traction control engagement to understand a situation on the roadway) are privacy-protected in certain ways. There are also tens of thousands of streaming closed-circuit television cameras on the ground, in police cars and maintenance vehicles, in the sky, and in bus stations that are collecting data. With the help of image and video processing capabilities, it is possible to predict where vehicles are going as they are tracked from one camera to the next.

Most of the CATT Lab's analytics are after-action review analytics or planning analytics to help people determine what to invest in or where to move assets to respond to a specific incident. In closing, Mr. Pack described several challenges the CATT Lab has faced with its data analytics tools:

- *Scalability.* With a limited budget, it is critical to optimize and try to predict user requests, so as to have data precomputed to lead to solutions more quickly.
- *Normalization.* Although there might be hundreds of sensors collecting information at different time intervals, all of the data ultimately have to look somewhat similar for the user to be able to use them to answer a question.
- *Ever-changing data landscape* with new technology and new sensors.
- *Private sector competition with the public sector.* The CATT Lab has to be aware of private sector data sets and be able to fuse them with public sector data sets. Issues with acceptable data use terms and conditions can arise during this fusion.
- Protection of people's privacy.
- *Ease of access and usability* with the development of compelling user interfaces.
- *Creation of buy-in* by convincing agencies to share data, with analytics that answered a question posed by someone of a senior level in the agency.
- Sustainable funding strategies.

Open Discussion

Dr. Drew observed that despite its challenges, the CATT Lab has successfully gathered, normalized, and scaled data. She asked about the framework used to integrate each data set and to build analytics. Mr. Pack said that when the CATT Lab first started to develop analytics tools, it built a common schema and expected agencies to provide their data in that format. Because no agency had the funding to convert their data, that approach was ineffective. Now, the CATT Lab accepts data in whatever format or transmission method the agencies choose, and an internal team is dedicated to the standardization and fusion of those data. Multiple review processes with the agencies ensure that data are mapped and fused appropriately, and an art and usability team is dedicated to continuous iteration and testing of the user interface. He emphasized that it takes a significant amount of time to normalize data (e.g., it could take several months to ingest one data set). Dr. Drew described this as a positive example of the centralized data governance concept championed by Dr. Chute.

Reflecting on the CATT Lab's indefinite date retention policy, Dr. Julie Ryan, chief executive officer, Wyndrose Technical Group, asked how it manages both the volume of data over time and the challenges of media degradation and technology migration. Mr. Pack noted that this data retention policy emerged because it was more costly to reintegrate data than to store them indefinitely. Technology migration, however, is expensive and can inhibit growth; it is difficult to keep pace with the changing technology and the need to convert systems. In response to a question from Dr. Drew about the size of the CATT Lab's data set, Mr. Pack replied that it is many, many petabytes, and growing daily. He added that Amazon Web Services is only used for backups; the CATT Lab found it more cost effective to build its own private cloud to host these data. Gen. James (Mike) Holmes (USAF, ret.), senior advisor, The Roosevelt Group, asked about the CATT Lab's processes for cleaning and presenting data. Mr. Pack explained that some of the data (e.g., incident data) cannot be cleaned; if the CATT Lab over-cleanses certain data sets, it obfuscates the truth of the data and could cause problems for the users. Therefore, the CATT Lab provides a visual overview of the entire data set, with the ability to zoom, filter, and view details on demand. Cleansing tools such as filters can be applied to user interfaces, however, to eliminate data that are likely suspect. When multiple data sets describe the same event in a different way, he continued, fusion becomes significantly more challenging. Dr. Marv Langston (USN, ret.), independent consultant, pointed out that Alabama has put all of the state's data on Google Maps ("Virtual Alabama"), and he asked Mr. Pack about using a similar approach to make data available. Mr. Pack responded that the CATT Lab has some secure data that cannot be made publicly available. He emphasized that the CATT Lab's system is a true fusion and analytics platform (as opposed to an open data.gov system) that helps people to address difficult problems.

Lt. Gen. Hamel inquired about the current status of zero-trust frameworks within the Department of Defense (DoD) and other large government agencies. Mr. Caron said that although he has yet to see a full implementation of zero trust, many of the agencies are pursuing that path. He suggested that agencies begin by developing a "playbook" to determine all of the key players and resources. He added that President Biden's May 2021 Executive Order on Improving the Nation's Cybersecurity emphasized zero trust, and all agencies in the Executive branch were required to submit their plans for zero trust within 60 days of the executive order. The Air Force in particular has taken a step toward zero trust at the enterprise level. He mentioned that the National Institute of Standards and Technology's National Cybersecurity Center of Excellence is developing a proof of concept for zero trust. He reiterated that because zero trust is a new way of thinking, it requires a culture change. Dr. Drew asked if any agencies have prioritized their most important assets in need of protection. Mr. Caron acknowledged that while progress is being made, this as an ongoing challenge, particularly when assets are miscategorized owing to a lack of information. Because it is usually the IT staff who are focused on zero trust, it is often viewed as a "technical" issue. However, the technology is the easy part; the integration, policy changes, identification of risk tolerances, baseline creation, and inventory of owned assets are difficult. To be effective (instead of merely compliant) in cybersecurity, he continued, these non-technical elements have to be prioritized.

Gen. Holmes asked how encryption and other advanced technologies relate to risk mitigation. Mr. Caron advocated for advanced encryption but noted that adversaries are leveraging the same technologies (e.g., quantum computing) as the United States—and the U.S. government is behind the competition. He explained that if security is so restrictive that it reduces performance, people will find ways to work around it. Instead, government agencies need to adopt an approach that is simultaneously sustainable, secure, and supportive of the mission.

Dr. Langston wondered how data governance forces a data schema across an organization as large as DoD and whether the medical field has a common schema. Dr. Chute noted that for many years, the healthcare industry did not have a centralized structure or coordination across its organizations. After the Office of the National Coordinator (ONC) was stood up in 2004, incremental details of information would be requested to be comparable and consistent across organizations. It was not until 2020 that the 21st Century Cures Act required electronic health record vendors and other organizations to conform with ONC specifications (i.e., common ways to exchange medications, laboratory results, and diagnoses). Each year, the ONC publishes an updated U.S. Core Data for Interoperability. He emphasized that common schema are enabling national-level data aggregation and integration in healthcare. He recognized that the process takes time but added that there are precedents in this and other large-scale industries that prove it is evolving. He suggested that the Air Force could begin with an ontological characterization of "things that fly," for example, and then delve into specific models. Each has metadata that are updated in near real time (e.g., flightworthiness, repair status), and dashboards could be used to make inferences about range of force projection, for instance. The goal is to begin with relatively discrete, achievable, feasible characterizations; create buy-in across the community on those assets and elements; and demonstrate the resulting value to the community. Confirming the feasibility of this approach for the Air Force, Dr. Drew shared an anecdote about when Boeing bought McDonnell Douglas, part of Hughes, and part of Rockwell International Corporation. Each of those companies had its own technical library and librarians who had created indices of reference documents. Those indices were used to create knowledge bases and a searchable ontology that became the core of the search engine, which became a unifying force for all four companies.

Dr. Annie Green, data governance specialist, George Mason University, added that data governance and common schema are effective, but the latter is usually at the application level (i.e., defining databases). The next step is to create data catalogues that include data lineage. She noted that many people have not adopted common schema because they want to move quickly, which is not possible at the enterprise level. Lt. Gen. Hamel asked how these processes became self-reinforcing in the healthcare industry. Dr. Chute explained that before regulatory mandates were implemented, "carrots and sticks" (i.e., rewards and penalties) were used to incentivize conformance to ONC standards. He envisioned that Air Force contractors could have their devices and resources generate and transmit metadata in a way that is conformant and relevant to the Air Force's needs for near-real-time situational awareness. He acknowledged that providing this level of electronic accessibility to enable inference could create serious new security vulnerabilities. Lt. Gen. Hamel observed that the mandates for protection of private health records have led to significant security measures. Dr. Chute commented that encryption and multiple-authentication for access are standard practices; cybersecurity is foremost in the mind of the chief information officer of any healthcare organization, which was not the case 25 years ago. He described this as a "co-existing cultural evolution" of the importance of security and the availability of the data. An unanticipated benefit is that the research community's ability to draw inferences about the healthcare system has advanced, owing to the availability and integration of these data sets across organizations. Dr. Drew clarified that having a common data schema does not necessarily mean that only one system exists or that everything will be protected in the same way. Data can be segmented and prioritized, and the security posture can be tailored to priorities and risk management.

Lt. Gen. Hamel wondered which users should be involved in creating data definitions and whether they need to map to communities of practice across the enterprise. Dr. Chute replied that this should be a team effort. Because "the experts" may not know how to *communicate* content, both domain experts and knowledge engineers are integral. He noted that unless senior leaders are trained to think in information-enabling terms, the potential and the opportunities of data for decision making might not be obvious. Once these opportunities are presented, the benefits are clear. He asserted that with top-level leadership understanding that knowledge and data are primary assets that could be coordinated, the organization could become more successful and efficient.

Dr. Langston asked about the role of blockchain systems in supporting the movement of healthcare data. Dr. Chute responded that blockchain is computationally intense and might not be practical for medical data; but that may not be the case for military data. Lt. Gen. Ted Bowlds (USAF, ret.), chief executive officer, IAI North America, asked about authoritative data sources. Dr. Chute noted that healthcare tends to be a more federated environment, and the ONC is responsible for standards and specifications. Patient management is a localized decision, he continued, which is very different from the centralized approach of the military. Mr. Alden Munson, senior fellow and member, Board of Regents, Potomac Institute for Policy Studies, added that there is a basis to allow consolidation of data from various sources for a position report, for example, even though some are of much higher quality than others. Lt. Gen. Bowlds underscored that there has to be a way to identify ground truth when data are coming from multiple locations or sources.

Mr. Munson pointed out that if the Air Force achieves its vision, it will become a more attractive cyber target—a security construct that is included in the architecture at a fundamental level and is matched to that challenge is needed. While he expressed his support for use cases, he emphasized the need for an underlying holistic architecture process, because the pilot programs have to be compatible with the evolving architectural vision.

OUT-OF-THE-BOX LEARNING: PANEL TWO

Mr. Chris Lynch, chief executive officer, Rebellion Defense, and former head of Defense Digital Services (DDS), observed a need to reshape the overall focus for defense and national security, including reconsideration of who serves as trusted advisors, builders, and creators. He described the cautionary tale of Healthcare.gov, which cost $1 billion yet only allowed six people to create accounts on its launch day. He expressed his frustration with the government spending so much on something that initially garnered so little value—a direct contrast to the progress in the software industry.

When the White House created the U.S. Digital Service, Mr. Lynch worked on medical record transfers from DoD to the Department of Veterans Affairs to ensure the best care for veterans. A simple file format conversion problem could result in the death of a veteran, a problem that was solved in 1 week by his team of software engineers who created file format converters. Motivated by this experience, he launched DDS, which recruited software engineering experts to address problems for which technology was failing a mission. This team worked on a ground-control system for the global positioning system; although hundreds of millions of dollars had been spent on this system, it was operating at a level comparable to that of 20 years prior. Because the ground-control system had 21 components, it took 3 months to test it. To address this problem, the team used DevOps to automate the process, reducing the testing time to less than 1 hour. The team addressed similar issues with the Joint Strike Fighter and its flight control system. During both projects, the team worked to secure the military's software (e.g., through challenge programs such as "Hack the Pentagon") using approaches that were standard in commercial software companies.

Mr. Lynch aimed to convince DoD senior leadership of the value of hiring technical people (with recent and relevant experience) in positions of authority to make decisions on technical problems. He emphasized that the world is entering an era with nearly unlimited compute and unlimited storage; software is going to transform the defense mission by creating competitive advantage as the industrial manufacturing era ends and the software superiority era emerges. The military currently solves problems with human capital; however, he asserted that because the scale of the global threat environment and the great power competition is too great for human beings, it is critical to leverage new technology to enable software superiority. Modern software will allow the military to see, decide, and act first at a scale greater than that of any one individual.

He explained that Rebellion Defense was created ~2 years ago with a vision for software superiority and a goal to enable better and faster decision making in a world in which the platforms, domains, Combatant Commands, and services have all been connected or collapsed. Rebellion Defense relies on unlimited compute and storage and uses artificial intelligence (AI) and data to lead to decision advantage (i.e., machines and humans each work to their respective strengths) in the era of great power competition. He shared several lessons learned from his experience in the commercial sector:

- *Awareness that different types of technology companies have different roles and attract different types of talent.* Hardware and industrial manufacturing companies build things, such as jets; services companies have conversations with the customer about what to build and follow through on making sure that it is built; and software companies build products.
- *Value of a connected ecosystem.* DoD would benefit from thinking about connections in terms of application programming interfaces (APIs), which make it possible to "rip and replace" other products when capabilities are introduced that better meet customer needs.
- *Need for continuous deployment of new models.* Most of the advantages of AI and machine learning (ML), computer vision, and joint all-domain command and control (JADC2) will only be realized by embracing the ability to continuously deploy new capabilities quickly and cheaply into the warfighting environments.
- *Value of leveraging the right resources.* Defense is a world-scale business that requires resources that far exceed the DoD research and development budget. It will not be possible to attract commercial software companies into defense if DoD infrastructure and technology is orthogonal to what they are already building—they have used commercial cloud for more than 20 years at scale, have billions of users, and process data at volumes that far exceed most missions within DoD.

In closing, Mr. Lynch advocated for creating disruption among processes that are fundamentally broken and doing them better, faster, cheaper, with more trust, and at scale. Despite the fact that DoD partners with many top tier universities, graduates choose jobs in other sectors because they fear that the government bureaucracy is untenable. He said that the government has to present opportunities to do incredible, forward-leaning work in support of the nation in order to hire the right people.

Col. David (Matthew) Neuenswander (USAF, ret.), Chief of Joint Integration, The Curtis E. LeMay Center for Doctrine Development and Education, explained that the Defense Information Systems Agency is responsible for U.S. Message Text Format (USMTF). Approximately 330 USMTF messages define air space coordination measures, fire support coordination measures, and defense coordination measures, and they identify the areas where business is conducted as machines communicate and attempt to exchange messages. The Theater Battle Management Core System (TBMCS), the Air Force's largest command and control system, wrote the air tasking order, air space control order, and air space control plan, and communicated with all of the other joint systems (e.g., the Army Tactical Air Integration System and the Air Defense System Integrator) using USMTF. In 2004, he continued, the Air Force replaced TBMCS with another system that ultimately did not work. In the interim, the funding stream for USMTF that was in TBMCS at the 2004 level was frozen. Since that time, the doctrine community created new doctrine and put it in USMTF; while the doctrine version is up to 2020 and there have been substantial changes to USMTF, none of those changes are in the machines. So, an important question emerged: Is the doctrine what is in the machines, or is doctrine what is written on paper?

Col. Neuenswander provided an example of a significant airgap that was recently revealed. The 2004 version of USMTF uses "restricted operation zone" ("ROZ"). However, "ROZ" is not in the 2004 version of TBMCS; only "ROA" (for "restricted operation area") is included. Thus, while ROA is found in TBMCS, only ROZ appears in the doctrine. Although a human could understand and navigate this mismatch in terms, a machine could not. He noted that first step to address this problem was to determine what command and control systems exist and what version of USMTF each is using. It became apparent that some of the air operations centers are still using the 2000 version because some of the allies did not want to update their machines to the 2004 version. The use of different languages to communicate with machines across the world creates significant issues for JADC2. He asserted that everyone should adopt the same format, but that requires first determining what formats are still in use. He anticipated that funding will be restored so that TBMCS can be updated.

Dr. Drew asked how likely it is that everyone would conform to the same format and, if not, how to solve the problem. Col. Neuenswander pointed out that there is already a standard directed by the Joint Chiefs of Staff, although not everyone is part of it. He added that in 2019, doctrine was demoted to "advice," which could be one of the reasons people use different systems. However, he underscored that if people want machines to take over certain tasks, it is imperative that everyone use the same language format. He hypothesized that the Chinese likely all use the same system and emphasized that this is a real problem for the United States; someone needs to take ownership and provide authoritative direction because it is crucial to update so as to have the capacity for all systems to communicate.

Dr. Cara LaPointe, co-director of the Johns Hopkins Institute for Assured Autonomy, described the role of autonomous systems in digital transformation. Echoing Mr. Lynch's perspective, Dr. LaPointe said that the national security enterprise is entering a software era, and autonomy and AI will be key to success. She emphasized that a level of trust has to be developed, as people who do not trust autonomy will not use it. The first step is to understand the ways in which AI and autonomy could transform an organization's ability to accomplish its missions by identifying the problems that need to be solved and how to approach solving them differently by leveraging these technologies.

She defined autonomy as anything AI-enabled that begins to interact without human intervention (e.g., cyber physical systems, decision algorithms). Autonomy is increasingly entering every realm of society. The first wave of AI included handcrafted knowledge and human-built models based on expert systems. In the past two decades, the technology progressed to machine learning, and now the focus is on contextual reasoning. Getting autonomous and AI-enabled systems to work safely, securely, and robustly is challenging, especially given that these technologies are expected to integrate into an entire ecosystem. She stressed that policy and other governance mechanisms are equally important, as is understanding the complex strategic feedback loops among all of these areas.

Dr. LaPointe highlighted several questions related to the unsolved challenges of autonomous systems:

- How do we ensure that autonomous systems will operate safely in an unconstrained world? How do we do more test and evaluation?
- How do we create better design tools to build more reliable autonomous systems?
- Do all autonomous systems need to be explainable?
- If accidents happen, how do we know what went wrong, and how are these systems auditable?
- How do we prevent systems from learning bad behaviors in data sets?
- How do we manage autonomous systems in a crowded dynamic ecosystem, especially in environments where people and autonomous systems are operating side-by-side?
- How do we monitor autonomous systems to ensure that they are operating as intended, while recognizing that it is impossible to eliminate all risk?
- How do we proactively create effective policy? It is important to understand both the policies for the actual use of the systems and the policies involved in the creation ecosystem in order to realize the full benefits of autonomy and provide "guardrails" against potential negative impacts of the technology.
- How could the technologies be attacked (e.g., via manipulating inputs to algorithms)?

She emphasized that building a holistic framework of assured autonomy is critical to achieving safe and reliable operations that are (1) secure and resilient to attack, (2) predictively and seamlessly integrated into complex human ecosystems, and (3) beneficial (e.g., saving money and time) and ethical. She said that many tools need to be created to fully realize the benefits of autonomy (see Figure 4.3), and challenges remain to collect and fuse underlying data.

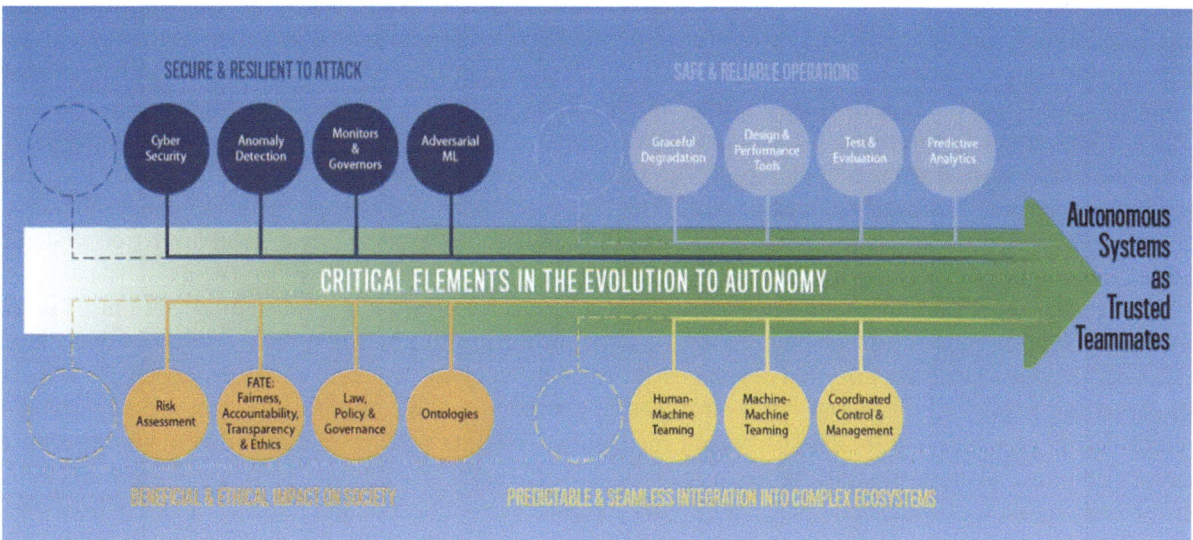

FIGURE 4.3 Building the tools of assurance. SOURCE: Cara LaPointe, presentation to the workshop, September 9, 2021. © 2021 The Johns Hopkins University Applied Physics Laboratory LLC. All Rights Reserved.

In closing, Dr. LaPointe shared several lessons learned and success strategies. Most importantly, digital transformation is a human challenge that will not be solved in isolation by technologists. Robust communication, cooperation, and feedback mechanisms are needed across organizational siloes (i.e., operators, users, and technologists). Contractors also have to be brought into the conversation to enable streamlined acquisition. Change is difficult, and cultural impediments are real, she continued. In DoD, the main challenge is that often no one "owns" the whole transformation process. Leaders who understand both the mission and the technology are critical, as is a human-centered approach that is inclusive of all stakeholders. She asserted that change management is essential to overcome cultural impediments. Technology is rarely the barrier in moving from proof-of-concept to solutions at scale—it is the enablers, assurance, and transformation of the entire "DOTMLPF-P" (doctrine, organization, training, materiel, leadership, personnel, facilities, and policy) ecosystem. She emphasized that government acquisition processes underestimate the sustainment needs of digital technologies and suggested adequate resourcing for digital sustainment and preparation to make trade-offs among priorities.

Dr. Langston asked if explainable AI can be used to mitigate any of the aforementioned challenges. Dr. LaPointe replied that the ultimate goal is to make the technology trustworthy and trusted; explainable AI is one approach, but it is not sufficient on its own.

Mr. Randall Hunt, director of developer relations, Vendia, described an evolution in business logic over the past 15 to 20 years from monolith, to microservices, to functions-as-a-service and ephemeral compute. A monolithic application is essentially one large code base that is expensive, and difficult to create and run. These applications are powered by monolithic databases that have complex entity relationship diagrams, which become even more complex when trying to add and share data with partners, vendors, customers, or users. He explained that managing these relationships is a full-time job, and the entity relationship models become tribal knowledge—understanding and contributing to these models requires a significant investment of time. Although schema-less data stores have made improvements, they have not solved this problem.

Approximately 20 years ago, Mr. Hunt continued, monoliths began to split into service-oriented architectures. For example, rather than residing within the existing monolithic layer, an authentication layer would live on its own server and communication would occur over XML and other early protocols that were parseable by machines. This allowed for individual services to be scaled and then abstracted, and it improved the pace of iteration for individual teams. Approximately 10 years ago, microservices became the primary method by which teams were building applications.

Mr. Hunt noted that because the same code was being written 100 times to do functionally the same thing, the focus shifted from the servers to the business-based, product-based logic between all of the foundational bricks. And because most were not running continuously, it was possible to invoke functions, leading to the use of functions-as-a-service. Functions-as-a-service models power telephone tree systems and text messaging, for example.

He defined DoD as a unique "business" that has a global platform and a substantial amount of work proceeding in thousands of different directions. As networking and compute continue to improve over time, DoD will need an infrastructure that leverages those improvements as soon as they happen. This core infrastructure, however, is already built—it exists in the commercial, private, and secured government sectors. He emphasized that there is no reason for DoD to reiterate or expand that infrastructure, because vendors continue to innovate and improve regardless of defense investment. Software is becoming the "differentiating factor" because it has the ability to make strides well beyond the fixed advances of hardware (e.g., changing one line of code can increase performance by 100,000) for minimal investment. He suggested that organizations like DoD focus on the logic and the software of their product instead of the logic and the operational infrastructure of their compute backends. People often dedicate too much time to building large operations teams; managing cloud resources; sharing; continuous integration/continuous delivery; and authorizing, complying, and auditing but not enough time on the data model—understanding the data model and how to create something from it drives improvement. With its focus on business logic, Vendia provides a GraphQL API when customers submit a data model, which allows customers to iterate quickly. In closing, Mr. Hunt underscored that any organization investing in or building a monolith in 2021 is making a mistake. The next generation of businesses will be those who take advantage of their data quickly and effectively to make decisions, move forward, and iterate.

Dr. Drew championed Mr. Hunt's advice to DoD to avoid investing time, energy, and resources in the creation of infrastructure that is already available, because doing so does not add value to the business or the mission. Dr. Langston asked about the differences between developing functions-as-a-service and developing microservices and containers. Mr. Hunt explained that each functions-as-a-service platform has advantages and disadvantages, but the primary benefit is that a single developer can focus on a single function and reason over a set of functions. To take advantage of functions-as-a-service, he continued, one should separate the area of interest and the data layer. When building with containers, there is concern about compute and memory usage given the individual number of containers that are deployed on a server; with functions-as-a-service, the only concern is roundtrip network latency. A case in which a container would be a better choice than functions, however, would be a live speech transcription. Dr. Drew inquired about the largest enterprise that has used functions-as-a-service as a substrate for its product development and whether this approach is being used in DoD. Mr. Hunt replied that a substantial portion of Amazon runs on functions-as-a-service, as does the Financial Regulatory Authority, for example. Several large organizations have built entire platforms on top of functions-as-a-service, and their business models have pivoted: they have become more resource effective and can iterate more quickly on smaller pieces of the application. There are a few functions-as-a-service deployments in the government sector more broadly. In response to a participant's question about blockchain, Mr. Hunt noted that much of the public chain is slow. He advised against DoD's investing significantly in any public chain, because it is unlikely to solve the specific problems in need of solutions. However, the concept of a ledger data store could be powerful.

WORKSHOP TWO CLOSING REMARKS

Gen. Holmes referenced an article[1] that considers the U.S. military's intent to connect every sensor and shooter to be the wrong approach. Because China dedicates resources to counter each U.S. effort (e.g., communications paths, electronic warfare systems), it is important for the Air Force to build systems that are resilient to attack as well as to be prepared to continue the fight when those systems fail.

In light of the Air Force's plans for digital transformation, Col. Scott McKeever, director, Chief of Staff of the Air Force Strategic Studies Group (SSG), mentioned a case study[2] about the challenges of the recent evacuation operations in Afghanistan. He said that the Air Force is a global organization with many components and many chiefs—achieving unity of effort is essential but is proving difficult. He noted that the first two workshops in the series have provided several useful paths forward for the Air Force—for example, via investments in people, processes, and technologies at scale.

Col. Douglas DeMaio, 187th Fighter Wing Commander, Alabama Air National Guard, provided an overview of the planned agenda for the final workshop of the series, and Lt. Gen. Hamel invited planning committee members and workshop participants to share their observations from the first two workshops of the series. Dr. Green said that with the exception of a few small integration case studies, too many stovepipes remain in the Air Force: the large-scale integration needed to move from data to decisions is missing. She noted that Mr. Caron's model of zero trust is a good first step, but it only addresses the security aspect of data (i.e., how to protect them), not necessarily the distribution aspect of data. She also observed that although presenters discussed "structure" and "taxonomy," there was no discussion of "knowledge." She explained that algorithms have to reference knowledge, which is actionable for decision making. She emphasized that AI and knowledge go hand in hand: intelligence creates information, and information

---

[1] C. Dougherty, 2021, "Confronting Chaos: A New Concept for Information Advantage," War on the Rocks, https://warontherocks.com/2021/09/confronting-chaos-a-new-concept-for-information-advantage/.

[2] A. Eversden, 2021, "Lack of Access to Data During Afghanistan Exit Shines Light on Tech Gap," C4ISRNet, https://www.c4isrnet.com/battlefield-tech/it-networks/2021/09/08/lack-of-access-to-data-during-afghanistan-exit-shines-light-on-tech-gap/.

creates data. In addition to these data challenges, Lt. Gen. Hamel noted that figuring out how best to *use* available technology and create the organizational constructs and governance to do so remains difficult. Dr. Green described this as an issue of the connection between the vision and the mission: the Department of the Air Force (DAF) has to determine what it wants to achieve and improve before creating a strategy.

Dr. Ryan shared her observations from the first two workshops in the series. She echoed Robert Tross's suggestion that the Air Force focus on the *how* rather than the *what* for digital transformation. The discussion about the value of managing change, monitoring progress, and reimagining processes instead of digitizing existing processes resonated: because data have become a major weapon system and the DAF plans to exploit data to an unprecedented degree, the DAF has to be prepared for those data to become a major target for the adversaries. Therefore, she continued, the Air Force has to translate its strategic needs for future competition and conflict into improvements to the data superstructure, without being overwhelmed by current acquisition processes but also by developing new system requirements and decision-making policies and processes. The barrier to achieving this vision is thinking about digitization in terms of only the data objects instead of the entire digital ecosystem. In a digital ecosystem, everything but the hardware is data. She cautioned that total digitization is not a simple process: a series of decisions has to be made about the target data format; sampling rates; storage strategy; and transition plan, which prioritizes goals, considers how data storage obsolesces, and maps how to migrate data from old to new platforms. She emphasized that it is critical for the Air Force to have a strategy for creating and maintaining minimum essential data sets that are immediately available for continuity of operations when data repositories, including cloud enclaves, are attacked physically or virtually. She explained that decision pathways (and their roadblocks) need to be considered as part of the overall digitization strategy. Human knowledge about how to use data appropriately is important, especially when operating in a degraded data environment—quality training and education thus become a higher priority than certification. Last, she remarked that the strategic use of data (particularly the logistics of data) needs to be studied specifically from a warfighting perspective. Dr. Green noted that all of these activities require the right people who understand strategic warfare and can develop the architecture. While operations are ongoing, the Air Force has to take a step back for planning.

Dr. Langston observed that not enough energy, time, or resources are being spent on data: data sharing has been a long-standing problem within DoD, one that has become worse as cybersecurity issues have increased. The DoD Instruction Series 8350 states that everyone must share their data, but people are not penalized for failing to do so—that has to change, he asserted. For example, Virtual Alabama ceased funding for people who did not add their data to the Google Earth Layer. Lt. Gen. Hamel asked whether the military's existing systems make it difficult to share data or if people are simply unwilling to do so. Dr. Langston suggested that the problem is multi-layered. Those in charge of funding will lose the money if it is not spent properly and quickly; if there is no "requirement" to share data, people may not want to focus what little money they have on that activity.

Dr. Paul Nielsen (USAF, ret.), director and chief executive officer, Software Engineering Institute, Carnegie Mellon University, remarked that with so much data flowing in and out of the system, sometimes decision making occurs at a high level where people are not in immediate contact with the problem and thus do not have the right context to make a decision. He supported Mr. Lynch's assertion that technical decisions need to be made by technically competent people. Dr. Langston noted that although some of the current senior leadership understand the need to reduce time cycles and become more efficient, an overabundance of Pentagon oversight remains a barrier to progress. Dr. Nielsen added that the Director of Defense Research and Engineering for Research and Technology staff grew substantially from 2000 to 2010, and Lt. Gen. Bowlds said that these additional staff are essentially generating work that does not need to be done. Lt. Gen. Hamel advocated for the active use of new tools and authorities, the empowerment of lower-level decision makers, and action on smaller and shorter time scales to better meet user needs—large programs of record often collapse under their own weight.

Lt. Gen. Hamel commented that because digital transformation affects every member of the organization, it is important to identify communities of practitioners and their responsibilities across the enterprise. He advised against using the Advanced Battle Management System (ABMS) as the "flagship of transformation." Dr. Langston said that in the Navy, progress is slowed by the requirement for program managers to report to the contracts and legal departments. Lt. Gen. Bowlds noted that the Air Force has made the same mistake by giving more power to the contracting officers than to the program managers. Dr. Langston suggested the adoption of something similar to Platform One across all of the services, and using it iteratively to build software programs. However, he cautioned against having all of its components maintained by the Air Force instead of by commercial providers.

Gen. Holmes perceived that the absence of Air Force Systems Command is palpable: under that system, it was possible to identify a threat, create a concept of operations, and acquire the needed platforms or networks. By connecting acquisition and sustainment, a focus on the acquisition process was lost: the Air Force Materiel Commander was removed from the loop, and the program executive officers (PEOs) worked directly for the senior acquisition authority without any real link to the operators, warfighters, or the threat. This model has essentially turned PEOs into contracting officers. Significant staff cuts in the Air Force have also reduced its capacity to think through a problem and deliver and execute a solution (e.g., the Air Force Materiel Command has lost 5,000 acquisition PEOs who are needed to manage existing programs). He noted that the Air Force has aging, ineffective, and expensive systems that have to be replaced because China and Russia have had 40 years to learn how to defeat these systems. Digital modernization provides the opportunity to leapfrog Russia and China and negate their investments. He advised against purchasing "next-gen" systems; they are too expensive and often function in the same way as the old platform. He emphasized that although there are many people in the Air Force who are interested in transformation and are trying to move forward, the coordination and cooperation needed to create a unity of effort are missing. The lessons learned from other large organizations and the commercial sector become meaningless if the Air Force does not develop this unity of effort. To leapfrog Russia and China, the Air Force has to lead a change management effort, which includes incentives, that allows for the acquisition of new capabilities in a reasonable time frame. He shared a motto from a former maintenance group commander that is still relevant today: "the purpose of analysis is insight, and the purpose of insight is to drive decisions. And anything that does not lead to insights to help with decision making is wasted time."

Dr. Rama Chellappa, Bloomberg Distinguished Professor of electrical and computer engineering and biomedical engineering, Johns Hopkins University, observed that in the case study on medical records, the strategy was driven by a clear goal (e.g., diagnose a disease, monitor patient improvement). Before it can consider how to do digital transformation, the Air Force needs to specify its goals. Dr. Green suggested that the goals be broken down into objectives that are aligned with functions. Instead of having technology drive the process, she continued, the emphasis should be *why* and *how* technology will be inserted into a current function to improve performance. Lt. Gen. Hamel added that it is critical to define problems so that they can be logically decomposed and reintegrated as solutions are identified.

Lt. Gen. Bowlds shared several themes that he noticed over the course of the first two workshops: (1) Senior leadership has to drive the culture change needed for digital transformation, and the strategy has to be consistent as these leaders change. Trust has to be decentralized—more data are exposed and people are given more tools, and the decisions are driven further down into the organization. (2) Stovepipes have to be removed to enable true integration. (3) A plan is needed to remove critical legacy systems without interrupting operations. (4) Digital transformation is about data. When acquisition programs generate their own data rather than sharing data, duplication emerges. It is important to instead identify authoritative sources and focus on data integrity. He emphasized that ABMS and JADC2 are not "strategies" to enable data sharing; an operational concept is needed.

Mr. Munson commented that when there is a difficult problem to solve, it is important to consider why the solution is elusive. He defined acquisition in two ways: "acquisition" includes the contracting programs and the budgeting staff from the agency, while "Acquisition" includes those with oversight in the Pentagon; the administration; and congressional committees, authorizers, and appropriators. He suggested that the Air Force create a team focused on "Acquisition" to increase program effectiveness. He also proposed that the Air Force pursue industrial-strength security for its enterprise; if it achieves a true digital transformation, it will become an even larger target for adversaries. Although many pilots and prototypes have been successful, Mr. Munson described them as "the enemy of the enterprise-level effort" because it is unlikely that any of these prototypes can serve as the foundation on which to build the needed architecture. Although prototypes provide a learning opportunity, the resources needed to fund prototypes detract resources from larger initiatives. He encouraged domains across the service to define their use cases: What result do they desire? What data do they need? What communications and connectivity do they need? He advocated for the creation of a "recipe" to define use cases, complete dozens of them, and learn how their integration could characterize the architecture that is derived from core mission needs. Last, he posited that the intersection of Air Force and Space Force needs does not extend beyond human resources functions and suggested a distinct separation between the ways in which the Air Force and Space Force think about their respective missions. Lt. Gen. Hamel recognized that the Air Force and Space Force have different missions, but he reiterated Gen. David Thompson's assertion that because the Space Force is small (in size and in funding), it is dependent on the Air Force beyond personnel. The common digital infrastructure has to come from the Air Force because it is funded at a higher level. He added that when done well, use cases are an effective mechanism to extend an abstract concept of operations. He suggested broadening the notion of "community of practitioners" across the whole of the services before identifying important use cases. Gen. Holmes said that policy, resource, and funding gaps prevent people from executing a strategy, which could be achieved if someone would take charge and issue the request.

Mr. Edward Drolet, deputy director, Chief of Staff of the Air Force SSG, suggested that the planning committee contact Maj. Gen. Michael Schmidt for his perspective on digital transformation. Mr. Drolet noted that an innovation ecosystem is being developed for the Air Force, as it works diligently to move programs to minimum viable products, demonstrate capabilities, and balance cost and scale. Gen. Holmes said that vice chiefs and chiefs sometimes create entities similar to the SSG when their own staff are underperforming. This approach often leads to resentment, in which case it could be difficult to achieve buy-in among those staff. These entities may represent an organization that is *not* functioning appropriately as opposed to an organization that is transforming. Mr. Drolet assured Gen. Holmes that the SSG is tracking several initiatives that provide overall direction and monitor digital issues for the transformation (see Appendix D).

Dr. Nielsen observed that companies that have had successful digital transformations, such as Walmart and Amazon, are DoD-size organizations. However, with the added challenge of legacy systems and processes, it will be difficult for the Air Force to transform—but doing so is essential to remain relevant in the future. He stressed that if the Air Force does not use modern software engineering techniques and modern systems engineering and architecture, the uniformed, civil service, and defense industrial staff will seek jobs elsewhere to do more innovative work.

Dr. Drew categorized the discussion from the first two workshops in the series into five themes: (1) Outcomes, decisions, and goals can be realized when there is a specified problem to solve, which is not currently the case for the Air Force. The Air Force could focus its work in areas of mission operation, acquisition/development, maintenance, and business support/administration. (2) Leadership and governance, as well as funding, are key aspects of the digital transformation. She suggested the creation of a "digital board" to carry out the governance of projects (versus retaining siloes). (3) A variety of approaches toward (e.g., starting with an enterprise view, seeking quick wins) and methodologies for (e.g., agility, failing fast, experimentation, change management) transformation exist. Focusing on data and mission logic instead of the backend infrastructure is critical, she continued, as are considerations for cybersecurity, zero trust, data governance, and cross-functional teams. (4) Several challenges remain for the Air Force, the first of which is that ownership of processes that span multiple groups needs to be determined. Other potential barriers include creating buy-in, incentivizing people to share their data, and balancing centralized and decentralized control. (5) Many case studies exist to demonstrate the "what" and the "how" of successful transformations.

5

Workshop Three, Part One

OPENING REMARKS

Workshop series co-chair Ms. Deborah Westphal, chairman of the board, Toffler Associates, explained that this final workshop in the series would identify gaps between what the Air Force is currently doing and what it could consider doing in the future.

THE FUTURE THREAT ENVIRONMENT

Dr. Brendan Mulvaney, director, China Aerospace Studies Institute, National Defense University, discussed China's progress in digitization and modernization. He explained that China conceptualizes things differently than the United States—for example, the information domain in China includes electronic warfare; cyber; spectrum operations; and intelligence, surveillance, and reconnaissance systems. Because China operates in a different framework, it can be difficult to make comparisons between the two countries for analysis. China does not have many of the same restrictions that the United States has in terms of collaboration and information sharing; thus, it uses information from many inputs for its large information system. This approach is often referred to as "informationization." As early as 1991, China understood both that information systems were key to modern warfare and that there was a sense of urgency to compete with the United States, which was more advanced at that time. China's first step of informationization was digitization (i.e., moving away from Cold War-era analog systems that had no cross-platform capability). The next step is "networkization" (i.e., free flow of information up and down the chain). China has begun to create an integrated command platform—a system into which all information could flow, with each user having an appropriate level of network access. At the same time, China is embarking on "smartification." According to Dr. Mulvaney, China strongly believes that if enough information is collected and analyzed correctly, any problem can be solved. As a result, China is beginning to dedicate science and technology investments to using machine learning (ML) and high-powered computing to analyze the information, signals, and intelligence emerging from all of its sources (e.g., space, cyber, on the ground, etc.). China also collects and stores encrypted information in vast data centers so that it will have an advantage when the quantum computer becomes operational and the encrypted information can be read. China is working to move the human to be "on-the-loop" (versus "in-the-loop") and eventually to remove the human completely from the loop. Dr. Mulvaney believes that the Chinese are more likely to turn life-and-death decisions over to artificial intelligence (AI) than the United States.

He explained that China conducts both 5-year and long-term planning, and as long as its economy remains stable, so too will the policy environment. China remains behind the United States in many key areas but is approaching parity in many others, and it continues actively pursuing partnerships and investments in Silicon Valley. China's Strategic Support Force (SSF), which was stood up in 2016, combines its space and cyber forces. He noted that if something can affect space operations, it can affect cyber operations, and thus the two are integrally linked. He said that Xi Jinping, the Chairman of the Central Military Commission for the Communist Party in China, expects that the next war will be won in the information domain. Therefore, China is investing in space and counterspace operations, including cyberspace operations. China's military still has some stovepipes, but it has a plan to transform by 2049. With the initial efforts in networkization, China's theater commands (similar to the U.S. Combatant Commands) already have more information and easier access to that information. China's theater commands are moving toward a joint model for staffing, authorities, and lines of communications.

Dr. Mulvaney mentioned that China has a substantial amount of fiber, which is protected, encrypted, and has backups from low-tech to quantum relays and satellites. All of that information is flowing into SSF Headquarters and down to the theater commands. The eventual goal is for the theater commands to have the ability to push tasking and information and intelligence to individual units that will move forward in operation. He cautioned that China is quickly closing the gap with the United States in its collection and analysis capabilities and might already be on par with some U.S. capabilities. China has also increased its training and exercises to practice networkization, with an emphasis on contested environments, and is working to improve the synchronization of its acquisition efforts at a national level.

Dr. Marv Langston (USN, ret.), independent consultant, asked Dr. Mulvaney about the prediction made in *AI Superpowers* that China will be ahead of the United States in AI by 2023. Dr. Mulvaney replied that China has surpassed the United States in some areas of AI, but the United States is still ahead in most areas of AI—although China is quickly closing the gap. Dr. Langston also wondered whether the Chinese have operationalized quantum communications and networks with Air Force Satellite Communications. Dr. Mulvaney noted that China has quantum encryption keys and key distribution through terrestrial networks but has not operationalized quantum communications in networks yet. He added that the Austrians are engaging in similar efforts and if they partner with the Chinese, there could be direct impacts.

Ms. Westphal pointed out that the Chinese are collecting data on individual U.S. citizens. She wondered about the need to rethink warfare if airmen's personal lives are targeted in an attempt to influence their decisions during operations. Dr. Mulvaney remarked that this is an area China considers to be part of the information domain, and it actively collects information on its own and U.S. citizens. He acknowledged Ms. Westphal's concern that U.S. airmen, who are in constant contact with their families, could lose focus on the battlefield if China has the power to interfere in a situation (e.g., financial or personal) on the home front. He added that the benefits of a free and open society such as the United States can become detrimental when adversaries have ready access to information. He expressed with certainty that China will use information to gain advantage. Ms. Westphal suggested that the Air Force spend more time thinking about its defensive posture as civilian life and military operations begin to overlap. Dr. Mulvaney agreed with Ms. Westphal that the Air Force should consider its role in protecting civilian infrastructure and communication nodes as well as individual airmen.

Dr. Langston questioned whether China has taken advantage of the Office of Personnel Management (OPM) hack on security background data. Dr. Mulvaney responded that the OPM hack revealed who has clearance, how old the clearance is, how often it is updated, and the level of the clearance as well as some background information (e.g., identities of friends and families). He hypothesized that China would have tried to compromise some of these sources by using the information to entice people to partner with a particular laboratory of interest to China, for example. Dr. Langston asked how China's digital money system has improved its ability to track its own citizens. Dr. Mulvaney said that China promotes its approach to domestic security as a "smart city" that will be safer and run more smoothly. Yet, people are constantly monitored (e.g., someone crossing a public street outside of an authorized crosswalk is captured with facial recognition on a camera and immediately receives an alert on his phone that he has been ticketed and fined for jaywalking; his fine is removed from his state-owned bank account and his social credit score reduced). He cautioned that China is exporting this smart-cities technology to other countries, and information from those countries flows back to China. Ms. Westphal wondered if there are strategies to prevent the United States from collecting information on Chinese citizens. Dr. Mulvaney explained that the Chinese view their "Great Firewall" as an effective way to eliminate threats. He said that the United States will have to find ways to counter the systemic differences between the countries' approaches to information. Dr. Langston asked if the Chinese Communist party is surveilled. Dr. Mulvaney replied that, to the best of his knowledge, although there are likely secure rooms for senior party officials, no one is exempt from surveillance.

Mr. Alden Munson, senior fellow and member, Board of Regents, Potomac Institute for Policy Studies, asked if the Chinese would make the Air Force a high-priority cyber target if it successfully creates a digitized force. Dr. Mulvaney emphasized that the Air Force is already a high-priority cyber target, but China will want to learn more about how the Air Force's digitized system works and how to disrupt it. He suggested that the Air Force enhance its training in a contested environment to be prepared for this situation.

Dr. Rama Chellappa, Bloomberg Distinguished Professor of electrical and computer engineering and biomedical engineering, Johns Hopkins University, pointed out that although China has far more data to train on, success with facial recognition does not translate to general progress in AI. He added that although China has made progress, a free society will survive—one can never underestimate free people's ability to win. Dr. Mulvaney acknowledged the difference between specific AI and generalized AI. He mentioned that the Chinese have emphasized "indigenous innovation," but it is difficult to convince free thinkers to do creative design in an environment like China where they will have no academic or political freedom.

Dr. Annie Green, data governance specialist, George Mason University, wondered if China is monitoring whether its personal tracking efforts add value to the economy or increase monetary sources for residents. Dr. Mulvaney replied that China is not tracking its citizens for added financial value; it tracks people to increase the party's control, which adds "value" to the society. China expects that if people know they are being monitored, they will be more likely to follow the party's rules.

Ms. Westphal asked Dr. Mulvaney about areas in which the Air Force could be paying more attention, given his perspective of China. Dr. Mulvaney asserted that the Air Force should be training to fight in a contested environment without satellite communications. The Air Force also needs to improve agile combat employment. Utilizing U.S. partners and allies will be the only way to succeed, he continued, so it is imperative to cultivate those relationships.

WHAT DOCTRINE, CONCEPTS OF OPERATIONS, AND TACTICS, TECHNIQUES, AND PROCEDURES DO WE NEED TO OPERATE IN A DIGITALLY TRANSFORMED AIR FORCE?
PANEL ONE

Maj. Evan "Switch" Hatter, Chief of Doctrine Outreach, the Curtis E. LeMay Center for Doctrine Development and Education, defined doctrine as agreed-upon best practices that are supported by history, debate, analysis, wargame exercises, and contingencies. Doctrine serves as official advice or guidance, and it is authoritative, not directive; thus, "should" is used instead of "shall" or "will." Doctrine provides guidance and stability for the Air Force, and the Air Force drives how doctrine proceeds over time. The two key pillars of doctrine are unity of command and mission command.

Maj. Hatter explained that between initial concept and doctrine, "emerging doctrine" describes something on the horizon to becoming a best practice. The LeMay Center's Chennault Series, in particular, pursues gaps and seams in the doctrine. The LeMay Center also forms doctrine writing subgroups, which are comprised of subject matter experts from the field, and conducts Joint All-Domain Operations Symposium wargames.

He noted that when the digital modernization strategy emerged in 2019, Gen. David Goldfein requested that the LeMay Center establish the joint all-domain operations (JADO) doctrine, which became the Air Force's first "doctrine note" (AFDP 3-99). In March 2021, Air Force Doctrine Publication 1 was a major effort to rewrite the Air Force's core foundational principles for air power. Gen. Charles Brown has requested that the LeMay Center also provide the service doctrine on agile combat employment, which is expected to be published as an Air Force doctrine note in mid-October 2021.

Maj. Hatter discussed Air Force Doctrine Publication 1 in greater detail, emphasizing that the focus has shifted from "phases of war" to "competition continuum at scale." "Airpower" has also been redefined as the ability to project military power through control and exploitation in, from, and through the air. Air Force Doctrine Publication 1 prioritizes the air domain, as well as the information environment, the cyberspace domain, and the electromagnetic spectrum. He stressed the importance of airmen understanding that any of their actions (e.g., written, spoken, social media) have informational components that communicate messages, which could be leveraged for operations and planning. The airmen's philosophy for the command and control of airpower (i.e., mission command) is centralized command, distributed control, and decentralized execution. Mission command is communicated through a commander's intent through mission-type orders, which require different authorities (e.g., conditions-based, delegated, or flexible command).

He emphasized that joint all-domain command and control (JADC2), referenced in AFDP 3-99 and in the doctrine note for agile combat employment, requires a level of redundant and resilient command and control nodes to ensure disconnected and distributed command and control when the higher-level command and control fails. JADC2 also requires edge computing and self-healing mesh networks. He said that airmen should be trained and equipped to employ communications equipment in distributed operations, and the system should be secure but simplistic enough to work in these environments. Commanders have to coordinate across domains, but the Chennault Series revealed a gap within command authorities—is direct liaison authority and tactical control or operational control sufficient to work not only in a joint environment but also in an all-domain environment? He remarked that doctrine is pursuing that and other key questions. For example, the LeMay Center considered what key elements need to be provided to an airman for mission command via a mission-type order. With the assistance of subject matter experts, an overall framework was developed. Commander's intent is provided throughout a mission-type order, but the pace plan is critical and posture is foundational—agile combat employment posture provides deterrence to the adversaries and assurance to the allies that distributed operations will be maintained in a disconnected environment.

Maj. Hatter referenced the doctrine, which explains that to operate disconnected in a distributed location, capability development should include accessible and redundant cloud-based systems that function seamlessly when disconnected and reconnect without interruption. The doctrine also suggests that secure, adaptable, interoperable, and integrated data networks provide information synthesis, distributed decision making, and assessment, which are essential to work with joint partners. The force should be optimized for these major combat operations in a contested environment, he continued, and this approach should work not only at main operating bases but also in the least capable, small contingency locations functioning as network nodes to generate combat air power. Both the agile combat employment and JADO doctrine notes address how AI and ML could enable decision superiority within agile distributed operations.

In closing, Maj. Hatter reiterated that doctrine is codified best practice. When the field determines that an emerging concept should be put into doctrine, the LeMay Center either codifies those best practices into existing doctrine, or works to develop a doctrine note and codifies the note into a living document that can be rapidly iterated (versus the traditional 2-year doctrine rewrite timeline). Since the initial JADO doctrine note was published in 2019, it has been iterated on three times.

Ms. Westphal wondered how best practices are codified if the Air Force is not yet training digitally. Maj. Hatter said that the LeMay Center could lead a writing group to determine whether a path forward exists, but he reiterated that the "best practice" has to come from the field before it can be codified. Mr. Munson asked if doctrine could be used to generate use cases to define the base features of a digitized force. Maj. Hatter noted that agile combat employment will only succeed with cloud-based architectures, mesh networks, and self-healing networks. Similarly, successful JADO requires AI, ML, and human-machine interfaces. Those components have to be functional for the JADO and agile combat employment doctrine to be successful. Mr. Munson added that issues need to be addressed on behalf of the entire force instead of by individual commands and activities. Maj. Hatter replied that doctrine is not meant to contain force requirements; however, vignettes could be presented (e.g., the use case for cloud-based architecture or edge computing) without having undergone doctrine testing. He stressed that the Air Force would not want to reveal specific requirements in its doctrine (e.g., how many gigs of transfer speed are needed for mesh computing).

Col. Charles Galbreath, Deputy for the Chief Technology and Innovation Office (CTIO), U.S. Space Force Headquarters, explained that the CTIO emerged in response to Gen. John Raymond's intent for the Space Force to become a digital service. The Human Capital Office, the Operations Office, the Strategy and Requirements Office, and the CTIO collaborate to achieve this vision. The CTIO's primary responsibility is to lead the digital transformation for the Space Force. For example, it pilots efforts from Headquarters and coordinates across the field commands and other L2s to infuse digital capabilities and processes into activities across the Space Force. In addition to the application of digital tools and the development of an enterprise IT infrastructure and data governance standards, the transformation includes science and technology and analytic components. The CTIO currently has 30 government billets but plans to have 80 to 90 over the next 2 to 3 years, and it has opportunities within four directorates overseen by Dr. Lisa Costa, the incoming chief technology and innovation officer: Innovation and Digital Transformation; Science, Technology, and Research; IT, Data, and Data Analytics; and Analysis.

Col. Galbreath noted that the first document to codify the Space Force as digital was the Chief of Space Operation's Planning Guidance, released in November 2020. The direction was to create the Space Force as a digital service to accelerate innovation. It also introduced four key focus areas for the Space Force: (1) digital workforce (i.e., education and cultural changes with the creation of the right attitudes and digital fluency), (2) digital engineering (i.e., an end-to-end digital thread of capabilities from design, to acquisition, to operational testing and evaluation, to development, to mission planning, to robust digital twins to support anomaly resolution and attack identification), (3) digital headquarters (i.e., decision making at all levels by producing streamlined capabilities to make informed data-driven decisions and using the available manpower to the best extent), and (4) digital operations (i.e., delivery of capabilities and effects in more rapid and meaningful ways).

In May 2021, the CTIO released the *Space Force Vision for a Digital Service*, which was built around those four key focus areas and defined what it means to be a digital service. He described the *Space Force Vision for a Digital Service* as an aspirational and educational document. Immediately after its release, a roadmap was developed to achieve the vision. While the roadmap (a living document) is not constrained by manpower or resource limitations, it expanded the four focus areas into a series of objectives, activities, and tasks that are now being evaluated for execution potential, and adjustments will be made based on available funding. He emphasized the need to confront the emerging threat, accelerate delivery of innovative capabilities, leverage the small size of the service to be more agile and adaptable, and override existing bureaucracies to compete. The *Vision* states that the Space Force should be interconnected, innovative, and digitally dominant—that is, turn the "cumulative technical prowess into potent force-multiplying effects to develop, field, and operate capabilities more quickly and effectively than any potential adversary."

Col. Galbreath commented on the CTIO's Software Development Immersive, which includes intensive coding coursework over several weeks, followed by an applications period and an internship with the Space Operations Command or other Space Force organizations. This program teaches government personnel with basic coding knowledge how to lead a coding effort as well as provides them with additional coding skills. The goal of this program is to increase DevSecOps activities across the Space Force. The CTIO has also created force multiplier courses through Digital University to educate everyone in the Space Force about digital tools and practices, and offers virtual sessions on various digital activities.

Dr. Pamela Drew, former executive vice president and president of information systems, Exelis, asked Col. Galbreath to elaborate on the CTIO's pilot efforts. He explained that there are pilot efforts across all four of the key focus areas. One effort relates to the creation of *digital engineering* capabilities for missile warning as part of the next generation of programs of record. In a *digital headquarters* effort, the CTIO is leveraging Rhombus Guardian and Brown Heron for displays of force readiness for the chief of operations and to support manpower decisions with the evaluation of the right personnel mix (i.e., backgrounds and experiences). Another effort uses a natural language processing algorithm with AI to evaluate resumes to enhance the *digital workforce*. In terms of *digital operations*, the CTIO is focused on JADC2 and the Advanced Battle Management System (ABMS) as well as leveraging AI to support space domain awareness.

A participant wondered how legacy systems are being addressed with respect to digital engineering. Col. Galbreath replied that consideration for the future force design includes an understanding of the current architecture and essential modifications. A macro-level representation of the legacy architecture is needed to compare any proposed modifications for the future force design against a known baseline. Achieving the detailed level of digital twin that will be possible for future systems is unlikely for the current system: that approach would not create a significant return on investment. He expected some amount of "grandfathering" to the guidance that all systems will have a digital twin by a certain milestone.

Mr. Munson asked if there is an effort to define how the Space Force will be different from the Air Force. Col. Galbreath noted that the Space Force has a strong partnership with the Air Force, in particular with the Office of the Chief Information Officer. Although the Space Force relies on the existing enterprise information technology system provided by the Air Force, it will define its own unique requirements as it moves forward with digital tools and processes. The Air Force is willing to work with the Space Force, and, because the Space Force is so small, it can experiment (e.g., with new tool sets) in ways that the larger Air Force cannot. The Space Force is also leveraging the Air Force's Digital University and providing additional courses. Because the Army, Navy, Marine Corps, and Coast Guard are also pursuing digitization, he continued, a digital engineering ecosystem would be beneficial so that all of the services can communicate and engage with open system architecture modeling and simulation. Mr. Munson inquired about relevant use cases that span important features of a digitized environment. Col. Galbreath said that the CTIO is utilizing use cases in all of its pilot efforts; because the CTIO has increased in size, it is important to have a specific focus.

Mr. Jay Santee (USAF, ret.), vice president, Strategic Space Operations, Defense Systems Group, The Aerospace Corporation, asked about the "digital ecosystem" and how it will support transformation efforts. Col. Galbreath expressed his hope that all current and future systems will have an associated digital twin. With adequate funding, these digital twins could work together in a virtual environment, where every detail is represented. In the meantime, the CTIO has several pilot efforts that initiate a set of digital engineering capabilities, which will grow over time and federate into multiple enclaves of capabilities at different security classification levels. He also shared a few examples of how the Space Force could leverage AI. He described a recent robotic process automation workshop that utilized AI tools to release operators and acquirers from more mundane tasks, which could be applied today. The Space Force also hopes to leverage AI for space domain awareness (i.e., to discern patterns of life and activity for satellites and determine if something is abnormal). Ultimately, the digital ecosystem could emulate an operator and a threat operator in a potential combat scenario.

Ms. Westphal wondered if enough time and effort are being spent to understand how authorities and decision making at the edge could change in a digitized force. Col. Galbreath replied that space has always been much more digitally inclined than any of the other domains. The Space Force will have to rely on AI and automation to support many of its activities owing to the associated time elements (e.g., latency has a bigger impact farther into the cislunar space). In the terrestrial sphere, AI tools help to sort large data sets rapidly and support decision making. AI can also categorize activities quickly, allowing humans to focus on more critical issues. Weapons release authority, for example, will always be in the hands of a human, but automation could be useful for identifying threats. He noted that during the recent evacuations from Afghanistan, data on how many people were onboard, how long people had been on the tarmac, and how long people waited once they landed were used to support decision making. Ms. Westphal emphasized that decision making in a timely fashion is about trust—delays arise in conflicts over who owns the data.

Dr. Andrew Stricker, analyst, Strategy and Concepts, the Curtis E. LeMay Center for Doctrine Development and Education, discussed his previous experience working on a digital transformation effort with several universities—Vanderbilt University, Harvard University, the Massachusetts Institute of Technology (MIT), Northwestern University, and the University of Texas at Austin. Although this effort was on a much smaller scale than what the Air Force is trying to accomplish, there are useful insights and commonalities. He echoed the notion that transformation is not about technology; it is about changing culture and establishing trust. He posited that the digital transformation cycle model used to help these universities transform (see Figure 5.1) could be utilized by the Department of the Air Force (DAF).

Dr. Stricker explained that these universities were motivated to transform to become more competitive on the international spectrum of new discoveries. Although they had a history of working in partnership, they had not established digital connections with federal laboratory structures, high-performance computing areas, and other new capabilities. Taking a "whole-of-government perspective," he continued, the universities began to establish new partnerships. However, just as the Air Force is now realizing, the universities recognized that it is difficult to focus simultaneously on a digital transformation and existing efforts. He emphasized that the digital transformation cycle is a continuous journey. An "all-hands" effort was required for the digital transformation to gain traction among the universities; the students and staff mattered tremendously in this effort, not just the administrators.

Similar to the Air Force's concern about competitive advantage on the world stage, the universities sought to revolutionize capabilities with AI and ML to augment teaching, research, and other areas of scholarship. Visualization was a powerful tool in transforming how researchers were developing theories, real-time insights, and new research directions. He observed that the Air Force is trying to implement similar visualization tools so that people on the functional lines can better understand patterns and challenges. As part of the university effort, real-time digitization tools and model-based reasoning were used across all disciplinary areas to create "what-if" scenarios with data-informed infusions of information from several federal data sets. The model-based reasoning "energized" the faculty and students, showcasing just how many more discoveries remained to be made.

Dr. Stricker noted that digital transformations have significant changes for people's day-to-day work. In the universities, people accustomed to exerting leadership were reluctant to expose the vulnerability of learning new things; a comfort level had to be created, with multiple entry points for engaging leaders, staff, and students. Small teams emerged across the universities to foster new ways of experimentation. It also became clear that a new infrastructure was needed to enhance connectivity. In the past, government laboratories and universities grew in stovepipes because the work was independent, creating robust infrastructure within some domains but creating barriers when trying to share data and connect resources across departments or disciplines. An enterprise-level architectural perspective was needed, he continued, which requires much patience to iterate and balance the use of legacy infrastructure capabilities and new capabilities.

Turning to a discussion of his work with the LeMay Center, he explained that he writes a weekly brief on translating cognition and AI efforts at universities across the world for military usage and applications. One important issue is the need for trustworthy data. Although data may be collected electronically, that does not mean they can be accessed, cleansed, or used. Cloud computing capabilities are fundamental in establishing areas to work with data. He noted that funding remains a challenge for universities and the Department of Defense (DoD) alike, especially in relation to small business efforts to simulate new capabilities. Finding the right security balance is also difficult: organizations have to protect assets but also have the ability to work within open systems. He underscored the need for DoD to harvest the "incredible ingenuity" taking place in the open-source community, vet it, and operationalize it to serve military needs.

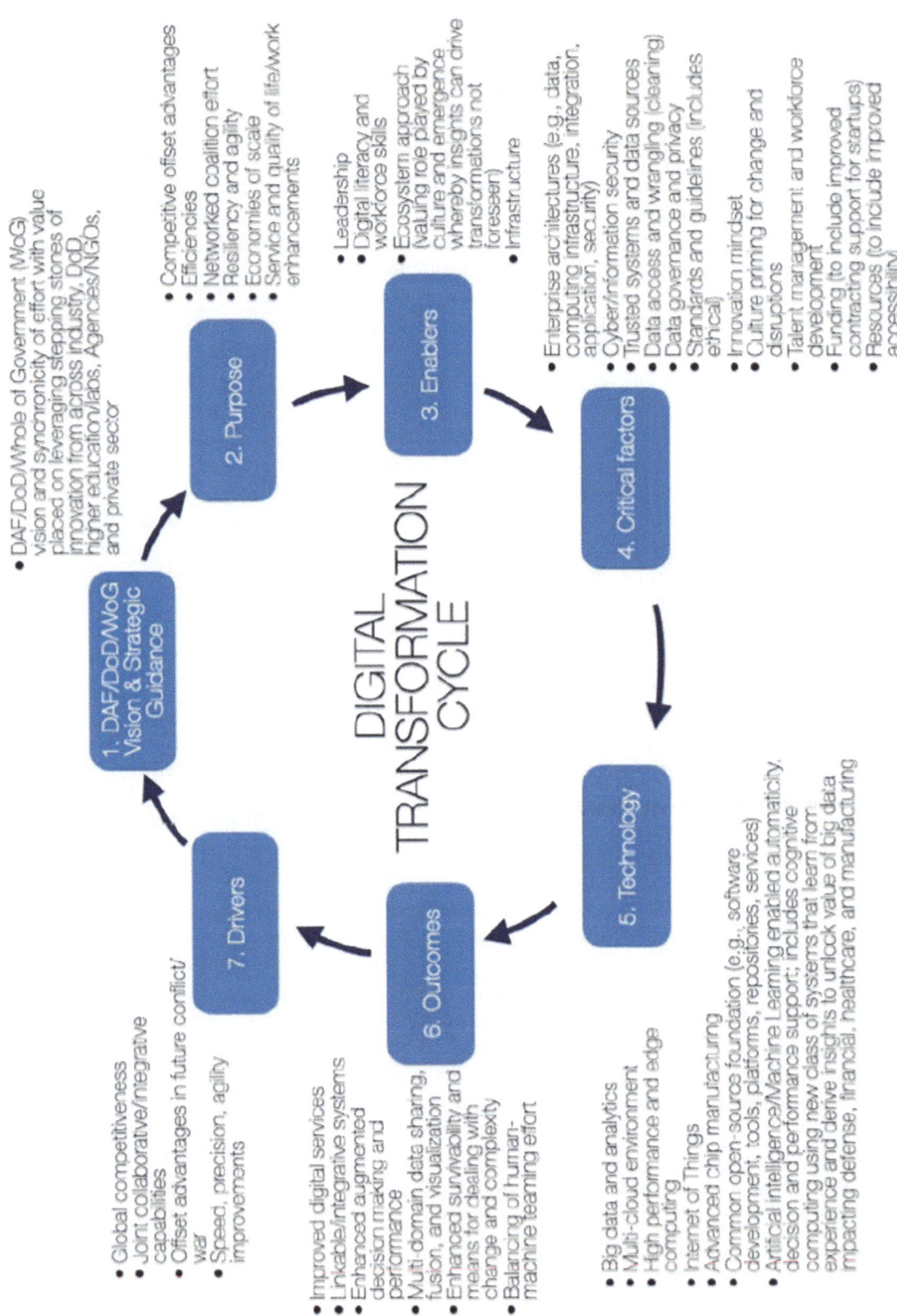

FIGURE 5.1 Digital transformation cycle. SOURCE: Andrew Stricker, presentation to the workshop, September 23, 2021, adapted from International Telecommunication Union, 2019, *Digital Transformation and the Role of Enterprise Architecture*, ITU Publications, http://handle.itu.int/11.1002/pub/81404388-en.

In terms of overall progress with AI, Dr. Stricker said that work remains to be done in assistance with common sense. Because humans can be overconfident and underestimate threats, this technology could aid decision makers in DoD, especially in the case of large data sets. A key part of realizing these technologies is having the right people in place who can work with the toolsets and in the data sciences, and help leaders to use and apply the tools for decision making. An important outcome of digital transformation is improving human-machine teaming, although this is challenging given that human teams already find it difficult to trust other human teams.

Dr. Stricker cautioned that the United States is in a "foot race" with China, and China has been able to leapfrog the United States in some areas. It is important for the United States to leverage its unique contributions to global competition. Agility and adaptability are key—accelerating digital transformation with AI will help to automate the speed at which data are processed and fused in support of decision making, which will also help to realign the human-machine structure. He emphasized that digital transformation should enable the use of AI and ML to stay in communication with dispersed forces and support reaggregation.

Dr. Langston asked about the value of model-based reasoning as well as whether general AI techniques could support human-intensive functions such as command and control. Dr. Stricker replied that general AI is taking place in "baby steps" (e.g., MIT's Lincoln Labs is working on one-shot learning capabilities; others are working on abductive reasoning developments). Model-based reasoning has revolutionized research, medicine, biology, and engineering, and he expected that it could revolutionize the Air Force in its ability to examine the "what-ifs" (e.g., to understand potential effects of model manipulations during wargames and simulations). He noted that the U.S. Department of Energy already leverages tools for building and manipulating models to identify gaps.

Ms. Westphal invited Dr. Stricker to identify a few areas on which the Air Force could focus to make the digital strategy successful. He said that the Air Force is a few years behind in developing the infrastructural components needed for digital transformation. It will take several levels of effort to get the appropriate infrastructure in place to work with data and use them in models. For example, Vanderbilt invested more than $120 million in infrastructural improvements for high-performance computing. He reiterated that the United States does not have much time to catch up in the foot race with China. In response to a question about a unity of effort across the Air Force, Dr. Stricker observed that the unity of effort is taking place on paper and in discussions but not in action. He asserted that the Air Force needs to realize that the digital transformation is much larger than project milestones and objectives.

Mr. Todd Carter, A2/6 Cyber Talent Management, mentioned the Air Force's challenges in developing the right level of workforce expertise and battling with the civilian sector to retain that expertise. He asked how to address these challenges, beyond traditional incentive structures. Dr. Stricker suggested directly engaging the best talent in an organization's biggest problems. Giving top talent small, insignificant tasks will discourage and disincentivize them. He also proposed that the Air Force consider new ways to associate with talent (perhaps for shorter-term assignments) beyond the civil service and uniform structures. Mr. Carter added that empowering people to take ownership increases retention, but hands-on leadership and management are essential. Dr. Stricker pointed out that this leadership style might be foreign to some members of the Air Force; the culture has to encourage creativity and minimize bureaucracy. Mr. Edward Drolet, deputy director, Chief of Staff of the Air Force Strategic Studies Group, noted that the Joint Artificial Intelligence Center is working to develop AI talent for the DAF.

WHAT DOCTRINE, CONCEPTS OF OPERATIONS, AND TACTICS, TECHNIQUES, AND PROCEDURES DO WE NEED TO OPERATE IN A DIGITALLY TRANSFORMED AIR FORCE?
PANEL TWO

Lt. Col. Brian "Dante" Burgoon, 561st Weapons Squadron Commander, Nellis Air Force Base, explained that the 561st is responsible for Air Force Tactics, Techniques, and Procedures (AFTTP) support and development for all Air Force documents. The 561st is currently developing 113 AFTTP 3-1s or 3-3s and is responsible for more than 200 manuals. The 561st is engaged in a continuous cycle of writing, publishing, and notifying end users. The current construct requires a 2-year rewrite timeline for manuals—during the 2-year process, end users codify new tactics that should be included in the manual, subject matter experts collaborate, and then the document can be updated. A working group meeting with end users and subject matter experts is hosted every week at Nellis, during which a PDF is created that can be pushed out to end users after editing and approval. During the 1.5- to 2-year gap between the rewrite of entire documents, flash bulletins are released to end users. He emphasized that, on this timeline, it is taking too long for many good tactical ideas to make their way into documents. Notification is also a problem, as only some end users are signed up for email alerts.

Lt. Col. Burgoon noted that the 561st developed the KNITE program to address two issues: (1) from the user perspective, cross-document knowledge was low and access was difficult; and (2) from the perspectives of AFTTP or doctrine writers, the writing process was difficult. The purpose of the KNITE program is to shift from taking months or years to capture ideas in documents and distribute them to end users, to developing a more iterative process.

In the KNITE program's proof-of-concept, a host service is used for the rewrite process and dissemination. He compared it to a Google search that leads into a Wiki page: the end user can search by keyword and find guidance in one place instead of sorting through multiple PDFs. When users log-in to this system, the system will know the person's credentials and background and provide the right level of access to information and search capabilities. People with more experience and a higher level of need-to-know will thus have a larger volume in their search results. A comment feature will be available to input desired changes, the contents of which will be captured and provided to the subject matter experts and adjudicators to consider for publication and updates. With this new approach, he continued, it would be possible to update ideas and new tactics quickly instead of waiting for 2 years to contribute to the publication of a rewrite. The KNITE architecture is useful not only for AFTTP development but also for doctrine.

Lt. Col. Burgoon revealed that the KNITE program has several goals: (1) transform how tactics are captured and disseminated; (2) streamline the creation and update of tactics through a knowledge curation tool, allowing rapid response to emerging threats and capabilities; (3) store data elements as nodes, allowing for robust semantic queries that can be output in several user-selectable formats; (4) standardize common content across communities and ensure that every operator has the most up-to-date tactics; (5) perform context sensitive queries based on tactician profile and viewing history; and (6) create a collaborative web-based content creation, editing, and approval environment, streamlining the tactics dissemination process. The Air Combat Command/A3 established KNITE as a requirement in March 2021, and the target goal for development at scale is June 2022.

Ms. Westphal asked about disconnects among planning, acquiring, and using systems. Lt. Col. Burgoon replied that the Air Force is trying to develop tactics as quickly as possible. Ninety percent of AFTTP is dedicated to rewrites and adapting to the enemy with new tactics. The 2-year cycle, however, is not adaptive—allowing subject matter experts to provide direct input in the new construct will drastically speed up this process. Ms. Westphal wondered if AI would be used to collect those inputs and present options for the best way to update tactics. Lt. Col. Burgoon mentioned that his team is working with MIT on AI initiatives to aggregate faster. However, the base architecture has to be developed first before AI can be injected and executed.

Mr. Munson asked if other Air Force users would benefit from having a similar tool and whether this capability could be hosted in the Air Force's digital environment. He also wondered if KNITE would serve as a helpful use case for the architects of that digital environment. Lt. Col. Burgoon responded that KNITE will likely be hosted on Platform One. He remarked that opportunities exist for other users to leverage the KNITE architecture for document publication. Gen. James (Mike) Holmes (USAF, ret.), senior advisor, The Roosevelt Group, expressed his concern that even with the application of digital tools, there will still be a shortage of subject matter experts to work through the material. Lt. Col. Burgoon recognized this challenge but said that the 561st is now linked directly to the weapons school instructor pilots, who are the subject matter experts for the rewrites, to enable monthly releases of information. Gen. Holmes suggested involving wing weapons officers, who can provide information about resource availability for execution. Lt. Col. Burgoon noted that the new system will promote cross-talk among the subject matter experts as opposed to only having occasional meetings. Gen. Holmes asked how the system will be secured, and Lt. Col. Burgoon emphasized that software is being developed inside the constraints of Platform One so as to adhere to its security standards.

Ms. Westphal asked if enough attention is being paid to the edges of the Air Force in terms of structural and cultural change. Gen. Holmes described the KNITE initiative as an example of the Air Force making a good decision to push authority and responsibility down to the experts in the weapons school and in the 561st. Now, the 561st needs the tools to make this new culture successful.

In response to a question from Dr. Green about whether auto-tagging and auto-classification methods are being used in the KNITE program, Lt. Col. Burgoon noted that there are search-based queries for each paragraph. Dr. Green added that even if the documents are parsed down to the paragraph level, there can still be categories for tag values that can be role based and pushed out to the appropriate people. Lt. Col. Burgoon explained that while it is possible to tag everything, doing so could be ineffective if people with lower levels of classification are accessing only portions of documents. Gen. Holmes remarked that natural language/ML tools could be helpful with this issue. Although such tools would be useful, Lt. Col. Burgoon described them as "higher ticket items" because more programming capability would be needed first. Ms. Westphal asked about gaps in Air Force effort that need to be refocused to operate in a more digitally rich environment. Lt. Col. Burgoon expressed his concern about maintaining the funding needed to continue improving—increased buy-in and sustained investment enable robust capabilities.

Mr. James Crocker, Chief Technology Officer, BESPIN (Business and Enterprise Systems Product Innovation), explained that BESPIN emerged to address two challenges: (1) how to build a software factory to target mobile application development, which had not been done previously in the Air Force; and (2) how to create a software factory that focused across all of the functional areas, within the policy constraints and hurdles of the government. BESPIN started ~2 years ago with eight people focused on the "art of the possible." They concentrated on user-centered design and quick resolution of pain points through automation and applications. He emphasized the value in having metrics to demonstrate impact and the ability to scale, which increase buy-in and a willingness to partner to improve overall manpower capabilities. BESPIN has paired Airmen one-to-one with industry, which helps capability to progress faster. BESPIN is able to capitalize on all of the functional airmen across the Program Executive Office to create the capability to focus on needs and direct them to meet the functional owners' requirements.

Ms. Westphal asked what BESPIN has accomplished thus far and what issues it plans to address in the future. Mr. Crocker said that since BESPIN received its second continuous Authority to Operate, it can push to any endpoint and deliver to any edge network or backend cloud infrastructure. He described the ability to facilitate different tech stacks as a significant achievement. Furthermore, there are efforts to democratize and understand data that are siloed between different systems (e.g., there are 2,000 data sources in the Air Force, none of which talk to each other). An enterprise-level effort, Data-as-a-Service, aims to make these data cross-functional. Twenty different applications and five enterprise efforts are in production, as well as Digital University, which has expanded from its grass-roots movement by airmen to facilitate operational capabilities and training. He remarked that the integration of DevSecOps has revealed a massive manpower shortage. In the coming year, BESPIN hopes to engage more with Digital University to address this issue, as Digital University is changing the framework of how the Air Force trains, assesses, and vets for Air Force capabilities. Another important BESPIN goal is to drive down the cost of developing software for squadrons, wings, groups, and flights, for example, and to drive down the time to production. He envisioned eventually driving down the 800 man-hours needed to deliver an application to cloud infrastructure to 100 man-hours, which would lower full-time equivalent costs and produce capabilities faster. Ms. Westphal wondered how this improvement would factor into the acquisition process and into companies and industry. Mr. Crocker acknowledged that acquisition presents a hurdle; BESPIN is trying to establish pre-vetted contracts focused on blueprinting application types, which could reduce contracting time from 90 to 30 days.

Ms. Westphal asked if there are any culture clashes between old and new processes as the organization matures. Mr. Crocker revealed that these clashes arise every day. He described the "frozen middle" that spends more time trying *not* to change than the time it would take to change. Repeated demonstrations of performance are key to showing stakeholders the art of the possible and "thawing" this frozen middle.

Dr. Green asked if BESPIN has an integrated platform-as-a-service so that when the data are integrated, a catalogue would show the classification levels of those data. Mr. Crocker said that BESPIN is working on the ingestion and virtualization layers to better understand metadata—everything being targeted is Impact Level 4 and is being tagged. BESPIN works with Palantir for some of the virtualization pieces, and meta-tagging efforts continue as the data are normalized. Dr. Green wondered if a data catalogue with data lineage exists. Mr. Crocker replied that this work is ongoing, but it is challenging given how much of the data are siloed.

Mr. Crocker explained that as BESPIN began to build applications, it realized that for 30 percent of each application, the development cycles were consumed by trying to get the data to work, trying to couple with data, trying to reach back for data, or trying to share data. He described this as a major pain point: the ~312 squadrons across the Air Force were spending an average of 100 man-hours each per week working with data. This was the impetus for moving Data-as-a-Service to an enterprise level effort, and a new contracting methodology made it possible to "double-dip" contract dollars for capabilities and realize substantial cost savings.

Mr. Santee observed that much of this work relates to process reform. He asked about BESPIN's process to move from a document-driven to a data-driven practice. Mr. Crocker noted that the first step was to consider how the user requirement could be addressed. He emphasized the value of involving people in solving problems instead of forcing them to adopt preconceived solutions. Once the problem was understood, solutions had been exhausted, and the best solution had been identified, a directive emerged. That then drove the process reform of the Air Force Instruction. He added that DoD's discomfort with policy change remains a challenge, but this is a better approach.

Ms. Westphal inquired about challenges or opportunities to accelerate to a digital force. Mr. Crocker replied that innovation efforts need more champions and should be vectored under a functional owner. Having topcover *and an established funding line for at least 3 years* for these innovation efforts would help to thaw the frozen middle overall, he continued. Ms. Westphal wondered if innovative people will stay with the Air Force or will seek more interesting careers elsewhere. Mr. Crocker noted that the Air Force needs to prevent industry from hiring its experts by providing relevant training, topcover for flexible innovation, and an empowering career path.

CONSTRAINTS AND CONSIDERATIONS FOR OPERATING IN THE FUTURE: A PANEL PRESENTATION

Dr. Julie Ryan, chief executive officer, Wyndrose Technical Group, and study lead for the National Academies of Sciences, Engineering, and Medicine report *Energizing Data-Driven Operations at the Tactical Edge: Challenges and Concerns*,[1] noted that the Air Force uses a significant amount of energy; in 2017, it used 48 percent of energy expenditures for the entire DoD. Of that, 86 percent was for aviation fuel and 11 percent was for installation expenditures. With 97 percent of expenditures being used for aviation fuel and installation, a question arises about the tactical edge. The conversation about the future revolves around everything being wired for sensors and communication and coordinated using AI and ML, and creating sense and process data for a highly coordinated decision cycle capability against adversaries.

She explained that the National Academies was charged to investigate and produce a report on energy challenges and opportunities for future data-driven operations. The study committee was expected to

---

[1] National Academies of Sciences, Engineering, and Medicine, 2021, *Energizing Data-Driven Operations at the Tactical Edge: Challenges and Concerns*, The National Academies Press, Washington, DC, https://doi.org/10.17226/26183.

investigate the current state of Air Force planning, research and development, and expectations related to energy usage for military operations in the 2030 time frame; investigate potential threats to energy assurance and access based on recent events and assumptions of future energy dependence that should inform Air Force/government planning for energy generation, storage, and use; investigate and describe current research and state of the art in energy efficient computation including hardware, software, and big data; investigate and describe the energy needs for advanced weapons platforms including the static infrastructure that provides support to ML, AI, and integrated operations; and recommend manpower, research, and expertise requirements needed for the future energy environment.

Dr. Ryan commented that we live in an energy rich environment where we take power flow for granted—a bad assumption for operating in a contested environment. With the explosion of IT within warfighting systems (e.g., wearables, and emerging concepts such as JADO and dynamic basing), two questions arise: (1) How will devices that enable the knowledge-based future be powered? (2) How will devices that are farthest from stable and permanent locations manage their energy needs? She emphasized that without power, there are no data, no communications, no data processing, and no collaboration. She described one of the models used by the study committee to explore these questions. The Energy Ecosystem model includes transmission (data and energy), protection (energy grid, mission/force), time horizon (today and 10 years into the future), and environmental controls (temperature, humidity, and particulates), all anchored by compute and storage capabilities.

The study committee came to consensus on 47 findings and 16 recommendations in its report, some of which Dr. Ryan summarized for workshop participants as follows:

- Energy needs associated with readiness are not expressly collected. No one knows how much energy will be needed for the functionality of data processing or to support combat operations at the tactical edge. Yet, the impact from loss of power is potentially devastating. The ability to execute mission requirements with knowledge-intensive systems must be reflected in both unit and mission readiness associated with the energy required. The committee recommended including energy needs in readiness reporting metrics for all weapons systems. The committee also recommended that resource and capability readiness assessments should include the availability of adequate and *appropriate* energy to ensure data capabilities at the tactical edge.
- Pull-the-plug activities are not included in most field exercises; in fact, most field exercises have extremely robust energy infrastructures. Yet, power and other infrastructures associated with power will be the targets of attack and will not be continuously available. Losses may stem from existing poor commercial infrastructure, enemy denial, lack of maintenance, lack of fuel, or human error. The committee recommended conducting pull-the-plug exercises for all realistic field exercises. Data from those exercises should be used by the mission planners, and the results of the pull-the-plug exercises on tactical edge data capabilities should be used to revise and update mission readiness assessments.
- Energy needs for computational support are not defined in any major weapons system or mission profile. The committee made the recommendation to include energy needs associated with data expectations, both for support and internal to the mission or system, as explicit requirements for all missions and systems. The contracts should include language that requires specific and complete descriptions of energy needs, types, and compatibility with logistics support. It is also essential to explicitly address the energy minimization, power consumption monitoring, and energy generation for the tactical edge information environment, including all small devices and Internet of Things capabilities.
- The manpower skillset needed to maintain, install, and upkeep energy at the tactical edge is rare. The committee recommended establishing a manpower program to recruit, educate, assign, and train both military and civilian personnel to address the energy challenges associated with data-driven operations, particularly those not likely to be solved by the commercial enterprise. The committee also recommended that energy engineers (particularly specialists such as antenna and

radio frequency engineers) should be incentivized with interesting work opportunities.
- Delivering energy to users (especially small users) is a challenge. The committee made the recommendations to develop an economic benefit model exploring the utility, opportunity costs, risks, and benefits for different energy delivery modes; explore alternative methods of harvesting, storing, and reusing power; and consider the logistics tail for the energy types and methods of delivery from the perspective of cost efficiency of energy delivery and operational costs associated with single energy sourcing. Dr. Ryan added that the Marines are experimenting with using drones to deliver batteries to small users (as opposed to conventional fuel convoys), which mitigates human risk and reduces opportunity cost if the drone is shot down and another needs to be sent.
- Technological interoperability is a concern for deployed American forces, particularly in foreign countries that have different energy infrastructures. The committee recommended considering interoperability with foreign nation power systems and partner military forces when designing power systems, including standardization of certain elements and plug-and-play capability.
- The energy implications of planning and design choices need to be understood. The committee made the recommendation to invest in future research (e.g., product and process technologies associated with reducing energy usage, minimizing energy logistics risk, and improving energy resiliencies; energy-aware algorithms in practical deployable software; and approximation techniques in software algorithms that are effective in energy reduction without compromising accuracy) and conduct experimental campaigns in realistic scenarios, including a variety of systems and deployment characteristics of tactical-edge units, to guide the research and implementation potentials.

Dr. Ryan described energy as an urgent consideration for the Air Force. She noted that because it will take a substantial amount of time to develop a comprehensive research program, these areas have to be prioritized. The committee suggested the following plan:

- *Near term*—energy needs and readiness, pull-the-plug exercises, explicit energy requirements, and manpower.
- *Midterm*—energy minimization, skillsets, energy resilience, and interoperability.
- *Longer term*—research.

Ms. Westphal asked which aspects of energy the Air Force could consider, given that it may have different energy sources in the future than it had in the past. Dr. Ryan said that it might not be possible to develop airplanes that run on batteries with the same thrust and capability as those that run on petroleum-based fuel. She explained that as global warming becomes an even more significant problem, petroleum-based fuels will likely be reserved for trucks and planes, while everything else will be forced to use renewable waste systems, kinetic energy generation, and transportable solar grids and wind systems. This transition would require new knowledge capabilities, implementation strategies, and transformers. Ms. Westphal inquired about operational partnerships around energy, and Dr. Ryan noted that potential conflict areas such as the Sahara Desert or the Himalayas create particular challenges because of the environments and the particulates (e.g., if the humidity is at the wrong level, technology does not function). Because the Air Force will operate in so many different environments, this as a nontrivial engineering challenge.

Ms. Westphal wondered if the study committee considered the relationship between energy and competition with China. Although the committee did not address this issue in its report, Dr. Ryan mentioned that Elizabeth Economy has done research on how China relies on Africa and other places to obtain energy and grow food for its people. China is resource poor, and its primary raw material for energy is coal, but in order to achieve the national priority to reduce pollution, coal use would need to be reduced. China has thus begun to embrace solar and wind energy. She explained that China is moving into energy independence faster than the United States; however, because China is pushing down the per-unit cost, the rest of the world now has more opportunity to become energy-independent.

Dr. Drew stressed that the Air Force has to invest in this issue because industry does not have a ready solution for the energy problem. Dr. Ryan underscored that the solution demands collaboration between civil engineers and operators, which is a challenge given that they speak different languages and work in different time horizons. Dr. Chellappa added that energy will be extremely important to enable AI-based systems in space. He also noted that AI would benefit substantially if low-power graphics processing units could be designed that are easier to cool.

Col. Jonathan Zall, ABMS Cross-Functional Team (CFT), Air Force Futures, Headquarters Air Force (HAF) A5, described ABMS as the DAF's contribution to the joint force's JADC2 effort. The ABMS CFT developed a campaign plan to address what the warfighters have identified as major capability gaps associated with command and control and battle management. Many of these gaps and opportunities relate to digitization; he asserted that when the outcome is increasing success on the battlefield and bringing airmen home safely, these opportunities to digitize become obligations.

Ms. Westphal asked about the role of the CFT as well as its relationship to the larger DAF architecture and technology effort. Col. Zall described the CFT as the bridge between (1) the warfighters and their capability needs; and (2) the acquisitions team and others who will develop the DOTMLPF-P (doctrine, organization, training, materiel, leadership, personnel, facilities, and policy) solution set. He emphasized that the CFT is not comprised of technologists; the CFT's role is to understand and codify capability gaps and accelerate the delivery of usable solutions. The CFT first assembles an operations planning team to address specific warfighter-required capabilities (e.g., communications, connectivity, decision making). After identifying gaps and opportunities, the CFT assembles an integrated development team to accelerate the delivery of solutions to the warfighter—instead of writing requirements and then providing a capability 10 years later. The goal is to emerge from this process with a list of requirements, a test plan, and the documentation to move forward quickly to achieve minimum viable products and prepare to transition to a sustainable program for the warfighter.

Ms. Westphal wondered whether the CFT has quantitative or anecdotal data to demonstrate that this approach has increased the speed of the process. Col. Zall replied that because this is a new effort, there are no measurable data available yet. The CFT is adjusting to the vision of the new leadership and is optimistic that once the campaign plan has full approval, the CFT can move forward and begin to measure success, which is important to demonstrate value.

Ms. Westphal asked whether ABMS is issuing warfighting capabilities in a way that embraces the desired operational speed and behavior of the digital transformation. Col. Zall explained that ABMS plans to leverage the efficiencies that the Rapid Capabilities Office can achieve in delivering capabilities, and translate those into broad, scalable, sustainable programs of record for warfighters to use operationally. However, limitations and constraints exist: instead of writing new laws, ABMS is trying to work within the existing framework and use efficiencies within the broader system. In response to a question from Ms. Westphal about priority areas for the CFT, Col. Zall stressed that addressing "the China problem," is a top priority, because previous approaches to executing battle management and command and control will not lead to the desired results in a competition with China. The CFT is considering how ABMS could provide operational advantage—particularly decision advantage. The CFT is also focused on data sharing as the key enabler for progress: data sharing will establish the information flow to achieve decision superiority. In response to a question from Mr. Munson about the Chinese DF-21D, Col. Zall said that owing to its organizational construct, the CFT views problems holistically instead of addressing specific threats. Mr. Munson suggested that focusing on that particular threat could lead to more expedited acquisition authorities.

Ms. Westphal asked if there is a unity of effort in the Air Force to become a digital force, which would enable solutions for the data-sharing problem. Col. Zall noted that while many people within the Air Force are working on this urgent problem, it is not happening under a single authority. Individual commands, geographic areas, and agencies are working on different solutions, and many efforts are duplicative. To achieve unity of effort, Col. Zall suggested establishing the credibility of the CFT (including the Rapid Capabilities Office and others involved in the process) as warfighter advocates who are capable of delivering something worthwhile before another problem emerges. At that point, he continued, it may be possible to expand ABMS and achieve coherence across efforts.

Col. Zall expressed his concern about balancing the optimization of the day-to-day office environment with the optimization of a dynamic combat environment, and wondered if others consider that tension when prioritizing efforts for the digital transformation. Mr. Santee noted that there is a difference between formatting data for a repository for future analysis and formatting data in motion, such as those for ABMS's purposes. The Aerospace Corporation is trying to determine the optimum trade-off between data in motion (e.g., weapons systems data) and data at rest (e.g., maintenance data) for the Space Force. Gen. Holmes encouraged the CFT to continue to optimize its approach to best support the warfighter. Dr. Paul Nielsen (USAF, ret.), director and chief executive officer, Software Engineering Institute, Carnegie Mellon University, posited that although digitization could improve almost everything in the Air Force, that does not mean that everything has to be on the same network or be fully integrated (e.g., things with different time scales of operations than the warfighter capabilities). Gen. Holmes cautioned against optimizing Cloud One for analysis at the expense of latency for warfighters and highlighted the advantage of having multiple providers.

Col. Zall asked workshop participants for their perspectives on decision advantage as well as on the optimization of data flow and data management for a human decision maker versus for analysis. Mr. Santee emphasized that while increased decision-making speed is critical, improved decision-making *quality* is even more important—with higher quality data from exquisite sensors and more data informing the decision. He said that The Aerospace Corporation is encouraging the Space Force to use the Unified Data Library but noted that using it in an ABMS environment might not be as effective. Col. Zall noted that speed often results from the elimination of unnecessary delays that have been baked into processes. He echoed Mr. Santee's assertion about decision-making quality, because if a person makes the wrong decision, it will not matter how quickly he did so. He added that ABMS is not only improving command and control processes but also creating a gap between the decision capability and the decision quality of the adversary.

Ms. Victoria Yan Pillitteri, acting manager for Security Engineering and Risk Management Group, Information Technology Laboratory, National Institute of Standards and Technology (NIST), explained that NIST's mission is to promote U.S. innovation and industrial competitiveness by advancing measurement science, standards, and technology in ways that enhance the economic security and improve overall quality of life. One of NIST's strengths is its reputation as a neutral technical entity. It strives for technical excellence and integrity; is uncompromising in its pursuit of truth; is rigorous in its processes and methodologies; and provides an unbiased industry-focused result of standards, technology transfer, and research outputs. Serving as a non-regulatory agency within the U.S. Department of Commerce, NIST promotes the competitiveness of U.S. companies worldwide. NIST cultivates trust in technology and cybersecurity through research and development, the transition of research products to practice, the development of standards and best practices, outreach, and interagency and private sector coordination and collaboration to ensure that the research and products developed serve relevant communities of interest. NIST's technical guidance is leveraged by the federal agencies, the private sector, industry, academia, and international governments and companies.

Ms. Pillitteri noted that NIST has three types of publications related to cybersecurity and privacy standards and guidelines: (1) the Federal Information Processing Standards (FIPS) are developed when required by statute and/or a compelling federal government requirement for cybersecurity; (2) Special Publications (SPs) serve as guidelines, technical specifications, recommendations, and technical reference materials; and (3) Interagency Reports are reports of research findings, including background information for FIPS and SPs. All three types of publications are intended to help organizations of any sector or size better manage risk. NIST's research staff also develops research papers for technical conferences, presents poster sessions, and issues white papers and green papers. She explained that a robust and participatory process is used for the research and development of NIST standards and guidelines, based on the following foundational principles: transparency, openness, balance, integrity, technical merit, global acceptability, usability, continuous improvement, and innovation. First, NIST identifies a research topic for publication or update. NIST then conducts research and seeks preliminary stakeholder input. The NIST staff will continue researching and begin to draft the publication. When ready, it will be published for a public comment period. At the end of the comment period, NIST collects *all* input received, and reviews, analyzes, and adjudicates it. A decision is made whether additional stakeholder input is necessary and, if so, whether additional research is needed before the final publication of the document. She emphasized that NIST is committed to vetting its publications thoroughly, and releasing timely and relevant information to support the needs of industry.

Dr. Chellappa pointed out that the NIST-800 series standards are too restrictive for universities. If the federal government were to require universities to follow NIST-800, universities would not be able to accept grants from the federal government. He wondered how NIST balances security concerns with the value of working in an open environment. Ms. Pillitteri replied that NIST guidance advocates that all organizations in all sectors do basic due diligence in protecting their systems and information. She said that many DoD organizations use NIST SP 800-171 to protect the confidentiality of controlled unclassified information, but she acknowledged the need to balance openness to allow critical collaborations with the protection of federal information. Although specific federal agencies determine their own security protocols for their partnerships, a university that is processing, sorting, or transmitting federally controlled unclassified information would have to follow the minimum safeguarding requirements in NIST SP 800-171, which are required by law.

Dr. Langston remarked that the NIST-800 series is human-intensive, and he wondered why automated penetration testing tools are not used to validate the security of systems. Ms. Pillitteri commented that there is no "silver bullet" to address all security concerns. She said that there is a place for the processes and procedures at the governance level, and a place for the specific technical tests. How tests are conducted at different organizations depends on each organization's system architecture, security architecture, solutions, and processes. Because NIST has no insight into many of these variables, when it writes technical guidelines, it is building a foundation that can be customized by environment. Dr. Langston expressed his concern about the cottage industry of "cyber experts" who are not true cyber experts and thus are unable to secure organizations. Ms. Pillitteri articulated that this reinforces the need for standards, which provide a common language and common principles.

Gen. Holmes observed that a compliance-based system measures *compliance*, not *security*. Although there are many opportunities for people to write standards and for consultants to ensure compliance, systems do not become more secure unless they transition to a zero-trust approach, in which the data are secured through encryption—and even then, no system is ever truly safe from potential violation. Ms. Pilliterri stressed that there is no one-size-fits-all solution for security. She stated that there is a role for compliance with the bare minimum level of security for all systems, but it is important to incorporate critical risk management concepts. Gen. Holmes pointed out that the Air Force has a non-functional network; it is meaningless if this system is compliant when the performance is so poor. Ms. Pilliterri described this as an example of the value of good system design and engineering: it is important to build better systems (e.g., with cybersecurity, privacy, functionality, safety) from the ground up.

Ms. Westphal noted that if the plan is to build well-designed systems, it is important to take a future perspective of design. She also said that "digital trade" has several interpretations, owing to different perspectives on privacy and data across the globe. She wondered if NIST's standards could address some of these issues. Ms. Pillitteri noted that in addition to developing standards, NIST's experts participate in international standardization activities to ensure that the United States' position is well represented. She explained that it is difficult to design systems that are "future-proof" because of the challenges associated with anticipating future needs.

Mr. Munson reiterated that the Air Force needs a clear understanding of how attractive of a cyber target this proposed digital environment would create. He wondered how to achieve the best industrial strength cyber defense capability and whether a partnership with NIST could be suggested to the Air Force. Ms. Pillitteri responded that NIST is always interested in working with any of the federal agencies. She noted that this is a difficult problem to solve, especially given the shortage of the cyber workforce across the government and the private sector, and the challenge of securing the supply chain. She underscored that it will never be impossible to commit a cyber breach. Mr. Munson stressed that if it is not possible to create defenses to protect this rich data repository with facilitated access and tools, the Air Force should not develop a highly integrated, highly facilitated data architecture to underpin its digitization; it should instead use physical separations where necessary so that it is impossible for someone to breach and access the entire combination of data sets critical to the Air Force's functioning. Ms. Pillitteri replied that the Air Force has to understand the value of its information and integrate protection that is commensurate with the associated level of risk, but it also has to understand that there are no security guarantees.

6

Workshop Three, Part Two

OPENING REMARKS

Workshop series co-chair Ms. Deborah Westphal, chairman of the board, Toffler Associates, welcomed participants to the final day of the workshop series and provided an overview of themes that emerged in the previous day's discussions. She described her observations about the many hidden risks and gaps in the Air Force's digitization effort, including those related to the Air Force's need to

- Consider energy at the tactical edge and an overall strategy for energy;
- Develop a strategy for semiconductors to leverage artificial intelligence (ai) and machine learning;
- Understand china's digitization strategy, which includes data collection on citizens;
- Emphasize privacy, transparency, security, accessibility, and usability of data;
- Avoid using doctrine only to document past successes;
- Recognize risk without limiting future possibilities;
- Train and retain personnel;
- Fund the future instead of pay for the past;
- Address both the time to transition and the clash with old ways;
- Embrace partnerships in a contested environment;
- Determine who has decision-making authorities and how to speed up those decisions;
- Differentiate between enterprise strategies and operational strategies; and
- "Thaw the frozen middle" so that bottom-up innovations can flourish.

Dr. Marv Langston (USN, ret.), independent consultant, suggested that the Air Force adopt Andrew Stricker's Digital Transformation Cycle to highlight gaps and opportunities. Mr. Alden Munson, senior fellow and member, Board of Regents, Potomac Institute for Policy Studies, expressed continued concern about the Air Force's cybersecurity challenges. Although the ideal system would have all of the data necessary to support Air Force operations catalogued in a digital archive with ready access, if it is not possible to implement capable cyber defenses, that type of architecture may not be feasible. Instead, the data may need to be partitioned with a firewall, behind which it is not possible to access the entire data set. Mr. Jay Santee (USAF, ret.), vice president, Strategic Space Operations, Defense Systems Group, The Aerospace Corporation, stressed that although the cybersecurity issue is important, it cannot be an excuse for inaction. The United States cannot afford to lose its ability to compete with the adversaries. Because much work is involved in securing and maintaining the desired infrastructure, he suggested that the Air Force hire contractors to govern and maintain the architecture. He underscored that the digital transformation is about process reform: processes have to collapse and change in the transition from document artifacts to digital artifacts. It is crucial to provide access to higher-quality information to make better decisions. To be successful, he continued, the Air Force cannot simply issue tools; it should let people *create* them. Gen. James (Mike) Holmes (USAF, ret.), senior advisor, The Roosevelt Group, explained that decentralized action is essential in a world where communications will be continually attacked; instead of having 1,000 people in an air operations center planning and executing operations, it is important to bring the data to the people at the edge and allow them to make decisions. This cultural shift is a massive piece of the transformation effort. Mr. Santee agreed with Gen. Holmes that the governance of who can make decisions at what level will be critical.

FUTURE CYBER AND ELECTROMAGNETIC SPECTRUM ISSUES: A PANEL PRESENTATION

Col. Lisle Babcock, former LeMay Center Commander, emphasized that if the Air Force focuses only on digitizing *cyber* capabilities, it could miss an important opportunity to use electromagnetic spectrum (EMS) capabilities to gain superiority.

He explained that in 2019, the LeMay Center was tasked with writing doctrine for joint all-domain operations, which was the first time the Air Force adopted a forward-looking perspective for doctrine. The goal of this effort was to consider how the force could be deployed 3 to 5 years into the future, and to look across all domains to find a way to converge and bring kinetic and non-kinetic effects to bear at the edge of the fight. The next step was to consider the expected loss of communications in a contested environment with a peer adversary and how AI and mesh networks could be used to bring available data to the right people at the forward edge to execute commander's intent. He referenced Gen. Charles Brown's intent to use doctrine to change the culture of the Air Force—breaking the paradigms of centralized control and centralized command; expanding pipelines of communications for cyber capabilities; and training flight, group, squad, and wing commanders to make decisions without additional command and control communications and based on the risks to force and mission and available data. Delegating control of both assets and authorities is key to success in a contested environment. He said that Gen. Brown also stressed that recording ideas on paper is insufficient; people have to be trained differently.

Col. Babcock remarked that a true digital culture promotes external versus internal orientation, comprises delegation of control, encourages boldness over caution, emphasizes more action and less planning, and values collaboration over individual effort. These five elements tie into the joint all-domain operations doctrine as well as to Air Force Doctrine Publication 1, which discusses mission command, centralized planning, and decentralized execution of capabilities. A culture change is also needed in teaching, executing, and exercising capabilities within the Air Force, he continued, so that airmen are prepared to fight in a contested environment.

Col. Babcock asserted that accessing exquisite information and delegating control for decision making requires using the full spectrum of the EMS to revive data and relay them between the Air Operations Center (AOC) and the forward edge. He reiterated that the Air Force will lose the fight if it focuses only on networks and frequency ranges for cyber capabilities, without consideration for the entire EMS as a capability. In 2019, HAF A5L was stood up to serve as the EMS Superiority Directorate within HAF A5.

This group is considering how to build a software-defined radio capability that would "plug-and-play" with all current systems. This digital radio would link to major communications and provide data in real time, and enable a quick hop rate through multiple frequencies to avoid jamming or exploitation by the enemy.

Ms. Westphal asked how Air Force Futures could provide more value in the 10- to 15-year time frame. Col. Babcock described a symbiotic relationship between the LeMay Center and Air Force Futures. Because the LeMay Center tends to focus on a 3- to 5-year outlook and Air Force Futures focuses on the 5- to 20-year outlook, Air Force Futures is reviewing the LeMay Center's lessons learned. Rear Adm. David Simpson (USN, ret.), chief executive officer, Pelorus Consulting; partner, Deep Water Point; and professor, Virginia Tech, pointed out that with the increased use of AI and airpower to respond to threats at machine speed, human-impacting decision operations will shift, with the human contribution to the OODA (observe, orient, decide, act) loop occurring weeks, months, or years in advance. He proposed that senior leaders shift similarly and focus on the data collection plan, the inference bias being generated, whether new threat observations from the adversary have been employed to adjust algorithms, and whether the AOC is responding to the trend to have more unmanned aviation in the battlespace (for which the algorithm will predetermine a response). Col. Babcock replied that expert adjudicators in the LeMay Center's Wargames Center discuss what war could look like in 2035. The vision for the OODA loop is transitioning from human-*in*-the-loop to human-*on*-the-loop, to ensure quality and accuracy of algorithms. This new vision can only be achieved, however, if people trust machine learning; this will lead to buy-in from warfighters on the forward edge, and then the "human on the loop" could eventually reduce involvement further. He anticipated that the AOC will serve as a "fuser" for all of the individual operating areas and as a manager for the battlespaces. He noted that the forward edge leader should be able to assess risk, make a decision, and continue to operate until told otherwise. However, senior leaders have to be trained to be comfortable with empowering subordinates, as this is a substantial cultural shift for the Air Force.

Brig. Gen. Greg Touhill (USAF, ret.), director, Software Engineering Institute (SEI) Cybersecurity Division, underscored the value of the warfighter's perspective in digital transformation. Encryption and cryptography are becoming more important, and quantum computing continues to show promise for the future. However, the Air Force's current encryption and cryptography capabilities are "elderly" from an Internet-age time frame. He stressed that the Air Force needs to increase its investments in encryption and cryptography to improve its cybersecurity posture.

He described rapid advancements in AI and machine learning—for example, robotic process automation (RPA) is being implemented across business functions that underpin the warfighting capability in the Air Force, and throughout the government and industry more broadly. There have also been developments in robotic coding. As a result, SEI is focused on "fuzzing": checking the code that is developed by machines for error and correction using AI capabilities. He cautioned that adversaries are using the same AI capabilities for automated polymorphic malware development. There has also been an increase in the employment of robo-hackers in the commercial sector, and he expressed concern that this technology could be used lethally by adversaries on the battlefield to interfere with operations. However, the U.S. military has experienced substantial advances in autonomous systems that could be useful in contested environments, and those systems will continue to evolve. Other nation states and commercial enterprises are also investing in autonomous systems.

Brig. Gen. Touhill also expressed concern about the "suspect supply chain" (e.g., What is in your code, who is in your code, and where did your code come from?), and he noted that the U.S. government does not have a firm understanding of the provenance of its code. There has been a significant amount of software reuse among commercial products over the course of decades. Although difficult to create, he advocated for a software bill of materials. Because the risk surface is so vast (e.g., firmware, operational technology, Internet of Things devices, weapon systems, embedded systems), the Air Force needs to increase its aperture as cyber risk is assessed with the supply chain of software. Another area of concern is cloud security. Migration into cyber clouds is drastically increasing and has essentially become a business imperative throughout the defense industrial base, industry, and the military. Thus, he continued, it is critical to ask the following questions about cloud security: Who is on the virtual machine next to me? Who is on the container next to me?

Dr. Langston questioned why the Air Force is not taking advantage of quantum technologies. Brig. Gen. Touhill said that although there is movement toward practical applications for quantum, it is still in the very early stages. A higher level of maturity in the technical stack is needed to build reliable applications. However, because the curve is accelerating quickly, he suggested that the Air Force invest in the technologies and be aware of how adversaries are investing in them.

Brig. Gen. Touhill turned to a discussion of zero trust, which he defined as a security strategy, not a product. Zero trust is a starting point in which breaches are assumed and trust has to be earned; a person only has access to particular content based on specific authorization. Using the Office of Personnel Management (OPM) hack as an example, he explained that organizations often fail to understand their own data. Unclassified OPM data were deemed unimportant, without consideration for the sensitivity of those data. OPM did not understand who owned the data, how the data were hosted, or who could access the data; and rules about who should see the data were not defined. He described this as an ongoing challenge across the military. As Air Combat Command leads a zero-trust initiative for the Air Force, it is important to understand the data: where they are, who owns them, who should access them under what conditions, and how they are managed. He asserted that zero trust is a critical component of national security and prosperity as the Air Force moves forward.

Ms. Westphal pointed out that understanding data requires insight about supply chains. Brig. Gen. Touhill replied that the scope and scale of the products, hardware, goods, and services create a difficult problem, but random sampling remains one of the best practices. Additionally, when companies ask third-party providers for data feeds from robotic process lines, it is possible to plug-in to some of the AI capabilities to evaluate the consistency and quality control of some of the product lines. He said that this use of machines to check machines will likely become more prevalent. Mr. Munson added that in the case of SolarWinds, penetration of a small company represented a major compromise for the nation. He asked if the supply chain problem should be treated as a major threat to national security. Brig. Gen. Touhill responded that the supply chain is a whole-of-government issue, and a government-private sector partnership could begin to address the problem.

Brig. Gen. Touhill's final topic of discussion was the value of the EMS. He explained that the "untethered world" of mobility and various devices has provided excellent capabilities but has also presented extreme risk. The U.S. military's outdated cryptography and encryption technologies continue to be employed throughout the fielded forces because there is a misplaced perception of legacy system security. He added that cyberattacks are under way, but the Air Force does not have methods to address an adversary attacking the EMS. He emphasized that as space-based intelligence, surveillance, and reconnaissance and communications platforms become critical elements of the warfighting capability, it is important to pay attention to how cyber and the EMS are connected, and to allocate resources to protect the EMS.

Dr. Langston wondered why there are no "hide-in-plain-sight" efforts for software-defined networking. Brig. Gen. Touhill said that networks are now at the level of people and their devices. A challenge for the future is to leverage technologies (e.g., software-defined perimeter) to burn through the contested cyber environment while maintaining a measure of mission effectiveness. Dr. Langston suggested applying resources that are being wasted on outdated technology. Brig. Gen. Touhill noted that although the interrelated mesh is very capable, there are still ways to take it down. It is important to maintain some independence as well as a dedicated communications capability with multiple layers that is resilient by design.

Mr. Steven Hernandez, Chief Information Security Officer, U.S. Department of Education, opened his presentation with a discussion of the threat scape in the federal civilian space. He explained that the adversary continues to be impressive in its ability to automate, orchestrate, and defeat U.S. defenses. When building these defenses, every "brick" in the "wall" has to be placed correctly; an adversary only needs to find a single gap in the construct to gain access. Compliance with security standards is also critical. While there is an increased demand for red teaming exercises, he pointed out that these efforts are only as effective as the expertise involved. Even though a red team may clear a system, it does not mean the system is completely safe; it just means that a particular aspect of expert knowledge has been exhausted. To address this issue, he rotates his red teams every year or every quarter. He reiterated that the threat fully understands that only one weakness needs to be identified to establish a presence. With the increasingly blurred line between the personal and the professional lives of warfighters, there has been an increase in the number of attacks that leverage warfighters' personal information for use against the government. He asserted that as a result, an identity management framework is needed to help warfighters understand the role of identity and its relationship to ensuring the protection of U.S. systems and missions.

Mr. Hernandez noted that disruption is the new currency for attackers, most often emerging via ransomware. He discussed a devolution of communication—for example, soldiers who have to buy local cell phones and download What's App just to complete a mission. He emphasized that warfighters should have secure and assured services when and where they need them. However, when this is not the case, it is essential to have a mechanism to secure communications on commercial civilian technology. He also described today's secure, encrypted traffic as the "decrypted fodder" for tomorrow's quantum computers. It is important to think about the type of information being sent, the type of encryption being used, and what quantum means in terms of risk when it becomes powerful enough to break modern encryption technologies.

Mr. Hernandez turned to a discussion of federal initiatives to build more resilient defenses, noting a disconnect between vendors' proposed security and the reality. For example, although 5G has security capabilities, because they are rudimentary and do not integrate well with other security technologies, 5G remains an untrusted network. He remarked that having access to high quality data is important. Although data do not need to be located in one place, visibility of the data across the data ecosystem is key to decision making. The Office of Management and Budget (OMB) Memorandum 21-31 creates a foundation—fidelity, robustness, and visibility requirements—for data logging. After the SolarWinds breach, OMB Memorandum 21-30 was released to ensure that it is possible to identify critical software assets throughout an enterprise as well as who has enterprise-level visibility.

Mr. Hernandez explained that the current federal civilian estimate for funding shortfall in cybersecurity is approximately $9 billion. In the Technology Modernization Funding for 2021, Congress allocated $1 billion, for which the agencies can compete. This funding approach helps determine how to release legacy infrastructure constructs because it provides an infusion of cash for acceleration of IT modernization, especially for those projects that push toward new security architectures and better civilian-facing services. For instance, his department is 100 percent cloud-based, and many other federal agencies are moving in that direction. The Cybersecurity Infrastructure and Security Agency (CISA) recently released a draft secure cloud migration document that will be used by federal agencies in an effort to establish trust. CISA has also released a maturity model for zero trust, with different capabilities at various levels. It can take decades to achieve a mature digital trust architecture: zero trust is a lifestyle and a journey, not a destination. Organizations with a strong credential access management approach and a strong data approach are now focusing on the control plane with Secure Access Service Edge as an intermediary step (i.e., agile, flexible edge in the cloud through which services are accessed; and always-on encryption) and with Security Orchestration, Automation, and Response (i.e., robotic processes, automation, algorithms, and rules are taking immediate action based on real-time observations by redefining a software-defined network, establishing a new perimeter, or moving traffic to a honeypot). In closing, he highlighted areas in which the Air Force is succeeding: the foundation for a zero-trust architecture has emerged but will continue to evolve, and Platform One has helped build foundational capabilities for DevSecOps. He encouraged the Air Force to continue to expand those efforts.

Open Discussion

Dr. Langston suggested the use of automated penetration testing, and Mr. Hernandez noted a distinction between automated vulnerability discovery and penetration testing, which would rise to the next level of exploitation. He commented that automated penetration testing is effective in that it serves as a stop gap and in some cases has a human element, in which discovered vulnerabilities are passed to researchers. However, a significant amount of trust in the vendor is needed for this approach.

Mr. Munson observed a vulnerability around the Air Force's commitment to encouraging small companies to offer products. Often, the cyber defenses of these small companies are limited owing to scarce financial resources. He wondered how to continue to encourage these companies without accepting the cyber vulnerabilities that might accompany them. Mr. Hernandez responded that if the government wants high-assurance systems and platforms, it has to be willing to invest in those spaces when they are critical to the mission.

Dr. Rama Chellappa, Bloomberg Distinguished Professor of electrical and computer engineering and biomedical engineering, Johns Hopkins University, said that the cybersecurity community is already worried about the potential vulnerability of a deep learning system that has not been implemented on a wide scale. Mr. Hernandez remarked that deep learning is siloed for the federal government. He added that it is not the concept of deep learning that is challenging; it is the capabilities of the vendors and how they can be applied across the enterprise. The important challenge now is to work on high-assurance data and data visibility so that deep learning has something to view. Brig Gen. Touhill explained that among the many types of data (structured data, unstructured data, semi-structured data, and metadata) throughout the life cycle, the three key foci are (1) data integrity (accuracy and completeness), (2) data quality (readable and compliant with organizational requirements), and (3) data security (unaltered). These three components are especially important in deep learning environments. He asserted that "Grade A" data and a "Grade A" process leads to "Grade A" conclusions.

Ms. Westphal asked if the EMS is an area of future conflict and whether technology development is enabling its more efficient use. Brig Gen. Touhill emphasized that the EMS is already a contested space: there is much congestion and demand for bandwidth, and there is a drive for competitive advantage, ongoing espionage, and leverage of the EMS for collection and gathering. Col. Babcock explained that China and Russia are leveraging ultra-high frequency technologies. However, ultra-wideband technology, which has been in existence for two decades, is used infrequently even though it enables the use of a larger portion of the spectrum at a lower threshold. Some technologies will require additional support from the commercial sector, but it is important to use and leverage existing technology to create a standard baseline across all capabilities. He underscored the need to change the culture of the administration, of capability development, and of the acquisition process, which has to become more streamlined and expeditious. Mr. Hernandez noted that the EMS will be available in the future in new forms. Starlink, for example, will likely become the premier data fabric for EMS. However, it is important to develop the right assurance and technology to leverage such a capability. Secure hardware development is also an important part of this discussion.

CREATING A SUSTAINABLE CAPABILITY FOR THE FUTURE: A PANEL PRESENTATION

Dr. Jake Sotiriadis, director of Operations and Engagement, Collaboration Laboratory and Research Faculty, National Intelligence University, said that the first part of digital transformation should be to determine whether the right questions are being asked and whether the entire range of possibilities is being considered. For example, even though the world is three- dimensional, senior leaders are still being given one-dimensional products to conceptualize complex issues. Another approach has been for everyone to coalesce around one vision of the future, which raises questions about an organization's ability to move forward. To build new concepts and develop new strategies for digital transformation, he emphasized the need to become comfortable with being uncomfortable. He noted how difficult it is to predict the future: history demonstrates that most assumptions about the future have been consistently wrong. Therefore, he stressed that it is critical to think about alternative future scenarios and to question assumptions as part of a "cognitive operating system," which is the systems-based approach to understanding interconnectivity and embracing analytic complexity in thought processes.

Dr. Sotiriadis posited that most people understand that digital transformation is a necessity to link antiquated platforms, make information ubiquitous, and overwhelm the adversary with thousands of kill chains. He pointed out that the Air Force has to begin "trading in the currency of uncertainty" because it cannot operate with definitive conclusions. It is important to begin to ask how alternative futures defy accepted probabilities to affect baseline assumptions. Although it is clear that all systems have to be networked (e.g., the Advanced Battle Management System and joint all-domain command and control [JADC2]) to overcome the digital connection deficit, the cognitive operating system plays just as important of a role. He explained that using the processes of strategic foresight and future studies allows for anticipatory thinking, rather than reactive action. Many countries in Europe and Asia are mandating that policies that impact digital transformation and human capital investments go through a process of "future proofing" (i.e., considering alternative future possibilities in terms of potential response and investments or divestments). This approach requires harnessing weak signals and emerging trends in the current strategic environment without being hindered by bureaucracy. For example, he asserted that the OODA loop, which is an inherently tactical approach that informs operational culture, does not lend itself well to the great power competition or to macro-level problems. Given the difficulty that private sector organizations have in anticipating change and crafting preferred futures, a hierarchical and bureaucratic organization with short-term budget cycles such as the Department of Defense (DoD) will face even greater challenges.

He underscored the value of considering the costs of inaction: a digitally connected, networked lethal force would be cognitively irrelevant if this new type of thinking is not embraced. If the focus on the future continues to revolve only around technology, strategic opportunities could be missed. The organizations best postured to dominate in a world of disruptive change are those that can adapt, learn, and anticipate. He emphasized that the most useful statements about the future should initially appear to be absurd. Part of embracing the notion of strategic foresight in planning includes tapping into virtual and augmented realities for training and helping decision makers better understand and consider potential responses to alternative future scenarios. Once this type of thinking becomes the norm instead of the exception, a cognitive operating system emerges at the enterprise level. In the past, these types of "futures" initiatives have been designated to a single office; instead, a more comprehensive approach would be beneficial, including the position of chief futurist to coordinate efforts across defense, academia, intelligence, and the private sector. In closing, he stated that more intellectual diversity is needed in the Air Force, as well as an acceptance that a national security metaverse is imminent.

Ms. Westphal asked if the Air Force should focus on addressing its lack of diverse thinkers before building the futures capability. Dr. Sotiriadis replied that both avenues could be pursued in parallel. Having the futures capability established as well as having a champion for futures thinking at the enterprise level will attract external voices. And then having the right people in the right positions evolving the capability will attract additional diverse thinkers.

Dr. Eneken Tikk, executive producer at Finland's Cyber Policy Institute, remarked that it has become costly economically, societally, and politically to be simultaneously a democratic society and an information society. She shared perspectives on cyber diplomacy and cybersecurity from different regions and countries.

First, she examined the perspective of the European Union, mentioning that even close allies have varied approaches to cyber operations. Europe has almost 100 percent connectivity, similar to North America. The Nordic countries, in particular, have very advanced information societies and have achieved a balance of dependence and resilience. However, these countries still confront challenges, in which parts of the population are so vulnerable that it becomes impossible for the government or military to defend them from threats. She noted that Europe does not perceive itself as a primary cyber operator or recipient of the use of military cyber capabilities. Europe has a high demand of administrative accountability for the development and use of information and communication technologies, and there are expectations of digital welfare states. There is also an expectation that the state guarantees that these services and solutions are reliable, trusted, and available. She explained that Europe has extraordinary privacy and transparency agreements, along with rigorous checks and balances, which limits the U.S./EU privacy shield. There are still conflicting attitudes across European countries toward more centralized cyber operations and the roles of cyber commands. There is also a strong pressure in Europe for the rule of law and for strict limitations on cyber operations. This law-centric thinking, she continued, makes it difficult to justify policy-driven agendas.

Second, Dr. Tikk remarked, Russia is a very moderate information society; it is far from 100 percent connected and does not aspire to become an advanced information society. Yet, it has been successful in destabilizing the Western narrative that information and communication technologies drive societal and economic benefits. Russia has successfully demonstrated the vulnerability of democratic processes as ideal landscapes for international cyber insecurity. However, Russia has for the most part been protected from Western cyber operations and is less exposed to inquiries of accountability than Western nations. She said that every Western cyber operation reinforces Russia's pursuit to convince the world that increased digital sovereignty and control over the national information space is needed.

Third, she shared the perspective of "Country N," which encompasses the outlooks of several countries. She explained that the average level of Internet penetration across the world is only ~60 percent, but there are many countries with 90 percent and many others with far less. "Country N" has an understanding of potential vulnerabilities and costs related to technological capabilities, but connectivity and technology dependence remain important issues. There is little international law on "Country N's" issues (e.g., capacity) and limited resources to deal with the issue independently. "Country N" is exposed to two different narratives—the Western narrative (the European Union and the United States) and the Russian narrative—and is pressured to choose between them. The Western problems of advanced capabilities and freedom of use are not well understood by "Country N." However, "Country N" is relatively untouched by advanced capabilities and is open to less advanced capabilities.

Based on these three perspectives, Dr. Tikk asserted that the future of military cyber capabilities and the limitations of their use remains unresolved; the most advanced countries are often at a disadvantage, and the United Nations charter does not divide the world into "good states" (democracies) and "bad states" (authoritarian regimes). There is a high risk associated with advanced capabilities to prompt international or bilateral control, and questions remain about return on and direction of investment. In closing, she noted that the world's technological capabilities are far less than those of Western societies, and the international community at large is increasingly becoming disconnected from these privileged countries. Thus, it is critical to consider both economic and political costs in discussions of digital transformation.

Dr. Julie Ryan, chief executive officer, Wyndrose Technical Group, asked how a country could identify a path forward in this situation. Dr. Tikk emphasized that the solution is different for every country. She cautioned against assuming that the most important agenda for one country would be the same for others. Western governments are increasingly disconnected from their own populations, which is especially problematic. Ms. Westphal wondered about the role of partnerships, especially in a contested environment, and Dr. Tikk stressed the value of alliances and cooperation but reiterated the need to think about cost. For example, a political tension has arisen because the United States and Europe have such different perspectives on privacy guarantees for individuals. However, political arrangements alone may not determine an outcome because there are still legal procedures to consider. The legal environment that may impose countermeasures to operations is no longer just an international issue; it is increasingly domestic. The more this affects populations, she continued, the more it affects industry or corporate actors, who can take action against U.S. policies or operations through domestic processes.

Mr. Patrick Sack, vice president and chief technologist, Oracle National Security Group, explained that Oracle supports organizations with the best and most trusted data to gain decision advantage. He said that with the evolution of cloud (which is replacing the need for organizations to have data centers behind their own firewalls and within their own perimeters), security is being taken seriously in commercial spaces for the first time.

He described cybersecurity as "asymmetric" because the attacker only has to be right once, while the defender has to be right always. With billions of dollars invested in cloud infrastructure and IT, and trillions of dollars invested in the sensitive content and intellectual property of cloud users, cloud providers have to think carefully about security. Therefore, cloud providers have many of the same concerns that the Air Force has about supply chains, security models, connectivity, insider threats, and trust. For example, because clouds are global and interconnected, disrupted communications on such a large network could be catastrophic. He pointed out that cloud providers have a responsibility for this critical infrastructure, including the money, lives, and jobs at stake.

Mr. Sack noted that data centers are interconnected with compute and storage and with redundant high-speed communications all over the world. Although Oracle and Microsoft Azure are competitors, they have connected their data centers to prevent increased threats that could emerge when data migrating among multiple clouds traverse other customer networks. Having these dedicated pipelines that can be monitored provides more confidence for data security.

He observed that customers seek a simple way to install software, without the responsibility of needing to patch or secure it. Customers request high levels of isolation and data protection for their systems. Although customers desire the highest level of security, they also want to delegate some of the most critical parts of security to the cloud provider. At the same time, cloud providers worry about attack vectors from the supply chain, hardware, software, and operating systems. In particular, cloud providers are concerned about the integrity of hardware and software; in the world of zero trust, nothing is trusted and everything is verified. For example, it is important to validate system integrity and ensure that hardware does not contain counterfeit parts. Furthermore, Oracle cannot automatically trust its customers because it does not know how they will behave once on the systems. In addition to its continuous security processes, Oracle has processes that protect against customers' data, processing, and access to infrastructure. This new approach is essential when hardware is reused. He emphasized that cloud providers have a responsibility to protect infrastructure and help customers establish better security practices so that their businesses can run smoothly and better decisions can be made.

Mr. Sack explained that many commercial customers do not have the level of expertise needed to understand their hardware, their operating system, or the way their architecture was connected. Many customers do not know how they are connected to the enterprise, to the Internet, or to other agencies. The cloud provider offers that level of expertise at each of these layers, with an understanding of offensive, defensive, and continuous monitoring perspectives of chip architectures. Cloud providers remain aware of executive orders around critical software to ensure that they provide their customers with the right information about software assurance. He pointed out that although encryption acts as a safeguard, it does not provide a safeguard forever, because quantum computers will be able to decipher encrypted information in the future. Because the National Institute of Standards and Technology has not settled on guidance for the use of quantum resistant algorithms, it is important to anticipate the future so as to be able to incorporate defenses—Oracle has a team focused on quantum capabilities. He cautioned that the transition to new cryptography algorithms could create an opportunity for customers to lose data, and cloud providers want to reduce that possibility.

Mr. Sack said that if the commercial cloud is not sufficient for the government, then it would not be sufficient for all of the banks and healthcare organizations, for example, that are currently using it. Cloud providers are investing billions of dollars to provide a level of security assurance so that customers can focus on their data. Of the six major cloud providers (Amazon Web Services, Oracle, Alibaba, Microsoft Azure, Google, and IBM) in the world, five are U.S.-based companies, which he described as a tremendous advantage for government partnership. Working together, it is possible to leverage investment dollars to improve the government and the world by raising the assurance level; having better insight into the supply chain, the software supply chain, and threats; and understanding how the cloud is being used by adversaries and nation states. He emphasized the need for trust in data, infrastructure, and algorithms, and confidence in the decisions they allow at a faster rate.

Given the prediction that 14 percent of the world's carbon emissions will come from data centers by 2040, Ms. Westphal pointed out that environmental responsibility is becoming an issue of national security. She wondered how cloud providers consider the environmental impact of their growth. Mr. Sack replied that Oracle has a green initiative to rethink how it builds data centers as well as how power is produced for them. Ms. Westphal also asked how the Air Force could be a good cloud customer, and Mr. Sack suggested increased cooperation between the Air Force and the cloud provider to share cyber threat information. In response to a follow-up question from Dr. Pamela Drew, former executive vice president and president of information systems, Exelis, about customer best practices and challenges, Mr. Sack said that Oracle has been working closely with the Air Force to bring data into a single data center, and to enable levels of compartmentalization with additional controls and networking. He noted that it is difficult for people to think differently, but learning occurs for both the cloud provider and the customer: Oracle has to learn new techniques, and the Air Force has to learn to trust new techniques. He added that risk management is a key aspect of the provider-customer partnership.

Mr. Munson asked if customers who have joined the Oracle cloud have significantly reduced their in-house IT staff. Mr. Sack responded that many customers who have moved to the Oracle cloud have reduced their IT staff's *amount of effort* or reallocated their time away from mundane tasks assumed by the cloud, but have not reduced the actual number of staff. He emphasized that because Oracle has service-level agreements around the mundane tasks, it is held accountable for those. Instead of focusing on infrastructure security and software installation and patching, in-house IT staff can now focus on data security and analytics and outcomes. Mr. Munson expressed concern that those IT staff become less knowledgeable and more dependent on the cloud. However, Mr. Sack confirmed that because trust has to be established, most enterprise customers still want a level of insight into the way the cloud works. Mr. Munson asked how cloud providers were affected by the SolarWinds incident, and Mr. Sack stressed that Oracle was not affected because it builds its own software. Approximately 90 percent of Oracle's work is within its own control. He added that there is a consortium of cloud providers who share threat information with one another in an effort to protect the industry as a whole. Mr. Santee inquired about the risk of storing data on-premises versus storing in the cloud. Mr. Sack noted that the safest approach is to store data more than once and in different places. Most enterprises now have more data in the cloud than on-site; this approach is safe, and the processing capability and cost outweigh some of the other risks.

A FRAMEWORK FOR DIGITAL TRANSFORMATION: PANEL ONE

Mr. Jason Brown, strategic cloud advisor, public sector, Google, explained that Google relies on zero-trust security, assuming that there is a breach in the network at all times. Google developed technology that depends on machine learning for device-level security to sweep the network in search of potential breaches. Because Google is a mobile organization, its level of risk for threats is high. However, he expressed confidence that Google is the most secure unclassified network on which he has worked.

Having served many years as a member of the Air Force, Mr. Brown described the military's perception of risk as outdated; people often focus on the military's tendency to be risk-averse, but the real risk is created by the military's "technical debt." Philosophies around perimeter defense, for example, are outdated risk frameworks. Technical debt is a challenge across DoD, the public sector, and the commercial sector, increasing risk for all.

He portrayed software and data as some of the military's most impactful weapons. However, despite the destruction from ransomware attacks that has shut down entire enterprises, some still refuse to believe that data and software are being weaponized. He emphasized that because of the Air Force's technical debt, it has been unable to fully understand the impact of COVID-19 on its ability to complete its mission, in terms of logistics and maintenance, operations, personnel, health data, supply chain, and training. For example, the A4 has more than 350 separate systems and databases, written in different codes, and the federal government has more than 12,000 operational data centers. Bad actors could easily take advantage of this environment. COVID-19 also revealed the fragility of the supply chain. The supply chain is being mapped for various weapons systems for several organizations and military units, and those data will feed simulations; therefore, it is critical to understand the level of resilience of these supply chains. He stressed that data are a strategic asset—data can reveal strengths and weaknesses of the United States and its adversaries, as well as serve as a source of deterrence. Technical debt could be reduced by taking an application programming interface (API)-first approach, he continued, which makes it possible to obtain data from one location and either move them to a data warehouse in a cloud environment or extract them for use. For example, the Air Force's Project Brown Heron pursues data sources, brings them into a data warehouse, and reveals trends to answer difficult questions about readiness.

Mr. Brown asserted that although transformation is a lengthy process, several success stories exist. One case study of value is that of Delta Airlines, which used an API-first strategy. Delta was one of the latest Internet adopters and had siloes between its business areas, but in the late 1990s, Delta initiated a transformative warehousing effort, the Delta Nervous System. By 2019, Delta had $6 billion in profit and had reduced maintenance cancellations from 5,000 in 2010 to less than 100 in 2018. Delta was successful owing to efforts to modernize its enterprise software architecture. The Lego Company provides another useful case study. About 20 years ago, its supply chain was a disaster; the company had to redefine operations to apply discipline to the supply chain via digital transformation. It started with maintenance, then moved to human resources, and then to manufacturing. He emphasized that those who transform the fastest start with logistics, like maintenance, instead of starting with operations, which is a highly complex area. Logistics and maintenance also have a much higher return on investment. For example, when Kessel Run digitized a process, moving from planning on a white board to using an app, it saved 300,000 pounds of fuel per day.

In closing, Mr. Brown emphasized his passion for education. He championed the Air Force's Digital University, which helps airmen to become familiar with technology or pursue commercial certifications. At Google, employees are encouraged and incentivized to upskill, which is a necessity as technology continues to evolve quickly. Upskilling is essential for anyone who has to make a decision around technical debt, not just for airmen on the front line, he continued. Whereas the A4 is spending ~90 percent of its IT budget to maintain existing systems and only ~10 percent on new systems, the private sector is spending 50 percent in each area. Thus, he underscored that the Air Force needs to adopt a different perception of risk as well as a better understanding of the technology needed to surpass its technical debt.

Dr. Langston asked if studies have been conducted to determine how much money the Air Force could save if it shifted its unclassified operations to Google. Mr. Brown replied that a recent Google study revealed that Microsoft has 85 percent of the public sector market (for Office and related products). Google has offered some government leaders a continuity of operations planning capability; several public sector agencies already use Google workspaces, but Google would like to do more business with the U.S. government. Dr. Langston also wondered why the Air Force does not store its unclassified data in a Google data center. Mr. Brown reiterated that Google is the most secure network on which he has worked. He described Google's self-service culture—its internal search engine, MOMA, makes it possible to find information internally on almost anything, although there are different levels of access. As a result, Google employees rarely send attachments; instead, information is found via a link to a Google drive. Documents that are created at Google are called assets and are added as links to asset libraries, which enables information-sharing. He emphasized that these non-complex approaches are attainable for the public sector—airmen are already using this technology in their personal lives on a daily basis.

Rear Adm. Simpson supported Dr. Sotiriadis's assertion that any useful statement about the future should at first appear absurd. He emphasized the need for the Air Force to change the way it plans, budgets, and executes. For too long, the Air Force has focused on China in terms of a peer-to-peer fight over the straits of Taiwan. However, China is planning for and investing in a different fight, which is for long-term advantage in the commercial global technology economy. Both Russia and China have been aggressively attacking U.S. routes of trust—essentially attacking democracy as an optimal way to organize a government and deliver for its citizens. If the United States believes that it is the "dynamism" from a capitalist economy of small business-led innovation that ultimately wins, he continued, it should be concerned that China may be executing to that strength, while the United States focuses only on the domestic supply chain. The United States is thus beginning to lose influence in the global market. He expressed concern that the United States is taking the wrong approach as the world shifts from the era of industrial manufacturing to the information era. He advocated for the United States to improve its relationships with international partners and allies instead of focusing only on U.S. supply chains. The signal the United States is currently sending to its allies is that it puts a premium on American products in an information economy where it wants to have global influence. In the past, the United States has been a leader in the global technology market because of trust from other nations, so it is not surprising that China and Russia are attacking that element of trust. He stressed that it is important to evaluate the "trust cost" in addition to the monetary cost as the United States develops power.

Rear Adm. Simpson described the Air Force's current priorities: multi-mission balance, efficacy in contested battlespace (air, space, and cyber), JADC2 and the communication challenge, and aircraft modernization. However, he suggested that the Air Force is missing a top-line priority: decreasing the defense spending return-on-investment gap between the United States and China. China spends one-third to one-half of what the United States spends on defense each year, yet in the past 10 years, China has built more capital ships, introduced more classes of combat ships, and successfully integrated aircraft carriers with attached air wings. China has made significant strides in space and is ahead of the United States in developing high-end robotic and AI capabilities for drone fleets. Thus, the Chinese get much greater return on investment on their defense spending than the United States, while closing capability gaps rapidly. He underscored that China is better leveraging the synergy between commercial and defense research and development, and it is leading in 5G, the Internet of Things, and the race to commercial AI. He remarked that the United States has ceded influence to China in the global economy and global strategic interest. To address this challenge, he advocated for the Air Force to embrace a new partnership with the defense industrial base to determine a path toward better, faster, and cheaper and added that supply chain risk has to be better managed. He noted that China builds most of the world's commercial ships today (in the 1950s, it was the United States). The United States is in a better position with commercial manned aviation, but China is closing that gap quickly. China's strategy to reduce or eliminate its supply chain dependency on the United States and the European Union stands to threaten the United States. Most concerning, he continued, is that China has a clear lead in commercial unmanned aircraft manufacturing (i.e., small drones). He proposed that the Air Force to prioritize transformation of its combat power, acquisition, and sustainment, as well as measurement of its defense spending return on investment against China's.

In closing, Rear Adm. Simpson turned to a discussion of tactical issues in the Air Force. Although the Air Force spends science and technology dollars on innovative technologies, he explained that the transition to better, faster, and cheaper capabilities has been somewhat ineffective. For example, DevSecOps is performed by DoD program managers, who then transfer a capability to the operators; however, in the commercial world, operators and developers are one and the same, creating a continuous process. He described Platform One as "usefully disruptive" and impressive; however, that effort is still somewhat siloed. He stressed that there needs to be a recognition that a structural reorganization is essential to create shared repositories and build on capabilities.

Open Discussion

Dr. Langston noted that, in its vision for digital transformation, DoD does not seem to be addressing the return-on-investment issue or the bureaucratic barriers to rapid progress. Rear Adm. Simpson suggested that the Air Force practice using AI for mundane tasks, with the goal of eventually eliminating legacy processes and repurposing legacy people. He articulated that the Air Force needs to focus on the *implementation* of innovation. Mr. Brown pointed out that some congressional sponsors still have a vested interested in prolonging the lives of legacy systems. As a result, some people on the flight line inefficiently first write on paper and then plug that information into a system later. He reiterated that there is ample opportunity to replace, standardize, and innovate around digital transformation in terms of logistics, thus generating a return on investment and building momentum before moving to the removal of legacy systems.

Ms. Westphal asked how the Air Force could better work with Congress on issues related to funding. Rear Adm. Simpson proposed that the Air Force to dedicate its best talent to determine how to increase the return on investment of combat power. Although members of Congress are focused on best representing and supporting their constituents, they could also consider the importance of preserving national power and the ability to fight and win the nation's wars. Repurposing defense dollars both creates returns and makes lives better for the constituents within a member's congressional jurisdiction—for example, standing up an AI factory or a software factory creates job opportunities for local community college and university graduates, and leads to combat value. Because current business processes can be a detriment to moving forward with digital transformation, Mr. Brown described the need for additional oversight from entities other than Congress. Gen. Holmes noted that part of the problem is time; congressional terms (2 years) are shorter than the time frame in which the Air Force operates, especially considering the nature of long-term competition with China. He also highlighted a particularly difficult bureaucratic hurdle in DoD: everyone has a voice and everyone has a vote, making it easier to reject proposals and slow progress.

Mr. Santee observed that data and communications are becoming a weapons system in the contested environment, and he wondered about the services' perspectives on this issue. Rear Adm. Simpson noted that China has decreased the separation between its economic and military power. He cautioned the United States against focusing on the speed of the OODA loop; instead, better decision making is enabled by the "quality of the trip" around the OODA loop. He suggested unifying the right knowledge at the right time to achieve the greatest defense return on investment and protecting that (as opposed to defending the tactical OODA loop, which prioritizes speed for human decision making). Mr. Brown championed technology that improves the quality of decision making, and he emphasized the need to consider what the increasing use of mobile devices means for operations in a tactical environment.

A FRAMEWORK FOR DIGITAL TRANSFORMATION: PANEL TWO

Dr. Annie Green, data governance specialist, George Mason University, perceived that the Air Force is still missing the foundation for digital transformation. To make better decisions, it is critical to understand how all of an organization's components work together. She explained that because systems are interconnected networks, levels of abstraction contextualize decision making. It is also important to have the ability to "encapsulate" in a sensitive realm and to restrict access. All of these considerations are part of the digital "ecosystem." All of the moving components in this ecosystem can best be managed with computers, which store more and process faster than a human. She emphasized that these are not new approaches: the original digital twin (i.e., a duplicate of a real-world entity) helped bring the astronauts of Apollo 13 home safely. She highlighted the need for both top-down (e.g., unity of effort) and bottom-up (e.g., use cases) approaches in the strategic realm of the Air Force as it develops a roadmap for transformation. Strategy formulation begins with environment scanning, where data that represent the reality can be used for machine learning or algorithm development.

Dr. Green described the supply chain and the work-centered analysis chain, the latter of which emphasizes where people fit in to the ecosystem of successful product delivery. Eighty-seven percent of value in any enterprise comes from intangible assets, such as innovation, relationships, expertise and competence, and structure. Leveraging the intangible asset of intellectual capital leads to improvement and decreases costs, creating a path for an organization's growth. Although organizations may already operate in this fashion, there is no *visibility* into how intangible assets could be used.

A 2018 study from MuleSoft revealed that corporate executives seek increased IT operational efficiency (83%), improved customer experience (71%), increased business efficiency (70%), quicker introduction of new products and services (58%), improved employee experience (51%), and improved partner experience (27%). Dr. Green explained that the vital functions of any enterprise include the employee (e.g., the warfighter), the partner, the information, the technology, the customer, and the competitor, as well as the product and the process. She pointed out that the competitor and the information are often not given enough attention, despite the fact that enterprises revolve around access to information. With knowledge management, a common language is created—and this enterprise taxonomy establishes a path for enterprise leadership and management to identify intangible assets, indicators, and measures ("enterprise memory"). This provides a foundation to construct a neural network of interactions as well as algorithms and machine learning for the strategy formulation process, which augments the thought processes of the enterprise leadership and management who are developing the enterprise strategic plan. She underscored that strategy is key to defining a network, asking the right questions, and determining how to answer those questions.

Dr. Green asserted that it is crucial to plan, and to know which data and information drive enterprise strategy. Data are how the enterprise "thinks"; therefore, it is important to ensure that the data captured and used in enterprise algorithms have purpose, authenticity, integrity, and completeness. Flawed data increase the risk of moving the enterprise along a destructive path, no matter which digital solution has been introduced. Thus, she continued, the sources of the data and information driving the strategic decisions of enterprise leadership and management should be validated ("data lineage"), and the data and information used in algorithms should be planned. She described Peter Drucker's "The Information Executives Truly Need" and the four categories of diagnostic information that provide insight: foundation information (e.g., measures of cash flow and liquidity projections), productivity information (e.g., measures of performance of key resources), competence information (e.g., measures associated with core competencies), and resource-allocation information (e.g., measures associated with the allocation of scarce resources, such as capital and high-performing people). This diagnostic information is defined based on the enterprise taxonomy, where it becomes possible to identify areas for decision making.

She outlined the imperative for the Air Force to make better decisions based on authentic data. Enterprise cognition can enable this practice, with a language to describe and understand the forces and interrelationships that shape the behavior of leadership and management; the capability to change systems to be more in tune with the processes of the natural and economic world of the enterprise environment; and the capability to establish goals and decisions based on what the enterprise knows or needs to know to implement and execute successful strategies. She explained that data emulate memory within a system, information is structured and aligned with familiar terms, intelligence highlights the relationships between them to illuminate places in need of actionable change, knowledge is actionable data, and cognition makes the decision that feeds back into a system. This cognitive enterprise system (see Figure 6.1) absorbs the information through a structure that identifies the functions, concepts, and elements of an enterprise.

Mental models make sense of the enterprise, and decisions and actions are uncovered to support enterprise decision makers. The context layers of an enterprise emulate the human thought process, but if the data ("the memory") are not correct, people have to rely only on perceptions to make decisions. This cognitive enterprise system has all of the components of a true system: (1) what, why, who, where, when, and how; (2) people, process, information, and technology; (3) knowledge, skills, and abilities; (4) risks, obstacles, outcomes, and benefits; (5) frameworks and methodologies; and (6) measurements and maturity. Moving forward, she continued, the next step is to build a digital transformation business case (see Figure 6.2).

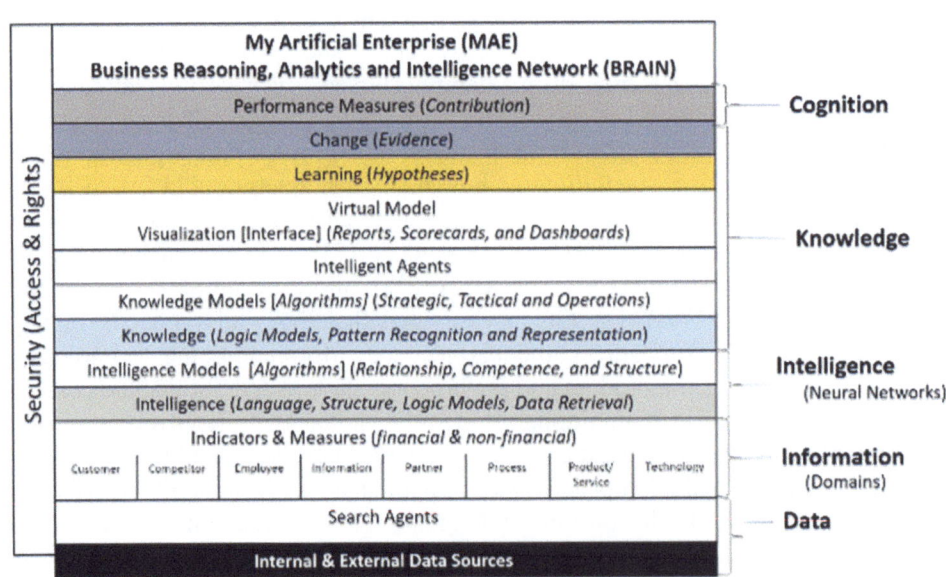

FIGURE 6.1 The cognitive enterprise system: an enterprise augmented reality platform. SOURCE: Annie Green, presentation to the workshop, September 24, 2021. All rights reserved.

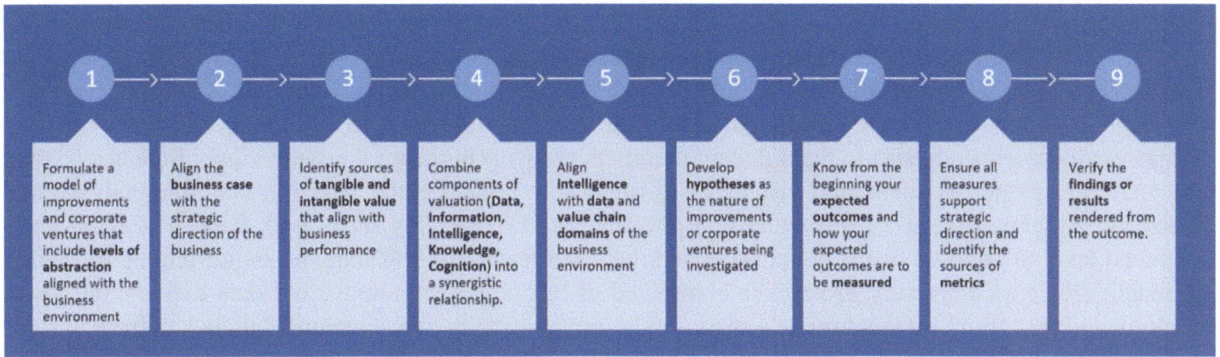

FIGURE 6.2 The digital transformation business case. SOURCE: Annie Green, presentation to the workshop, September 24, 2021.

Mr. Jay Zaidi, founder, AlyData, identified four tenets of successful digital transformation:

1. Organizations cannot solve complex challenges (e.g., digital transformation, governance, risk, compliance, or supply chain transparency) without defining the business value chain and the associated data supply chain.
2. Organizations have to be able to visualize the business value chain and the data supply chain based on ontologies and taxonomies, and then link operational data and operational metadata to the supply chain for better insight.
3. Organizations need the ability to link the metadata and the data to develop a dynamic view and to interrogate the underlying data for insights.
4. The business value chain and the data supply chain coupled with relevant operational metadata can provide timely, actionable insights to mitigate risk, reduce operational costs, and enable better governance.

Mr. Zaidi posited that data are a proxy for the operations of any digital organization. In other words, if an organization is engaging in a digital transformation, it is either creating more data or reorganizing existing data for new uses. Many organizations face challenges related to important processes of regulation, governance, and optimization, all of which have an underlying data component but occur in different dimensions. For example, governance addresses data privacy, security, and access, and optimization requires understanding the full data supply chain to reduce time to value.

However, he continued, it is difficult to increase speed of action when the lines of business, technology, data, and people remain siloed. He asserted that a new approach is needed to navigate this "invisible landscape of fragmented tribal knowledge" to discover, understand, and utilize data and ensure robust governance, analytics, and AI. The data architecture, data catalogue, data privacy, data lineage, data quality, and data science are all key components for data management and governance. The data and AI governance are layered on top of these foundational pieces to ensure accountability and oversight, and the metadata (i.e., contextual information related to each of these components) connect to capture significant relationships.

Mr. Zaidi described a case study on the use of the global positioning system (GPS), the purpose of which is to enable movement from Point A to Point B as efficiently as possible. This technology could be useful for organizations that want to do future state planning; conduct "what-if" scenarios; do impact analysis; do discovery work; understand gaps in the ecosystem; or make changes to applications, processes, or technical components. "GPS for Data Assets" is a dynamic enterprise data ecosystem visualization and management layer that includes many of the underlying components (e.g., data quality and observability tools and metadata, enterprise architecture-related artifacts and tools, customer data platform, data privacy tools) to provide a holistic view. Given that research shows that 90 percent of information transmitted is more effective when conveyed visually and 40 percent of people respond better to visually represented information, visualization of information from different siloes and in different formats is an important part this effort. Current models are translated, digitized, and transformed into visual lineage-type views to display environments and ensure that all team members are working from the same view of the ecosystem. The goal is to gather, connect, and visualize information to enable better decision making, analysis, and discovery. By capturing all of the underlying metadata and overlaying those with data, it is possible to conduct a level of analysis that is not possible in siloes. To reach this end state, he suggested the following approach: create a community of practice comprised of business, technology, and data experts; define an ontology and taxonomy for the domain and modify it; automatically ingest technical metadata from various data sources (e.g., file stores, databases, spreadsheets, data warehouses, data lakes) using prebuilt harvesters; and crowdsource missing business metadata or tribal knowledge that is not documented but is owned by associates.

Dr. Anthony Rhem, chief executive officer, AJ Rhem and Associates, described how to leverage AI-powered knowledge delivery to enable to digital transformation. He defined digital transformation as the process of using digital technologies to create new or modify existing business processes, culture, and customer experiences to meet the changing business and market environments and thus to fundamentally change operations and value delivery. AI-powered knowledge delivery is facilitated by the knowledge-as-a-service framework, which blends knowledge management and AI to deliver the right knowledge to the right person in the right context and enable fast, efficient, and accurate decision making.

He explained that knowledge-as-a-service uses a distributed computing model; connects tacit and explicit knowledge through ontology management and knowledge mapping; blends tacit and explicit knowledge (which are constantly updated, adhering to the organization's content life cycle management processes); makes use of AI through predictive analytics and knowledge flow optimization; and provides a dynamic, accurate, and personal delivery of knowledge. He posited that knowledge-as-a-service is most useful in the following cases: (1) an organization has an abundance of information and knowledge and needs a mechanism to understand it; (2) knowledge needs to be accessed in a timely manner; (3) access to the collective knowledge of an organization needs to be improved; (4) workers need personalized knowledge that responds to their specific needs; (5) workers need to be more productive by executing tasks and learning more efficiently and effectively; and (6) workers need to collaborate and share knowledge to foster innovation. AI plays an important role in knowledge-as-a-service by elevating how the delivery of knowledge occurs to the people who need it. He noted that AI is used to scale the volume and effectiveness of knowledge distribution; to predict trending knowledge areas that knowledge workers need; and to leverage supervised learning algorithms that will learn over time, which will deliver more personalized knowledge to an individual to solve a particular problem. AI also facilitates the delivery of Smart Search, which enables search to take advantage of ontologies between the tangible content and the people conducting the search. AI also makes it possible to leverage RPA to deliver personalized knowledge.

Dr. Rhem remarked that knowledge-as-a-service can be implemented through the digital workplace (Figure 6.3). The business case for the implementation of the digital workplace in digital transformation is that it enables personnel to be more productive and effective. The digital workplace could be used to ensure that those on the ground in the Air Force have access to the knowledge they need to complete their missions. The digital workplace aligns technology, employees, and business processes to improve operational efficiency and meet organizational goals; is the platform that staff members would use to access all corporate knowledge to execute their jobs; is enabled by cloud services, mobile, and AI; and removes geographic barriers from collaboration and processes and ensures that knowledge is available any time and any place. The digital workplace prioritizes personnel through improved collaboration and employee engagement; new staff workstreams via the use of personas; more productive business relationships within and beyond natural working groups; increased employee productivity; improved business processes and content management to facilitate the intelligent delivery of knowledge; and alignment with the organization's digital transformation goals.

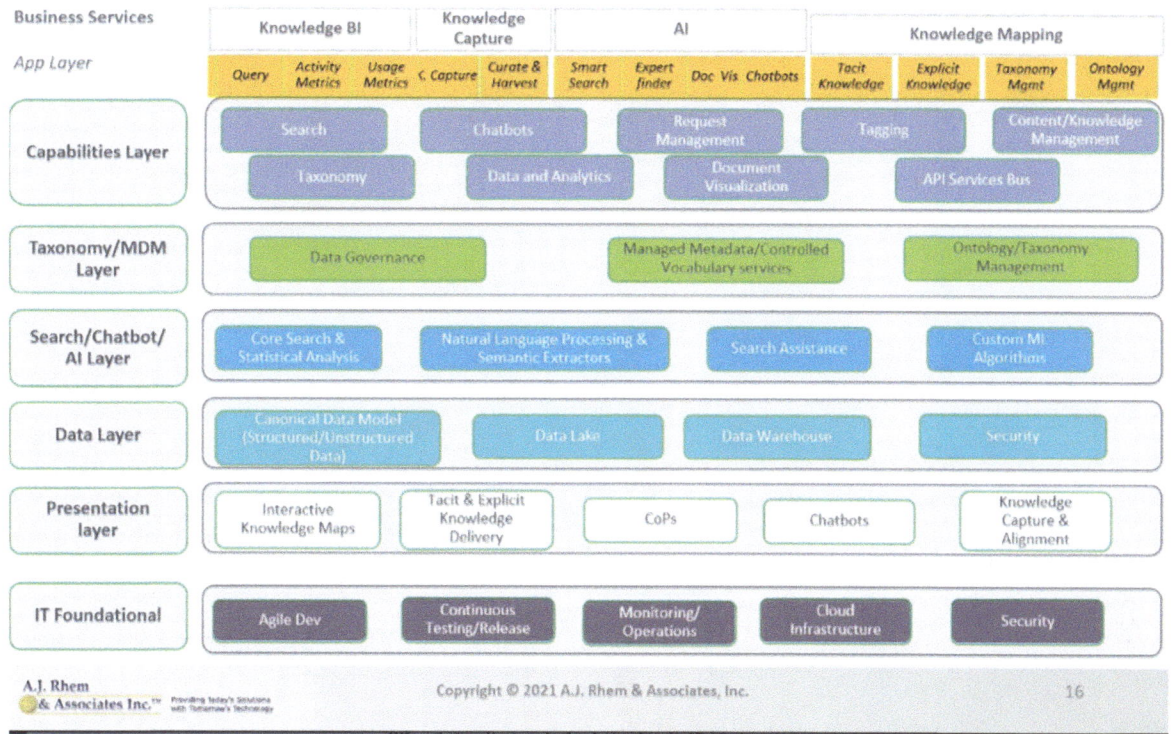

FIGURE 6.3 Knowledge-as-a-service and digital workplace framework. SOURCE: Anthony Rhem, presentation to the workshop, September 24, 2021.

In closing, Dr. Rhem noted that the benefits of knowledge-as-a-service in the digital workplace include

- Enhanced communication and innovation by creating a more collaborative culture;
- Increased productivity executing tasks and learning more efficiently and effectively;
- Personalized knowledge access;
- Prediction of trending knowledge areas that knowledge workers need; and
- Identification of targeted knowledge for real-time engagement and content consumption to aid in decision making and improve outcomes.

Appendixes

A

Statement of Task

The Air Force Studies Board (AFSB) of the National Academies of Sciences, Engineering, and Medicine will convene senior representatives from government, military, and industry to discuss risks associated with the technical, programmatic, organizational, and governance challenges facing the Department of the Air Force's (DAF's) enterprise-wide digital transformation strategies. Workshop participant's questions will reveal organizational and management gaps and weaknesses, as well as, technical shortfalls associated with DAF digital transformation strategies—for example, the issue of cybersecurity within the context of the DAF's proposed digital strategies. Proven organizational and management practices from both the public and private sectors will be discussed that can be adapted and adopted within the DAF.

To accomplish this, the Digital Strategy Workshop Series (DSWS) will host a series of three 2-day virtual workshops:

(1) Presenters at the first workshop will explain and discuss the DAF's digital transformation strategy—in particular, the proposed Digital Architectures and the systems, programs, organizations, and missions to be supported.
(2) The second workshop will feature information systems experts and managers from industry and other government agencies to discuss their experience with digital transformations and their views of best practices.
(3) The third workshop will focus on discussions of the potential applicability of lessons from Workshop #2 to the DAF's Digital transformation strategy and architecture.

A recording will be made available immediately following each workshop, to be followed by a single rapporteur-authored proceedings that will include all three workshops in the series prepared in accordance with institutional guidelines.

B

Workshop Agendas

WORKSHOP 1: SEPTEMBER 1–2, 2021

Virtual Conference

Day 1: September 1

11:15–11:30 ET	Opening Remarks Ms. Deborah Westphal/Lt. Gen. Mike Hamel, Workshop Series Co-Chairs
11:30–11:45 ET	"The Digital Air Force" Honorable Gina Ortiz Jones, Under Secretary of the Air Force
11:45–12:00 ET	Q&A
12:00–12:30 ET	"Digital Transformation" Gen. David W. Allvin, Vice Chief SAF Gen. David D. (DT) Thompson, Vice Chief SO
12:30–12:45 ET	Q&A
12:45–13:45 ET	Lunch Break
13:45–14:30 ET	"Why Digital Transformation" Lt. Gen. Bradley "Salty" Saltzman, HSF Chief Operations Officer Brig. Gen. Robert Lyman, Headquarters Air Force A2/6

APPENDIX B

                    Mr. Ed Oshiba, HAF A4

14:30–14:45 ET	Q&A
14:45–15:00 ET	Break
15:00–15:45 ET	"Digital Transformation Plans and Programs" Col. Jeff Mrazik, Deputy Chief of the ABMS Cross-Functional Team, Air Force Futures, HAF A5 Col. Sean Kern, HAF A8 (cyber panel chair) Mr. Wayne Schatz, SES, AF/A9
15:45–16:00 ET	Q&A
16:00–16:45 ET	"DoD Digital Modernization Strategy" Mr. John Sherman, acting DoD/CIO Mr. Jeff Jones, Vice Director, Joint Staff J6
16:45–17:00 ET	Q&A

Day 2: September 2

10:00–10:15 ET	Day 1 Recap and Day 2 Introduction Ms. Deborah Westphal/Lt. Gen. Mike Hamel, Workshop Series Co-Chairs
10:15–11:00 ET	"Leadership for Transformation" Mr. Anthony Reardon SES, SAF/Administrative Assistant Mr. Rich Lombardi, Chief Management Officer
11:00–11:15 ET	Q&A
11:15–12:00 ET	"Organization and Technology for Transformation" Ms. Lauren Knausenberger, CIO Ms. Eileen Vidrine, Chief Data Officer
12:00–12:15 ET	Q&A
12:15–13:00 ET	Lunch Break
13:00–13:45 ET	"Learning for Transformation" Brig. Gen. Shawn Campbell, Deputy Human Capital Officer, CSO Lt. Gen. Bill Liquori, SF Chief Strategy and Resourcing Officer Ms. Gwendolyn DeFilippi, Assistant Deputy Chief of Staff, Manpower, Personnel and Services (HAF/A1) Melissa Cunningham—HAF A2/6 Stand In (for Ms. Theresa Sanchez)
13:45–14:00 ET	Q&A
14:00–14:45 ET	"Executing Transformation" Col. Heather Blackwell, Air Combat Command/A6

                        Lt. Gen. Tim Haugh, 16 AF
                        Mr. Steven Wert, PEO Digital

14:45–15:00 ET   Q&A

15:00–15:15 ET   Break

15:15–16:15 ET   Discussion among Workshop and Study Participants

16:15–16:45 ET   Reattacks, Follow-Ups, and Closing Remarks

WORKSHOP 2: SEPTEMBER 8–9, 2021

Virtual Conference

Day 1: September 8

10:00–10:15 ET   Opening Remarks
                        Ms. Deborah Westphal/Lt. Gen. Mike Hamel, Workshop Series Co-Chairs

10:15–11:45 ET   "Why Digitize"
                        Robert Tross, Principal, Deloitte Digital
                        Danielle Ullner, Partner and Managing Director, BCG Digital Ventures
                        M. Nadia Vincent, Digital Transformation and Innovation Executive Advisor,
                            Digital Transformation Leaders
                        Dr. David Bray, Executive Director GeoTech Commission, Atlantic Council,
                            Former CIO at the FCC

11:45–12:00 ET   Q&A

12:00–12:45 ET   Lunch Break

12:45–14:45 ET   "Lessons from Others 'Like the Air Force' "
                        Rahul Welde, EVP Digital Transformation, Unilever
                        Dale Tutt, VP A&D, Siemens Digital Industries Software
                        Charles Rybeck, Co-Founder, Digital Mobilizations

14:45–15:00 ET   Q&A

15:15–16:45 ET   "Lessons from Others 'Like the Air Force' Continued"
                        Margaret Palmieri, Special Assistant at U.S. Navy
                        Jay Walsh, Interim Vice President for Economic Development and Innovation at
                            University of Illinois System
                        Jan Neumann, Digital Media Transformation, Comcast

16:45–17:00 ET   Q&A

APPENDIX B

Day 2: September 9

10:00–10:15 ET	Day 1 Recap and Day 2 Introduction Ms. Deborah Westphal/Lt. Gen. Mike Hamel, Workshop Series Co-Chairs
10:15–12:00 ET	"Out of the Box Learning" Gerald J. Caron III, CIO, Asst. Inspector General for Information Technology (AIG/IT), Office of the Inspector General (OIG), Dept. of Health and Human Services (HHS) Dr. Chris Chute, Johns Hopkins University Mr. Mike Pack, Digital Transportation Data and Analytics at The University of Maryland
12:00–12:15 ET	Q&A
12:15–13:00 ET	Lunch Break
13:00–14:45 ET	" 'Out of the Box Learning' Continued" Chris Lynch, CEO, Rebellion Defense. Former Head of Defense Digital Services (DDS) Col. (Ret.) David Neuenswander, USAF, Chief of Joint Integration, The Curtis E. LeMay Center for Doctrine Development and Education Cara LaPointe, Co-Director of the Johns Hopkins Institute for Assured Autonomy; AI-X Deputy at Johns Hopkins University Randall Hunt, Director of Developer Evangelism, Vendia
14:45–15:00 ET	Q&A
15:00–15:15 ET	Break
15:15–16:15 ET	Discussion Among Workshop and Study Participants
16:15–16:45 ET	Reattacks, Follow-Ups, and Closing Remarks

WORKSHOP 3: SEPTEMBER 23–24, 2021

Virtual Conference

Day 1: September 23

10:00–10:15 ET	Opening Remarks Ms. Deborah Westphal/Lt. Gen. Mike Hamel, Workshop Series Co-Chairs
10:15–11:45 ET	"The Future Threat Environment" Brendan Mulvaney, Director, China Aerospace Studies Institute (CASI), Air University
11:45–12:00 ET	Q&A

12:00–13:30 ET	"What Doctrine, CONOPS, TTPs, etc., Do We Need to Operate in a Digitally Transformed Air Force?" Col. Charles Galbreath, USSF HQSF AF/SF/CTIO Maj. Evan "Switch" Hatter, Doctrine Development, LeMay Center Dr. Andrew Stricker, Strategy and Concepts, LeMay Center
13:30–13:45 ET	Q&A
13:45–14:15 ET	Lunch Break
14:15–15:45 ET	"What Doctrine, CONOPS, TTPs, etc., Do We Need to Operate in a Digitally Transformed Air Force? Continued" Lt. Col. Brian "Dante" Burgoon, 561st Weapons Squadron Commander James Crocker, CTO, BESPIN (Business and Enterprise Systems Product Innovation)
15:45–16:00 ET	Q&A
16:00–16:15 ET	Break
16:15–17:30 ET	"Constraints and Considerations for Operating in the Future" Dr. Julie Ryan, Study Lead for the National Academies of Sciences, Engineering, and Medicine Energizing Data-Driven Operations at the Tactical Edge: Challenges and Concerns (AFSB Planning Committee Member) Col. Jonathan Zall, ABMS CFT, AF Futures, HAF A5 Victoria Pillitteri, Acting Manager for Security Engineering and Risk Management Group, Information Technology Laboratory, NIST
17:30–17:45 ET	Q&A

Day 2: September 24

10:00–10:15 ET	Day 1 Recap and Day 2 Introduction Ms. Deborah Westphal/Lt. Gen. Mike Hamel, Workshop Series Co-Chairs
10:15–11:45 ET	"Future Cyber and Electromagnetic Spectrum Issues" Col. (Ret.) Lisle Babcock, Former LeMay Center Commander Brig. Gen. Greg Touhill (Ret.), Director, Software Engineering Institute (SEI) Cybersecurity Division Steven Hernandez, Chief Information Security Officer at U.S. Department of Education
11:45–12:00 ET	Q&A
12:00–12:30 ET	Lunch Break
12:30–13:45 ET	"Creating a Sustainable Capability for the Future" Dr. Jake Sotiriadis, Director of Operations and Engagement, Collaboration Laboratory and Research Faculty, National Intelligence University

APPENDIX B

                Dr. Eneken Tikk, Executive Producer at the Cyber Policy Institute (Lieksa, Eastern Finland, Finland)
                Patrick Sack, VP and CTO Oracle National Security Group

13:45–14:00 ET	Q&A
14:00–14:15 ET	Break
14:15–15:30 ET	"Bringing It All Together—A Framework for Digital Transformation" Jason Brown, Strategic Cloud Advisor, Public Sector, Google Rear Admiral (Ret.) David Simpson, CEO, Pelorus Consulting; Partner, DeepWaterPoint; Professor, Virginia Tech Dr. Annie Green, Digital Transformation, Data Governance Specialist at George Mason University (Planning Committee Member), and Dr. Anthony "Tony" Rhem (AJ Rhem and Associates) and Jay Zaidi (AlyData)
15:30–15:45 ET	Q&A
15:45–16:45 ET	Discussion Among Workshop and Study Participants
16:45–17:00 ET	Reattacks, Follow-Ups, and Closing Remarks

C

Biographical Information for Planning Committee Members

MICHAEL A. HAMEL (USAF, retired), *Co-Chair*, is an independent consultant in the military and national security space, with a career in government and industry spanning more than 40 years involving space policy, planning, development, and operations. Most recently Lt. Gen. Hamel served in Lockheed Martin as Vice President of Commercial Space. Prior to that he was Senior Vice President of Corporate Strategy and Relations for Orbital Sciences Corporation leading strategic planning, product and business development, and government relations. Lt. Gen. Hamel served in the U.S. Air Force for more than 30 years in a broad range of space operations, development, acquisition, policy, and command positions, concluding his military career in 2008 as Commander of the Air Force Space and Missile Systems Center and Air Force Program Executive Officer for Space. Prior to that he was Commander of the 14th Air Force and served in senior command and staff positions at U.S. Air Force Headquarters and Air Force Space Command and was Military Advisor to the Vice President. Lt. Gen. Hamel holds a bachelor's degree in aeronautical engineering from the U.S. Air Force Academy and a master's degree in business administration from California State University. He is a graduate of the Industrial College of the Armed Forces and the program in national and international security at Harvard University. He is a member of the Council on Foreign Relations and a fellow of the American Institute of Aeronautics and Astronautics. He also serves on the boards of several corporate and advisory groups.

DEBORAH L. WESTPHAL, *Co-Chair*, is chairman of the board of the strategy advisory firm Toffler Associates. Recognized globally for her expertise in strategy, innovation, and organizational transformation, Ms. Westphal helps organizations understand the forces that drive change in their industries and the world and identifies the best courses of action to create enduring success. Ms. Westphal came to Toffler Associates in 1999 after 13 years as a senior government official in the U.S. Air Force (USAF). Her work in the area of technology and advanced concepts for air vehicles, missiles, and space systems has been recognized with numerous awards from the California Air Force Association (AFA), a USAF Meritorious Civilian Award, an AFA Los Angeles Chapter Civilian of the Year award, and an AFA Medal of Merit. Ms. Westphal has also served on the U.S. Army Science Board, the National Defense Industrial Association Greater Los Angeles Chapter Board of Directors, and the AFA Schriever Chapter 147 Board of Directors.

TED F. BOWLDS (USAF, retired) is currently the chief executive officer for IAI North America. In this capacity, he is responsible for program management, engineering, and technology transfer. Prior to this job, Lt. Gen. Bowlds served as the chief information officer (CIO) for FlightSafety, International. As CIO, he was responsible for the planning and execution of a $30 million annual budget and maintained a steady 99.9 percent system reliability. He also served as the chief technology officer responsible for innovation and the introduction of market-leading capabilities. During his 36-year career in the USAF and subsequent experience in industry, he led multiple large-scale, complex procurement activities, each dependent upon strong ethics and solid research foundation. The programs include the F-117 stealth fighter, B-2 bomber, and C-17 transport. As Commander of the Air Force Research Laboratory (AFRL), he was responsible for the diverse research undertaken by AFRL including microelectronics, human factors, medical, aeronautics, computers, satellites, and power generation. His last assignment on active duty was as the Commander of the Electronic Systems Center and Program Executive Officer for Air Force information technology procurements, applications, and systems. The portfolio of programs being executed included command and control, surveillance, and information technology. Lt. Gen. Bowlds is the chairman of the board of the Air Force Retired Officers Community (a continuing care retirement community). He is also a member of the Mississippi State Research Technology Advisory Group and the Department of Defense (DoD) Systems Engineering Research Council. Lt. Gen. Bowlds holds a Master of Science in electrical engineering, a Master of Science in engineering management, and a Ph.D. in systems engineering; he is a graduate of the USAF Test Pilot School Flight Test Engineer course and has attended numerous leadership and management courses.

CHARLES "CHUCK" BROOKS is a globally recognized thought leader and evangelist for cybersecurity. LinkedIn named Brooks as one of "The Top 5 Tech People to Follow on LinkedIn." He was named by Thompson Reuters as a "Top 50 Global Influencer in Risk, Compliance," and by IFSEC as the "#2 Global Cybersecurity Influencer." He is also a cybersecurity expert for "The Network" at the *Washington Post*, visiting editor at *Homeland Security Today*, and a contributor to *Forbes*. He has also been a featured author in technology and cybersecurity blogs by IBM, AT&T, Cylance, and many others. In government, Brooks has received two senior Presidential appointments. Under President George W. Bush, Brooks was appointed as the first Legislative Director of the Science and Technology Directorate at the Department of Homeland Security. He also was appointed as Special Assistant to the Director of Voice of America under President Reagan. He served as a top advisor to the late Senator Arlen Specter, covering security and technology issues on Capitol Hill. In local government he also worked as an auxiliary police officer for Arlington, Virginia. In industry, Brooks has served in senior executive roles for General Dynamics as the Principal Market Growth Strategist for Cyber Systems, at Xerox as Vice President and Client Executive for Homeland Security, for Rapiscan as Vice President of R&D, for SRA as Vice President of Government Relations, and for Sutherland as Vice President of Marketing and Government Relations. In academia, Brooks is adjunct faculty at Georgetown University's Applied Intelligence Program and graduate Cybersecurity Programs where he teaches courses on risk management, homeland security, and cybersecurity. He was an adjunct faculty member at Johns Hopkins University where he taught a graduate course on homeland security for 2 years. He has an M.A. in international relations from the University of Chicago, a B.A. in political science from DePauw University, and a certificate in international law from The Hague Academy of International Law. In media, Brooks is the featured Homeland Security contributor for *Federal Times*, featured cybersecurity contributor for the High Performance Counsel on Cybersecurity, and an advisor and contributor to *Cognitive World*, a leading publication on artificial intelligence. He has also appeared in *Forbes* and *Huffington Post* and has published more than 180 articles and blogs on cybersecurity, homeland security, and technology issues. He has 59,000 followers on LinkedIn and runs a dozen LI groups, including the two largest in homeland security. Brooks's professional industry affiliations include being a member of the August USA Chapter of EC-Council Global Advisory Board for TVM (Threat and Vulnerability Management); EC-Council is the world's largest body in cybersecurity training and certifications. He is on the Massachusetts Institute of Technology's Technology Review Advisory Global Panel, a member of The AFCEA Cybersecurity Committee, and member of the Institute of Electrical and Electronics Engineers Standards Association (IEEE-SA) Virtual Reality and Augmented Reality Working Group. Some of Brooks's other activities include being a subject matter expert to The Homeland Defense and Security Information Analysis Center, a DoD-sponsored organization through the Defense Technical Information Center; a featured presenter at USTRANSCOM on cybersecurity threats to transportation; and a featured presenter to the FBI and the National Academy of Sciences on life sciences cybersecurity. He is an advisory board member for The Center for Advancing Innovation, the Quantum Security Alliance, and a member of the CyberAvengers, a group that promotes safe cyber-hygiene. Brooks was also appointed as a technology partner advisor to the Bill and Melinda Gates Foundation.

RAMA CHELLAPPA is Bloomberg Distinguished Professor of electrical and computer engineering and biomedical engineering with Johns Hopkins University (JHU), Baltimore. He holds a secondary appointment in the computer science department. He received the B.E. (Hons.) degree from the University of Madras, Madras, India, in 1975; the M.E. (Distinction) degree from the Indian Institute of Science, Bangalore, India, in 1977; and the M.S.E.E. and Ph.D. degrees in electrical engineering from Purdue University in 1978 and 1981, respectively. He is also affiliated with the Center for Imaging Science, the Center for Language and Speech Processing, The Malone Center for Engineering Health, and the Mathematical Institute for Data Sciences at JHU. Before moving to JHU in August 2020, Dr. Chellappa was a Distinguished University Professor and a Minta Martin Professor of Engineering with the University of Maryland (UMD). He was a professor in the department of electrical and computer engineering and the UMD Institute for Advanced Computer Studies. He held the position of a College Park Professor in the Electrical and Computer Engineering Department at UMD. Prior to joining UMD, he was an assistant (1981–1986) and associate professor (1986–1991) and director of the Signal and Image Processing Institute (1988–1990) with the University of Southern California, Los Angeles. Over the past 40 years, he has published numerous book chapters and peer-reviewed journal and conference papers. He has coauthored and coedited books on Markov random fields, face and gait recognition, and collected works on image processing and analysis. He has served as a co-editor-in-chief of *Graphical Models and Image Processing*. His current research interests are computer vision, artificial intelligence, machine learning, image processing and pattern recognition with applications in face and gait analysis, markerless motion capture, 3D modeling from video, image and video-based recognition and exploitation, compressive sensing, and hyper spectral processing. Professor Chellappa has received several awards, including a National Science Foundation Presidential Young Investigator Award, four IBM Faculty Development Awards, an Excellence in Teaching Award from the School of Engineering at the University of Southern California, Los Angeles, and several paper awards from the International Conference on Pattern Recognition and Biometrics. He received the Society, Technical Achievement and Meritorious Service Awards from the IEEE Signal Processing Society. He also received the Technical Achievement and Meritorious Service Awards from the IEEE Computer Society. At UMD, he was elected as a distinguished faculty research fellow and a distinguished scholar-teacher, and he received the outstanding Faculty Research Award and the Poole and Kent Teaching Award for the Senior Faculty from the College of Engineering, an Outstanding Innovator Award from the Office of Technology Commercialization, and an Outstanding GEMSTONE Mentor Award. In 2010, he was recognized as an Outstanding Electrical and Computer Engineer by Purdue University. He is a fellow of the IEEE, Association for Computing Machinery, the Association for the Advancement of Artificial Intelligence, the American Association for the Advancement of Science, the International Association for Pattern Recognition, the Optical Society of America, and the National Academy of Inventors. He has served as an associate editor for four IEEE publications and as the editor-in-chief of the *IEEE Transactions on Pattern Analysis and Machine Intelligence*. He served as a member of the IEEE Signal Processing Society Board of Governors and as its vice president of awards and membership. He served as a general and technical program chair for several IEEE international and national conferences and workshops. He is a golden core member of the IEEE Computer Society and served a 2-year term as a distinguished lecturer of the IEEE Signal Processing Society. Recently, he completed a 2-year term as president of IEEE Biometrics Council. His Google Scholar h-index is 129.

DOUGLAS D. DEMAIO is the Commander of the 187th Fighter Wing, Dannelly Field, Alabama. As commander, he oversees the operations of more than 1,000 personnel and 22 permanently assigned F-16C+ Fighting Falcons in support of the State of Alabama and the federal government. The wing also provides support to four geographically separated units. Col. DeMaio earned his commission from the United States Air Force Academy in 1991. Upon completion of Under Graduate Pilot Training at Sheppard Air Force Base, Texas, he was assigned to Luke Air Force Base, Arizona, as the 56th Transportation Squadron Vehicle Maintenance and Vehicle Operations flight commander. Upon completion of F-16 training at Luke Air Force Base, he went on to serve in a variety of roles at the squadron, group, and wing-level. The colonel has served as a squadron commander, the director of staff, and the Director of the Deployable Air Operations Center. Col. DeMaio attended the Eisenhower School for National Security at the National Defense University, Fort McNair, Washington D.C., where he earned his master's in long-term strategy development. Prior to this assignment, he served as the Vice Commander and Director of Doctrine Development at the Curtis E. LeMay Center, Maxwell Air Force Base, Alabama. He is a command pilot with more than 2,800 flight hours in the F-16 and a veteran of five combat deployments to Southwest Asia.

PAMELA A. DREW has recently completed her service as Executive Vice President and President of Information Systems at Exelis. This organization provided full life cycle support of critical networks. These services were provided across government agencies including the Federal Aviation Administration (FAA), U.S. Air Force, U.S. Navy, U.S. Army, Defense Threat Reduction Agency (DTRA), and the intelligence community. Before joining Exelis, Dr. Drew was the senior vice president of Strategic Capabilities and Technology at TASC, leading an enterprise-wide team that provided systems engineering and integration, cybersecurity, financial and business analytics, and test and evaluation solutions to intelligence, defense, and federal and civil customers. In a prior role at TASC, she led the Enterprise Systems business unit that served defense and federal civil agencies including DTRA, the Department of Homeland Security, and the FAA. Prior to that, Dr. Drew was sector vice president of business development for Northrop Grumman's Mission Systems sector. Before joining Northrop Grumman in 2008, Dr. Drew was vice president and general manager for Boeing's Integrated Defense and Security Solutions organization heading strategy and business generation in homeland and global security markets. While at Boeing, Dr. Drew also served as vice president and general manager of Boeing's C3ISR business unit serving the U.S. Air Force, U.S. Navy, and several international customers including the United Kingdom, the North Atlantic Treaty Organization, Australia, and Turkey. In a prior role, she led a significant portion of Boeing Phantom Works developing and transitioning technology across the commercial airplane and military businesses. Dr. Drew has held several leadership roles with National Research Council boards and committees, including as the vice chair of the Air Force Studies Board and on the "NextGen" Air Traffic Management committee for the Transportation Research Board. She also serves on the board of directors for the University of Washington's Applied Physics Lab. Dr. Drew has been named an associate fellow of the American Institute of Aeronautics and Astronautics (AIAA). She also serves on the Strategic Advisory Councils to the Chancellor and Dean of Engineering at the University of Colorado, Boulder, where she earned her Ph.D. in computer science.

ANNIE GREEN is a digital thought leader and knowledge strategist/architect. She has a D.Sc. from George Washington University and a Master of Information Systems from George Mason University. Green is currently working as a data governance specialist for George Mason University and adjunct faculty at several universities. As a strategist/architect, she helps organizations see the "big picture" to provide a more holistic solution to building a cognitive enterprise. Her many years of expertise have resulted in a harmonious blend of theory, practice, and continuous learning focused on optimizing business/IT alignment, knowledge management, digital transformation strategies, change management, and governance in commercial, public, and government sectors. She is an advisor, professor, lecturer, speaker, journal reviewer, and author.

JAMES M. HOLMES (USAF, retired) retired from the Air Force in October 2020 after nearly 40 years of service. He is a member of the Council on Foreign Relations, an adjunct fellow at the Center for a New American Security, a senior advisor at The Roosevelt Group, the Chairman of the Board at Red 6, and an advisor to several defense and tech companies. He completed his Air Force service leading the transformation of Air Combat Command, a global organization operating and sustaining more than 1,000 aircraft and 11 Air Force bases with an annual operating budget of $7.4 billion. As the Air Force's Deputy Chief of Staff for Strategic Plans and Programs, he led a team that shifted Air Force strategy to respond to a new national security environment and built and defended the USAF's input to three $600 billion, 5-year Defense Plans with DoD and the U.S. Congress. As the Deputy Commander of Air Education and Training Command, he directed all aspects of USAF education and training, from basic and technical training to advanced degree programs. As the Air Force's Assistance Deputy Chief of Staff for Operations and Requirements, he coordinated global Air Force operations and requirements with the Joint Chiefs of Staff and regional military commanders. As Principal Director for Mid-East Policy in the Office of the Secretary of Defense, he formulated regional defense policy with the National Security Council and Department of State and coordinated U.S. defense relationships and activities with international partners. Before assuming his strategic role, he commanded Air Force teams in positions of increasing complexity, responsibility, and accountability at the squadron, group, and wing level, including 1 year in command of Air Force forces in Afghanistan. Gen. Holmes graduated from the U.S. Naval War College National Security Strategy program with highest honors and completed both the U.S. Air Force's School for Advanced Air and Space Power Studies program and the Fighter Weapons Instructor Course. He was the Graduate of the Year in the University of Alabama's M.A. in history program at Maxwell Air Force Base and received a B.S. in electrical engineering from the University of Tennessee. He is a fighter pilot with more than 4,000 hours in the F-15 and T-38, including more than 500 combat hours, and continues to fly general aviation aircraft.

MARV LANGSTON (USN, retired) is an independent consultant, focusing on new technology adoption, enterprise architecture and engineering, organizational strategy, and acquisition leadership. He has been serving the DoD and U.S. Navy community for the majority of his 50-year career, where he has focused primarily on Navy Command and Control. During his last public service SES positions, Langston served as Department of Defense Deputy Chief Information Officer, Deputy Assistant Secretary of Navy for C4I, first Navy Chief Information Officer, and as Director of the Defense Advanced Research Projects Agency Information Systems Office. During his 22-year Navy military career, Langston served as an enlisted nuclear power electronics technician and retired as a Commander, Engineering Duty Officer, where he served as an AEGIS Combat System Assistant Program Manager, a Special Assistant to RADM Wayne Meyer helping to establish Battle Force Engineering, and as a plank owner of the Space and Naval Warfare Systems Command. Following his public service career, Langston was the chief operating officer of a small high-tech startup company, chief technology officer of a large business practice, and was a senior staff engineer at the Johns Hopkins University Applied Physics Laboratory, where he helped establish today's AEGIS Ballistic Missile Defense capability. During his career, Dr. Langston earned a Master and Doctorate of Public Administration from the University of Southern California, a Master of Science in electronic engineering from the Naval Post Graduate School, and under the Naval Enlisted Science and Engineering Program, a Bachelor of Science degree in electronic engineering from Purdue University.

ALDEN V. MUNSON JR., is an advisor to government and industry in defense and intelligence. He is a senior fellow and member, Board of Regents at Potomac Institute for Policy Studies, and serves on the Defense Science Board. He was the Deputy Director of National Intelligence for Acquisition from May 2007 until July 2009. Previously, he was a consultant in defense, space, and intelligence and was associated with the investment banking firm Windsor Group. He was the Senior Vice President and Group Executive of the Litton Information Systems Group, leading information technology, command and control, and intelligence businesses for defense, intelligence, civil, commercial, and international customers. Mr. Munson was vice president at TRW, in the System Integration Group, the Space and Electronics Group, and the Information Systems Group (the former TRW Credit Business). In these assignments, he led numerous space, intelligence, and information technology organizations and activities. He began his career at The Aerospace Corporation, where he provided system engineering support to many space and intelligence programs. Mr. Munson received a bachelor's degree in mechanical engineering with distinction and departmental honors from San Jose State University (SJSU) and a master's degree in mechanical engineering from the University of California, Berkeley. He later completed extensive coursework in computer science at University of California, Los Angeles and attended executive programs at Harvard (Competition and Strategy; National and International Security) and Stanford (Management of High Technology Enterprises). In 1997, he was named a Distinguished Graduate of the SJSU College of Engineering, and in 2000, the National Reconnaissance Office named Mr. Munson in the first group of Pioneers of National Reconnaissance. He received the National Intelligence Distinguished Service Medal in 2009. Mr. Munson serves on the board of DigitalGlobe, a commercial imagery company. He was a founding director of Paracel Inc. (now part of Aplera) and has held board positions with BD Systems, the Armed Forces Communications Electronics Association, and the Manhattan Beach Education Foundation, and is an active member of the Intelligence and National Security Alliance.

PAUL D. NIELSEN (USAF, retired) is the director and chief executive officer of Carnegie Mellon University's Software Engineering Institute (SEI). SEI is a federally funded research and development center sponsored by DoD. SEI develops and transitions technologies in software architecture, integration and interoperability, cybersecurity, process improvement, real-time systems, and systems engineering related to software. Prior to joining SEI, Nielsen served in the U.S. Air Force, retiring as a major general. He served primarily in research and development assignments related to space and C3I. In his final assignment, Dr. Nielsen was the commander of AFRL and the Technology Executive Officer for the Air Force. He is a fellow of both AIAA and IEEE and a member of the National Academy of Engineering. He is a past president of AIAA and has served on the Defense Science Board. Nielsen received a Ph.D. in applied science from the University of California, Davis, and an M.B.A. from the University of New Mexico.

JULIE J.C.H. RYAN is the chief executive officer of Wyndrose Technical Group, having retired from academia in 2017. Her last position in academia was professor of cybersecurity and information assurance at the U.S. National Defense University. Prior to that, she was tenured faculty at The George Washington University and a visiting scholar at the National Institute of Standards and Technology. Dr. Ryan came to academia from a career in industry that began when she left government service. Upon graduating from the U.S. Air Force Academy, Dr. Ryan served as a signals intelligence officer in the Air Force and then as a military intelligence officer with the Defense Intelligence Agency. After moving to industry, she worked in a variety of positions, including systems engineer, consultant, and senior staff scientist with companies including Sterling Software, Booz Allen & Hamilton, Welkin Associates, and TRW/ESL. She is the author of several books, including *Defending Your Digital Assets Against Hackers, Crackers, Spies, and Thieves* (McGraw Hill, 2000), and is a fellow of the American Academy of Forensic Sciences. At Wyndrose Technical Group, she focuses on futures forecasting and strategic planning with an eye on technology surprise and disruption. She holds the degree of D.Sc. in engineering management from The George Washington University.

JAY G. SANTEE (USAF, retired) is vice president, Strategic Space Operations, Defense Systems Group, The Aerospace Corporation. In this role, he oversees the company's support of the U.S. Air Force's Space Warfighting Construct, which combines transformational and warfighting-focused command initiatives to maintain space superiority in the 21st century. He also leads the corporation's support to the Space Security and Defense Program and U.S. Strategic Command. Prior to joining Aerospace, Santee was outcome leader for Resilient Affordable Space at MITRE, where he was responsible for directing and shaping MITRE's contributions to the national security space enterprise's fielding of a resilient, affordable space force. Santee served 33 years in the United States Air Force, retiring as a major general in 2014. Santee's last assignment was as deputy director of DTRA. In this capacity, he played a key leadership role in the removal and destruction of declared Syrian chemical weapons materials aboard the MV Cape Ray. Santee's other assignments in the Air Force included, among others, acting Deputy Assistant Secretary of Defense for Space Policy, Vice Commander of the 14th Air Force, Director of the Space Operations Center (now the Joint Space Operations Center), Commander of the 21st Space Wing, and as an operations division chief at U.S. Space Command. Santee earned a bachelor's degree in geography from the U.S. Air Force Academy, an M.B.A. from Golden Gate University, and a master's degree in national security strategy from the National War College. Santee also completed the Program for Senior Executives in National and International Security at the John F. Kennedy School of Government, Harvard University. Santee was awarded the 2014 Ellis Island Medal of Honor, and was invested as a Chevalier de la Légion d'Honneur (Knight of the Legion of Honor), France's highest honor, in 2012. Santee serves on the U.S. Strategic Command's Strategic Advisory Group and on the Advisory Committee for the Secure World Foundation.

JAMES D. SYRING leads the auto and property insurance lines of business for USAA that include more than 8 million members, 14.6 million vehicles in force, and more than 5.9 million homeowner's and renter's policies in force. The USAA P&C Insurance Group continually sets the standard for exceptional service in personal lines insurance. Prior to this role, Syring served as USAA's Chief Administrative Officer (CAO). As USAA's CAO, Syring oversaw Corporate Real Estate and Workplace Services, Enterprise Security Group, Global Sourcing and Procurement, and Information Technology. These functions are foundational in serving, supporting, and protecting USAA's employees and members. Syring joined USAA in July 2017 after a 32-year career in the U.S. Navy. Reaching the rank of Vice Admiral, Syring served in numerous engineering duty officer assignments culminating with his selection as the 9th director of the Missile Defense Agency (MDA). In this capacity, he oversaw the MDA's worldwide mission to develop a capability to defend deployed forces, the United States, allies, and friends against ballistic missile attacks. A 1985 graduate of the U.S. Naval Academy, Syring earned his Bachelor of Science degree in marine engineering. In 1992, he graduated from the Naval Post Graduate School with his Master of Science degree in mechanical engineering. Syring joined USAA to continue serving the military that protects our country.

D

Chief of Staff of the Air Force
Strategic Studies Group Project and Study Ideas

AFWERX
    Collider Events, Connect-a-thons, Ask Me Anything (AMA), Spark Tanks
CYBERWERX
Joint Artificial Intelligence Center (JAIC) and National Mission Initiatives (NMI)
    AI for Humanitarian Assistance / Disaster Relief (AI4HADR)
    AI Workforce Subcommittee—developing AI Human Capital Transformation
USAF MIT AI Accelerator
Software Factories (17)—Federated
    BESPIN, Kobayashi Maru, Section 31, Space Camp, Corsair Ranch, Tesseract, TRON,
    Rogue Blue, Mad Hatter, LevelUp, SkiCAMP, Sonikube, Red 5, SWMGs at AFLCMC
Kessel Run and Project MAVEN
Project Holodeck
Project Brown Heron (PBH)
Pandemic Case Management Suite (PCMS)
MAJCOM/Wing SPARK Tanks/Cells
Computer Language Initiative
Digital University
Digital Talent Task Force (DTTF)
Digital Force—full lifecycle management for a digital career field workforce
Air Force Enlisted Force Development Strategy
Air Force Innovation Ecosystem (pipeline, strategy, charter, framework, etc.)
Innovation ecosystem continued development (MG)
Squadron Innovation Funds (SIF) and Momentum Funds (MF)

Vice Chief's Challenge (VCC)
Airmen Generated Innovation "Wins"
Projects ORSUS and MAVEN—OAR/OAW
COVID DAFACT Task Force (SBIR/STTR/DPA Title III)
425 Innovators
Strategic Innovation and Incubation Cell (SI2C) Project MORPHEUS
Bullpen / Gig-Eagle / Blue Point
Blue Horizon Scholars / AF Fellows
Vault, PBH, Rhombus Guardian, Envision, Warp Core
Platform One, Cloud One, EITaaS
Allies and Partners Working Group
Exchange Officers (EXO) and Foreign Liaison Officers (LNO)
NATO ACT innovation and collaboration engagements
Tri-lateral Strategic Studies Group (TSSG) and Trilateral Steering Initiatives (TSI)
Human Machine Teaming
Digital Airmen of the Future
AI for Coalition Information Sharing
AI Ethical Framework
Agile Combat Employment
Multi-domain Command and Control (MDC2) and Resilience
Mission Partner Environment (MPE)
JADC2 and ABMS Planning with coalition partners
Air Force Futures—ABMS JADC2
Nellis Shadow Operations Center (ShOC-N) ABMS Battlelab and MPE Center
Robotic Process Automation (RPA)
Senior Leader Digital Airman Course
Joint Staff Innovation Steering Group
Economic Warfare Operations Center (EWOC)
DAF Energy Campaign
DAF Debt Equity Strategy
Dual Use Strategy—Enhancing the defense industrial base
Project 300—PEO Airmen—Total Force
Dual use public/private digital talent partnership
Artificial Intelligence and Machine Learning (AI/ML)
Chief Execution Officer
Disruptive Innovation Group—DetX Incubator
Digital Strategy Workshop Series (DSWS) with the NAS
Accelerate Change or Lose—Action Orders A-D (Airmen, Bureaucracy, Competition, Design Implementation)
Sandbox Quantum Science Overview Seminar (Google)
Advancing Quantum capabilities
Hypersonics capabilities
AF Priorities and influencing outcomes of the NDAA
Defense Industrial Board (DIB)
Defense Innovation Unit (DIU)
Operation Flamethrower
SW Factory direct support to the Air Staff
Telework, Remote Work, and Hoteling
DAF Performance Metrics Innovation
AI Initiatives—AI Strategy
Rapid Development Experimentation Fund (RDER)

Air Force Gaming
Air Force PFPA COVID Project
Supply Chain Vulnerability—Logistics Under Attack
Industry Engagement for Digital Transformation and Innovation Development

E

Workshop Series Recap Meeting

After the final workshop of the series concluded, the planning committee met virtually on October 4, 2021. During this meeting, each participant described themes that he or she observed during the workshop series and shared additional thoughts about the Department of the Air Force's (DAF's) digital strategy. The following commentaries should not be interpreted as conclusions or recommendations; rather, they are reflections, insights, and ideas for future activities shared by planning committee members and representatives from both the Department of the Air Force and the National Academies of Sciences, Engineering, and Medicine's Air Force Studies Board.

Mr. Alden Munson, senior fellow and member, Board of Regents, Potomac Institute for Policy Studies, discussed considerations for and impediments to acquisition. He referenced an article that he published in 2015,[1] which presented the systematic barriers to effective acquisition programs: acceptable cost, schedule, and technical performance. He suggested several actions to improve the acquisition process:

- Do not begin acquisition programs that are not affordable.
- Do not award contracts at other than the cost, schedule, and performance baseline captured in a credible government "should cost" for the program.
- Do not run competitions for major development programs unless there are at least two fully qualified candidate suppliers.
- Depend only on mature technology for major programs or commit to rigorous technology maturation programs (e.g., Apollo).
- Professionalize the government acquisition workforce and make acquisition personnel decisions consistent with the expected challenges and durations of all programs.
- Rigorously manage program requirements and fund the program to those requirements.

---

[1] A. Munson, 2015, "Why Can't We Get Acquisitions Right?" Potomac Institute for Policy Studies, https://potomacinstitute.org/featured/706-why-can-t-we-get-acquisitions-right-by-alden-munson.

- Conduct regular, thorough, objective reviews on all development programs.
- Avoid the "conspiracy of hope," which can lead to several distortions—for example, contracts are sometimes let at a small fraction of an independent cost estimate for the programs; contractors are selected without evidencing the required domain knowledge or experience; leadership personnel are cycled through a challenging program like interchangeable parts of a machine; success is assumed in a critical technology development without commitment of money and time for its maturation; growing execution shortcomings are allowed to linger without being specifically addressed; increasing cost overruns and schedule erosions are played down; and a program is not staffed as indicated by independent estimates.

He next examined the use of commercially produced components in a government system. He explained that defense procurements are conducted under a very specific, scripted business model. When the government bureaucracy directs the business of acquisition, there is no common mediating construct. Although companies in the defense industrial base (DIB) have developed the ability to succeed under this model, the business model used in commercial markets is very different. For instance, economic value is the common medium through which affairs are mediated, profit is based on the economic value the product creates for the customer, intellectual property rights are paramount, formal competition is not used universally, successful suppliers are rarely replaced in the absence of strong market drivers, and bureaucracy or other considerations that do not improve the economic value to the participants are rejected. Firms engaged in business with the U.S. government are pressured to accept government terms: records are open to government auditors; profits can be limited; intellectual property may not be protected; and decision making can be labored, slow, and unpredictable. Many commercial firms, especially those that are opening new markets with new products and are being richly rewarded for the economic value that their customers can create, are not interested in doing business with the U.S. government under these terms. He emphasized the orthogonality between the two business models—the U.S. government cannot abandon its formal procurement system, and commercial firms are not incentivized to accept the terms driven by this system. Therefore, he continued, if the government wants access to products and services produced in response to commercial market forces, it needs to develop mechanisms to "harmonize" these two business models so that neither makes unacceptable concessions.

Mr. Munson shared a list of government best practices for the inclusion of commercial products in government systems: (1) recognize that the choice to include commercial-off-the-shelf (COTS)/non-developmental items (NDIs) in government systems cannot be pursued under the assumption that commercial suppliers would be compelled to operate according to the traditional government rules, regulations, and conventions; (2) harmonize the differences between the two diametrically opposed business models to achieve win-win outcomes; (3) recognize that to gain the benefit of COTS/NDIs (i.e., reduced research and development and maintenance over the life of the program), the product would need be used essentially as-is, because major modifications risk erasing the desired economies; (4) add a "go-back step" in the requirements and architecture processes (i.e., after the COTS/NDI components have been selected as the best fit available, the requirements and architecture trades would be revisited); and (5) develop and apply appropriately a new generation of security criteria around cyber defense throughout the commercial software and hardware supply chains.

He expressed an additional concern about whether the traditional acquisition system could execute such a program with the speed, agility, and efficiency required by the Air Force's digitization community. He proposed the following to address this issue: (1) the "thicket-like" system of regulations, approvals, and permissions around the acquisition program could be "pruned," or programs that need fast, agile, efficient execution could be allowed to waive elements that impede progress; (2) budgeting for such programs could provide multiyear funding, and reprogramming should be permitted more flexibly; (3) organizations could be flattened to shorten the "distance" between those executing the program and those with review and approval authorities; (4) roles of outside organizations could be mediated at the top of a program's approval chains; and (5) acquisition could become a career specialty, and acquisition assignments could reflect domain knowledge and be for durations credible for the challenges.

Dr. Julie Ryan, chief executive officer, Wyndrose Technical Group, championed the suggestions provided by Mr. Munson. Dr. Pamela Drew, former executive vice president and president of information systems, Exelis, reiterated Mr. Munson's assertion about the benefit of leveraging existing commercial capabilities instead of trying to tailor products. Lt. Gen. Ted Bowlds (USAF, ret.), chief executive officer, IAI North America, remarked that although the use of COTS could enable speed, he cautioned that the security around COTS products may not be as strong as the U.S. government requires. Dr. Marv Langston (USN, ret.), independent consultant, observed a failure in the U.S. Navy's past two classes of surface ships, likely owing to the fact that program managers are no longer in charge of programs (i.e., legal and contracting lead instead). If the Department of Defense (DoD) does not begin to rely on the use of Other Transaction Authorities and prototypes (similar to the Defense Advanced Research Projects Agency), he said that it will continue to experience failure. Ms. Deborah Westphal, chairman of the board, Toffler Associates, referenced a National Academies report on owning the technical baseline,[2] which found that moving program manager responsibility to contractors was a negative inflection point. Lt. Gen. Michael Hamel (USAF, ret.), independent consultant, noted that when program managers are disempowered, accountability and progress lag. He added that accepting COTS as-is is not the only option for the government; he suggested working more closely with the private sector in the development of products. To generate funding for and to gain critical capabilities, he continued, DoD would need to take more risks. Gen. James (Mike) Holmes (USAF, ret.), senior advisor, The Roosevelt Group, commented that the acquisition process suffers without the voice of the warfighter—owing to personnel cuts, operators are no longer part of the Program Executive Offices.

Lt. Gen. Hamel reviewed the purpose of the workshop series and the charge to the workshop planning committee: to examine the operational, technical, programmatic, organizational, and governance challenges, opportunities, and risks facing the DAF's enterprise-wide digital transformation strategies and plans. Top questions from the workshop sponsors included the following: What is the best sequence/synchronization for digital initiatives? Are there experiences from industry/others that demonstrate which actions achieve the biggest impact across workstreams? Is the vision for digitization on the right track? Are the right investments being made at the right time? He recapped the "Digital Transformation" presentation from the first day of the workshop series: Gen. David Allvin noted that speed is of the essence ("accelerate change or lose"); and Gen. David Thompson said that the Space Force is dependent on the Air Force, intends to be a truly digital, small service; and has a vision for a digital workforce, digital engineering, digital headquarters, and digital operations. Mr. Jay Santee (USAF, ret.), vice president, Strategic Space Operations, Defense Systems Group, The Aerospace Corporation, pointed out that because there are so many parts to sequence in the digital ecosystem, governance will be just as important as investments—thoughtful policy and an overarching orchestrator are needed for this effort.

Col. Scott McKeever, director, Chief of Staff of the Air Force (CSAF) Strategic Studies Group, expressed his hope that the observations shared during the workshop series would help move the DAF's digital transformation efforts forward. He echoed the importance of speed, as well as understanding the risk-reward calculus and the right sequence/synchronization of efforts. Personnel who understand both strategy and underlying technologies are also a key component of the success of the digital transformation. Lt. Gen. Hamel pointed out that the DAF includes three distinct sectors (the Secretaries, the Air Force, and the Space Force) with varying needs, and Col. McKeever replied that this is precisely what makes achieving unity of effort so challenging. Before describing some of the Strategic Studies Group's activities (see Appendix D), Col. McKeever emphasized the need to focus on the competitive environment (using China's progress as a guidepost) and highlighted the value of data. Several large data efforts are under way at the headquarters level—for example, Project Brown Heron utilizes a cross-functional team to consider the decisions that need to be made and to pursue relevant data. Because resources are limited, it is critical to prioritize within the framework of the Air Force's "compounding data asset." The cross-functional team

---

[2] National Academies of Sciences, Engineering, and Medicine, 2016, *Owning the Technical Baseline for Acquisition Programs in the U.S. Air Force*, The National Academies Press, Washington, DC, https://doi.org/10.17226/23631.

creates ontologies and knowledge graphs, and considers how contracts and finances connect to readiness. He also provided an example of ongoing data challenges faced by the Air Force: it took three Major Commands (MAJCOMs) and 3 weeks of communication with the Defense Information Systems Agency (DISA) to access data and systems that the Air Force already owns. In this federated system of decision making, connecting multilayered systems can be difficult. He reiterated the need to find people who can think digitally and cross-functionally to serve as "integrators" for these efforts. Dr. Langston noticed that even though enabling technologies are available, military systems never seem to share data—primarily because no one has the power to enforce data sharing. However, he stressed that data sharing is fundamental to digitization. Lt. Gen. Hamel wondered how effective capabilities would be integrated into the mainstream and how this system would become self-sustaining. Col. McKeever said that when resources are available, it is helpful to provide enterprise capabilities that incentivize people to work on these challenges. This creates a bottom-up transformation, which has proven more successful then orders from the top.

Gen. Holmes offered his observations of themes that emerged throughout the workshop series. He said that multiple threat analyses indicate that the DAF faces a growing need to improve information systems and processes for both warfighting (e.g., to improve capability, capacity, and command and control decision speed/tempo) and institutional tasks (i.e., to make decisions required to gain efficiencies/savings and to support recruitment/retention). He emphasized the need to "do better work and make work better" and explained that similar processes have been successfully implemented in civilian and government spaces. The DAF could learn lessons from others' transitions, allowing them to shape the digital transformation effort instead of beginning from scratch. He noted that the DAF's most pressing challenge is empowering and maximizing the impact of its people. This transformative level of empowerment aligns with the DAF's new warfighting and institutional doctrine and processes, which prioritize mission command via centralized control (CC), distributed command (DC), and decentralized execution (DE). Ongoing digital transformation efforts are unlikely to be successful without improved unity of effort that is consistent with this construct, he continued. A unified strategy would (1) appoint an appropriate leader (i.e., the Air Force works best under MAJCOM leadership), (2) provide DAF intent and required direction while empowering innovative approaches to execution, (3) prioritize and apply required resources, (4) measure and reward progress, (5) consider unplanned/unpredicted consequences, (6) direct or allow process and institutional changes required to permit transformation, and (7) be routinely reevaluated and updated. The best results in other organizations' information transitions were obtained by first improving the current state through agile processes (i.e., DevSecOps approaches and application programming interfaces for universal data visibility and access), and then providing the guidance and resources required to enable expansion of efforts.

Dr. Drew shared her key takeaways from the second workshop in the series. She referenced examples of success and lessons learned across multiple digital transformation application areas that the DAF is pursuing (e.g., mission/operations, acquisition, development, maintenance, and administration or business support). She observed that many of the workshop speakers described the importance of governance, leadership, and critical success factors. For example, Danielle Ullner of the Boston Consulting Group (BCG) noted that it is important to have an appropriate oversight structure with a cross-functional group and the authority to make decisions, as well as integrated management of budgeting decisions and cycles. Dr. Drew also mentioned the BCG study that revealed that 70 percent of digital transformations fail and of those that succeed, 80 percent relied on six critical success factors (i.e., integrated strategy with clearly defined transformational goals, leadership commitment from the chief executive officer through middle management, deployment of high caliber talent, agile governance mindset that drives broad adoption, effective monitoring of progress, and a business-led modular technology and data platform). During Workshop Two, several best practices of "how" to implement digital transformation were presented. The majority of successful cases had quick wins or incremental approaches; fail fast and agile methodologies were preferred over waterfall or other monolithic concepts; change management was key, particularly for the user community; implementation occurred through cross-functional teams; data and logic management capabilities were present; and zero trust was critical for cybersecurity. Speakers also shared key strategies to avoid failure: establish ownership and manage end-to-end processes; reduce barriers such as resistance to process, technical, or operational change; get early buy-in from key stakeholders; determine appropriate oversight design (e.g., centralized versus decentralized). In closing, she summarized three overarching themes from the workshop series:

1. The DAF's goal for digital transformation is to accelerate decision making in a relevant time frame and to maintain (or regain) the edge against adversaries (via operational/mission decisions, command and control, the Advanced Battle Management System, joint all-domain command and control, internal investments, acquisition, administration, and human capital).
2. Progress is being made toward digital transformation—for example, the squadron level now has the same data view as the chief of staff; the ties between mission requirement to aircraft availability leading to a funding requirement demonstrates improved planning, spending, and execution; a top-level digital foundation, zero trust, and a data strategy are in progress; integration of intelligence, surveillance, and reconnaissance and cyber electronic capabilities are under way; and some level of agile DevOps is being achieved, although barriers remain in true integration with the DIB in digital acquisition.
3. Potential gaps or barriers include a lack of prioritization that is unique to the Air Force and Space Force (i.e., data priorities against use cases and operation in a contested and energy-constrained environment with interrupted services); a lack of end-to-end process ownership and funding management; and an inadequate risk assessment by role for data access.

Dr. Langston emphasized that the world is on the edge of a massive change, as a result of digitization and advanced technological capabilities. He referenced a 2019 Air Force white paper,[3] which stated that "… victory in combat will depend less on individual capabilities, and more on the integrated strengths of a connected network of weapons, sensors, and analytic tools. Today's Air Force must transform to employ the data, technology, and infrastructure we need to prevail … To compete, deter, and win over our great power adversaries, we are forging a digital Air Force that will field a 21st century IT infrastructure responsive to the demands of modern combat, leverage the power of data as the foundation of artificial intelligence and machine learning to enable faster decision making and improved warfighter support, [and] adopt agile business practices that improve the effectiveness and efficiency of our management enterprise." He described a response to that white paper from Maj. John P. Biszko,[4] which challenged the following four assumptions about the digital Air Force: "The world can best be understood as entering into phases of technological advancement as a coherent whole; the most effective way for a military to win over great-power adversaries is to evolve its own capabilities in lockstep with the changing character of the technological landscape; the best way to attack or defend an increasingly digital entity is with increasingly digital weapons and defenses; and that government-sourced innovation is appropriately equivocal with military technological advances." He shared Maj. Biszko's explanation that "whereas the paper assigns technological advancement as the defining characteristic of a global community's evolution, changes in economics, climate, and politics may be even more salient drivers of how military power is applied to cope with global evolution. … As a force emphasizes its technological edge more than its human edge—its (artificial) reasoning over its will, opportunity, or creativity—it makes the adversary's problem increasingly scientific and less human. All the adversary has to do is determine how best to undermine something digital, which is relatively easy compared to how best to undermine another's creativity." Dr. Langston also highlighted the value of the Workshop Three presentation from Andrew Stricker of the LeMay Center and recapped some of his main assertions: " … digital transformation is dependent upon underlying architectures, human creativity, and culture to create dynamic opportunities … the digital transformation effort is highly dependent on addressing each of the seven areas [of the Digital Transformation Cycle] …

---

[3] U.S. Air Force, 2019, "United States Air Force White Paper," https://www.af.mil/Portals/1/documents/2019%20SAF%20story%20attachments/USAF%20White%20Paper_Digital%20Air%20Force_Final.pdf?ver=2019-07-09-181813-390&timestamp=1562710801965.

[4] J. Biszko, 2020, "Understanding and Challenging 'The Digital Air Force' USAF White Paper," https://media.defense.gov/2020/Jul/07/2002449935/-1/-1/1/BISZKO.PDF.

synchronicity of effort by DAF/DoD involving whole of government is critical … clearly communicating purposes that impact not only warfighting capabilities but quality of life and work among personnel will help to motivate/inspire/engage innovation mindsets and effort broadly across DAF." Dr. Langston observed a dearth of workshop discussion about the following: how the Air Force would synchronize with DoD, other government agencies, nongovernmental organizations, or the private sector on digital transformation efforts; competitive offset advantages; infrastructure or an ecosystems approach to improve productivity; the potential of the digital Air Force to displace workers; use of cloud, artificial intelligence (AI)/machine learning (ML), and data analytics (other than for data access); cognitive computing; improved digital services as an outcome (i.e., if it makes jobs easier and gets results, it will be implemented); and joint collaborative/integrative capabilities (i.e., even if the Air Force creates processes, it still has to integrate with the other services to affect the way we fight). He described another relevant article, "Complementary Actions Define New DISA Strategy,"[5] which defines information security as paramount to fight against the adversary and command and control as a "no fail priority." The article also discussed the plan to conduct "a zero-based review of all the C2 requirements needed by Defense Department personnel ranging from senior leaders to warfighters. This entails a revalidation to understand whether these requirements are being met, either from an acquisition standpoint or an operational standpoint. Other criteria include whether a program exists to improve requirements, if the correct resources are aligned, and what the operational team leveraging these capabilities needs. … " In closing, Dr. Langston articulated his final impressions of the workshop series, first describing the vice chief's desire to make better decisions as an assigned goal for the IT department, not a strategic objective for the entire Air Force. He added that strategic goals that do not impact funding resources are hollow goals. He expressed concern about "business as usual" continuing with the current digital transformation strategy, owing to a lack of discussion about tying the digital transformation goals to productivity changes aligned with IT infrastructure or industry best-of-breed process changes. He noted that Dr. Stricker's Digital Transformation Cycle represents a more coherent set of digital transformation objectives coupled with needed IT and process changes, but most of the elements in the cycle are only being partially addressed (if at all) by the Air Force. He underscored that bureaucratic proclamations without a means to quickly improve the jobs of airmen and the civilian workforce will not generate the desired outcome, and distributed budgets ensure that most of the Air Force acquisition and operations will function with little change.

Lt. Gen. Bowlds described an early release program effort in 2005, the Expeditionary Combat Support System, which was intended to digitize logistics, support, and supply. However, it was cancelled in 2011 after $1 billion had been spent with no results. He defined this cautionary example as a failure in organizational change management (i.e., "culture eating strategy for breakfast"). Reflecting on the three workshops in the series, he championed culture change as the key enabler for digital transformation in the Air Force; everyone has to be on board, especially at the middle management level. Another key tenet of digital transformation is the concept of operations (CONOPS)—using the old CONOPS with new data is not the right approach. Data security, data sharing, and digital operations are becoming increasingly important for the Air Force; data security in particular has to be considered early in system development. He echoed Dr. Langston's observation that there was not enough discussion during the workshops about how the Air Force plans to modify its infrastructure to support digital transformation and enable data movement. He added that with the amount of data being generated, now and in the future, AI/ML efforts should support decision making. He pointed out that although many of the workshop speakers emphasized the role of digital engineering (i.e., an acquisition tool to iterate the design with requirements input), it is imperative to take the next step of connecting platforms for campaign efforts. In closing, he encouraged the Air Force to move from using "buzz words" to focusing on true digitization, instead of creating modern stovepipes.

Dr. Ryan provided her final thoughts on the workshop series:

---

[5] R. Ackerman, 2021, "Complementary Actions Define New DISA Strategy," *Signal*, October 1, https://www.afcea.org/content/complementary-actions-define-new-disa-strategy.

- *Data writ large as a "big, juicy target"* (e.g., advanced persistent attacks, coordinated criminal gangs, physical attacks, and accidents). The Air Force cannot afford this risk, yet it is currently taking the wrong approach toward funding, people, coordination, and security.
- *Evolution versus revolution.* Data are claimed to be vitally important to the operational vision of the Air Force, but they are not being treated accordingly. If data are as important to the future battlespace as stated, that warrants data personnel who are uniformed members of the services, and data being treated with the same level of infrastructure attention as a major weapons system with concomitant life cycle support; otherwise, the evolutionary path will lead to extinction.
- *Security.* Security is more than just secrecy, and confidentiality is more than just secrecy from bad actors. Integrity is more than just truthiness, and availability is more than just access. Security engineering includes protection, detection, reaction, and correction. Security attributes apply not only to data; transactions should also be protected. Metadata, traffic analysis, emanations, operational patterns, and signatures are also important. People who are not deeply competent in information security aspects should not be allowed to make decisions without competent advice—it is too easy for charlatans to trick smart people into poor choices.

In closing, Dr. Ryan asserted that a true digital strategy requires competent funding, a whole-of-government approach, investment in the growth of personnel capabilities, and treatment as the most important national security issue.

Dr. Paul Nielsen (USAF, ret.), director and chief executive officer, Software Engineering Institute, Carnegie Mellon University, asserted that balance is needed in the digital transformation. For example, although putting all of the Air Force's data in one place creates an attractive cyber target, that is not an excuse to avoid modernization; new strategies to protect the data have to be developed. He observed that the vision for digital transformation presented by the vice chief of the Air Force was understood and echoed by other workshop presenters. Digital transformation could enhance all aspects of Air Force operations (e.g., warfighting, intelligence, acquisition, logistics, and business operations); however, he expressed concern that there appears to be no next-level plan for how to achieve this—no priorities, no architecture, and no funding. The Air Force has introduced some efforts that will enable this transformation (e.g., DevSecOps, software factories, containerization, cloud services), but he noted that there is something unfortunately familiar about this initiative with respect to previous Air Force initiatives—great vision without execution. This is especially discouraging for new Air Force recruits, who are digital natives but are expected to use 20th century tools to complete their missions. Reflecting on the vice chief's statement that the Air Force seeks improved decision-making capabilities, Dr. Nielsen pointed out that digitizing current processes may not improve decision making and, in fact, could make it worse. He stressed that the Air Force should understand how it makes decisions now, what the issues are, and how it would like to make decisions in the future, not just with speed but with quality. One fundamental requirement for digital transformation is a supportive 21st century infrastructure (i.e., hardware, software, and technical talent), and the Air Force will have to grapple with its legacy infrastructure, culture, and policies to achieve true digital transformation. He posited that most of the success stories from industry are directly applicable to the Air Force. The talent that the Air Force needs to make this transformation will require support from academia and industry (both defense and non-defense). He emphasized that agile governance and continuous development, integration, and deployment will be important to early and continuous progress.

Dr. Rama Chellappa, Bloomberg Distinguished Professor of electrical and computer engineering and biomedical engineering, Johns Hopkins University, underscored that digital transformation is 25 years old; he wondered what took the Air Force so long to reach this point and why it is not catching up at a fundamental level. He proposed that the Air Force integrate with other branches of DoD as well as with Silicon Valley and non-DoD entities in this transformation effort. He stressed that the Air Force cannot spend 20 years trying to achieve its vision; digital transformation is swift and changing. A 5-year master plan with well-defined metrics for measuring progress is needed. Most importantly, the technology talent base has to be developed. He explained that 60–70 percent of graduate students who specialize in technologies such as data science, AI, and ML are foreign nationals who are unable to work for DoD (although they can work in Silicon Valley and earn a $300,000 entry-level salary). He added that, as a result, there is a need to enhance the participation of U.S. citizens in these technologies.

Dr. Annie Green, data governance specialist, George Mason University, reiterated that structure, content, and competent people are critical to transformation.[6] In the first workshop of the series, she observed a saturation of topics (e.g., although AI was discussed, it was not discussed in the *context* of how it could be used in the Air Force environment). Initiatives and projects seem to be based on intriguing innovation and new technology opportunities; however, the Air Force is situated in a complex, adaptive system and has to think about refocusing its direction. Engineering and management are critical, she continued, but the Air Force has failed at engineering. For example, if the architecture is not yet established, it is not possible to determine how the pieces fit together and there is no way to drive strategy. And if there are no metrics to measure success, it is not appropriate to claim success. Representation, data integration, data valuation, and governance are also critical but not apparent in the Air Force's plan. She emphasized that a holistic structure is needed; it is crucial to be able to sustain processes and renew them when they have decayed.

Col. Douglas DeMaio, 187th Fighter Wing Commander, Alabama Air National Guard, posited that if the Air Force involves its people in the right way and creates the right messaging, digitization is achievable. He emphasized the following requirements for digital transformation, from an operational perspective: an enterprise vision, mission, and objectives; technology; culture change; and a method. He described the current state of digital transformation in the Air Force as nascent, including several enterprise initiatives without a comprehensive effort. He said that the Air Force lacks mature strategy, doctrine, CONOPS, method, and tactics, techniques, and procedures (TTPs); has little emphasis on culture change; focuses primarily on technology; and searches for perfect, centralized connectivity in the cyber domain. Although airmen want to digitize, they are not involved in the process of digitization. He noted that the Space Force has effective digitization efforts, with a comprehensive move toward culture change and technology; however, China also has impressive efforts in digitization, networking, and machine intelligence. He shared several observations from the workshop series: culture is critical in digital transformation; adversaries will likely focus on centralized decision making; the Air Force will fight for connectivity in peer-level combat; there is a new Air Force mission command (CC, DC, DE); and decision making may be focused at the tactical edge. To achieve an enterprise-level transformation effort, he suggested the following steps:

- Create a CSAF-driven culture change with digital Air Force doctrine notes and by developing and publishing a digitization doctrine.
- Implement digitization, networking, and machine intelligence across the entire electromagnetic spectrum, and develop a related CONOPS.
- Focus and empower people at tactical levels, via agile combat employment (ACE). For example, he described an upcoming ACE exercise in which airmen will have the opportunity to innovate with connectivity and logistics to identify unique solutions.

Digitization requires both top-down and bottom-up approaches with the embodiment of CSAF's mission command culture and joint all-domain operations, he continued. Headquarters Air Force (HAF) A3 is developing an operational method and TTPs to enable prioritization of data access at the tactical edge.

Mr. Santee recapped the Space Force's vision for an interconnected, innovative, digitally dominant force via digital headquarters, digital engineering, digital operations, and digital workforce. He expressed his support for this approach but still questioned how to achieve it. The Space Force described the vision for the digital ecosystem as a cloud-based, MLS domain that is remotely accessible and secure (with containerization and infrastructure as code as well as common, portable, and scalable tools and applications). The goal is to integrate seamlessly with other Air Force and DoD efforts and link integrated,

---

[6] A. Green, 2018, "Structure, Content, & Humans: Critical 'Planks' When Building Artificial Intelligence into a Business," Georgetown University School of Continuing Studies, https://scs.georgetown.edu/news-and-events/article/7282/structure-content-humans-critical-planks-when-building-artificial-intelligence-business.

authoritative data to engineer all domain capabilities. He emphasized that the services use funding, requirements, and program offices to govern and procure capabilities like the digital ecosystem. He wondered what the digital ecosystem would look like as a minimum viable product to support digital headquarters, digital engineering, and digital operations. He asserted that the Space Force needs data and thus needs to incentivize data sharing and penalize those who do not share data, and it needs to rely on policy and governance for collection and protection of these data. He cited an example of a 2002 mandate from Jeff Bezos that said that any employee not using select interfaces would be fired. The next question for the Space Force is what a minimum viable set of data would look like hosted in the digital ecosystem minimum viable product. Once the workforce has access to the minimum viable products, interconnection, innovation, and digital fluency, cognizance, and dominance become possible. The resulting change in the culture and CONOPS could be significant.

Mr. Charles Brooks, adjunct faculty, Georgetown University, offered several key takeaways (via Ms. Westphal) from the workshop series: there is a need for a larger digital transformation with a budget behind authority to demonstrate commitment; legacy systems embedded in both procurement and operations are adversarial to digital transformation; layers of bureaucracy in decision making impact agility; there is a need to be more tech-savvy, especially in AI, 5G, and computing; turnover of leadership is an issue as are siloes in the Air Force culture, which make it difficult to share information; investment in digital automation tools is necessary; and it is not easy to scale transformation among different programs in missions. He described the requirements for successful transformation, including a data-centric and digitized user experience; coordinated data flow and access management; security and transparency throughout supply chains; unified training; understanding of digital governance; and adoption of models, strategies, and best practices that have already proven effective in other agencies and the private sector.

Ms. Westphal emphasized that culture change starts with leadership and underscored that culture will not change if the Air Force does not change what it does on a daily basis. She expressed that although the Air Force talks about a sense of urgency, it has not *created* a sense of urgency for change. Because synchronization becomes desynchronization when leadership rotates every few years, creating a sense of urgency for transformation is even more important. To increase speed, different and bold actions have to be taken by leadership to signal urgency. For example, the right leader is one who is truly committed to bold change instead of committed only to the actions that will lead to a promotion. She supported the creation of a temporary transformation office as a centralized location for programs and activities. She stressed the need for this office to direct the vision, communicate the future state, celebrate quick wins, and signal urgency. A unity of effort is needed to sequence plans for transformation, she continued.

Mr. Munson communicated his takeaways from the workshop series. He described a "recipe" for success, from the perspective of a program manager: pursue a set of actions that will resonate with people and stimulate more action, consider how budgeting and oversight will occur, define the level of centralization required to scale, and position to be scalable and extendable. He emphasized the need for security and suggested an approach based on the activities already under way to create use cases for future pilots. It is possible to distill from these use cases basic elements of the architecture and implementation, and evolve the use cases to better reflect implementation in a digital world. He proposed creating an architecture framework, derived from the analyses of the use cases and the pilots, that includes a data strategy. He then suggested using the pilot with the most support to build the architecture that supports the use case. The current level of security, even with zero trust, is not sufficient to allow everything to be connected: difficult decisions need to be made about partitioning. He presented the goal to build an infrastructure that can accommodate new technologies—implement based on commercial infrastructure with the flexibility to change TTPs as necessary, and reserve custom Air Force development for the areas in which there are no commercial analogues.

As the meeting drew to a close, Dr. Richard Hallion, senior advisor, Science and Technology Policy Institute, submitted a written summary of his meeting commentary (see Box E.1), and Lt. Gen. Hamel provided the following list of general observations and themes from the workshop series:

- Digital transformation touches the Air Force's organization, operations, and activities—an

- extremely complex and challenging, but imperative, enterprise-wide effort.
- The workshop series engaged participants from a broad cross-section of the Air Force—not comprehensive but representative of the range of issues and challenges. The workshops benefited from diverse participants and dialogue but were limited by time, participants, protocols, and synthesis.
- There is a growing recognition that information capabilities will be a vital "center of gravity" in all future international competition and conflict—and may become the leading (decisive) edge of combat.
- Many good things are occurring within the Air Force, from doctrine, to technology, to innovation, to processes/application, to systems, to people, to partnering—but transformation has not reached a "tipping point," nor is the rate of change at the pace of the broader information advances in private sectors and by adversaries.
- Speed, agility, innovation, and resilience are essential attributes in digital capabilities and methods—increasingly being led by industry, commercial, and academia—that the Air Force needs to harness.
- There is an ample supply of information technologies and proven practices. The challenge is to adapt and scale across the services and truly commit to, resource, and implement needed capabilities—particularly enterprise infrastructure, data management, and security.
- Cybersecurity needs to be a top priority—"zero trust" appears to be the accepted methodology but should be designed in and based on "risk management" principles and practices. A top-level chief information security official is important.
- Rigid DoD processes present big impediments to digital transformation—requirements; planning, programming, budget, and execution; and acquisition. New tools, authorities, practices, and processes could be applied to digital transformation.
- There are many new authorities and tools that could assist the definition, design, fielding, and use of modern information/digital capabilities—the Air Force should aggressively push to define its preferred models and practices to leverage them.
- The Air Force's shift to CC, DC, and DE has profound and far-reaching implications—affecting all "organize, train, and equip" functions. Digital transformation is essential to enabling it but should also be a top practitioner.
- Hierarchical organizations and processes are the antithesis of modern information systems—federated, loosely coupled, open systems and "action teams" serving diverse communities of use are essential.
- Resourcing (i.e., dollars, talent, and leadership engagement) is critical to driving organization and culture change. It is not clear that the Air Force knows what it is spending or how best to shift resourcing from legacy capabilities to future desired capabilities.
- Stovepiped programs and efforts are widespread—new forums and regularized engagement/collaboration, organized around and within traditional lines of effort (e.g., operations, mission support, business activities) and new critical capabilities (e.g., infrastructure, data, security), are needed to create connections.
- The classical purpose of strategy is to link "ways and means to achieve desired ends"—there does not appear to be an articulated, department-wide strategy guiding its digital transformation. A deliberate strategy could be an important tool to capture, communicate, and evolve through learning.
- There is much room to improve "unity of effort" in the digital transformation across the Air Force.

BOX E.1
Hallion Thoughts Regarding the October 4, 2021, Meeting

Richard Hallion, senior advisor, Science and Technology Policy Institute, submitted the following written summary of his October 4, 2021, meeting commentary:

Overall, the workshop illuminated the contradictions and challenges within what is otherwise a quest—digital transformation—that we all regard as both desirable and absolutely necessary for the future of USAF/USSF and, in a larger sense, DoD. There are issues here with infrastructure; matching words with actions; security; threat analysis and response; strategy, doctrine, TTPs; corporate culture; whether to start small (evolution) or big (revolution); and prioritization that must be addressed, and very quickly at that.

My thoughts regarding the individual speakers and their presentations are as follows:

I thought that Mike Hamel raised a succession of very interesting points beginning with his statement and question that "We haven't gotten to a tipping point. There are a lot of good things going on, but when does it become self-sustaining?" Another point he raised subsequently, in reaction to Pam Drew's comments, was the absolute necessity of capturing those "nuggets" (as he termed them) of DT efforts/developments/accomplishments that have gone right. (And the pessimist in me would add we need to capture those things that went badly as well.)

The review of Workshops I and II by Mike Holmes and Pam Drew was very useful as it served to both trigger and focus the discussion of a number of issues by subsequent speakers, in addition to the comments both themselves raised. Overall, Holmes (and Cinco as well, later) brought a very important MAJCOM/warfighter perspective to the discussion. Holmes captured succinctly the importance of pursuing DT by empowering and maximizing the potential of AF/SF people, as that is at the very heart of centralized control, distributed command, and decentralized execution. I generally accept his idea that the "best transformation starts small, then accelerates rapidly," as well as his follow-on point that the USAF and USSF "should resist the temptation to build a giant system to get this [DT-ed] done: start small and build on that."

Pam Drew pointed out that the DAF "needs to focus on prioritization of that which is unique to the Air Force," adding (importantly I think) that one of the "extremely unique" aspects of USAF (and I would add USSF) operations is that those operations take place in contested environments, in the face of enemy threats, counters, and other actions, and as well in an environment where the availability of power and connectivity is not assured.

Marv Langston offered a very provocative view of DT and its social and cultural impacts, and if some of it seemed removed from the narrowly defined purposes of the workshop, I nevertheless think it is worth mentioning in the final report, particularly such aspects as likely future workforce realignment, reduction, and unemployment; robotics, work patterns, and possible future societal transformations stemming from space, solar energy, fusion energy, virtual work, social life, etc. Most interesting of all to me were the deficits he perceived in thinking about DT, notably that too little attention is paid to (1) changing the infrastructure, (2) integrating USAF/USSF DT efforts with DoD as a whole, and (3) cloud AI and data analytics.

Ted Bowlds stressed culture and CONOPS, both of which I think are critical. I liked (and agree with) his quote that "culture eats strategy for breakfast—the culture piece is number one and right behind that is the CONOPS." Bowlds raised security which was addressed by subsequent speakers as well, using the example of Pearl Harbor where, as he put it, "We concentrated all our airplanes to protect them from one threat [saboteurs] and thereby made them a target for another [Japanese naval aviators]." He raised the old Cold War-legacy TAC Brawler analysis tool to evaluate capabilities against threats, and that resonated with me, as I believe strongly we need to Red Team DT efforts so that the architectures, strategy, doctrine, and TTPs we employ to improve our efficiencies don't as well furnish potential foes with centralization leading to vulnerabilities offsetting any advantages we may enjoy. (A good example of where DT could be examined is as a means of helping address the challenge of defense against high-speed weapons, subject of an NAS study in 2017.)

In the same vein, Julie Ryan reminded us all that "data writ large is a big juicy target" and offered examples—Georgia, the Ukraine, and Colonial Pipeline—where Russian cyberattacks served either as prequels to kinetic attack or as a means to criminal exploitation. Her conclusion that "data needs to be treated equivalent to a major weapon system" is a crucially important point that I believe should be captured in the final report, as well as her follow-on point that "security is more than secrecy," and that we are embarking on an effort where there are many self-proclaimed experts, some of which are frauds and charlatans.

Paul Nielsen raised an issue that other speakers later alluded to, namely the mismatch between vision, words, and actions, noting, "We have great words and vision but then we fail to execute." He quite rightly reminded us all that "if we don't do this right we can just deluge people with more data," noting, "We need not only faster solutions but also higher quality decisions," and stressing that "we've got to start delivering soon. Perhaps with things that help airmen in their everyday lives and follow with weapons systems later."

He raised one point that is controversial, namely whether it is desirable for the USAF/USSF to attempt doing all this on its own, or by partnering with industry and academe, stating that he did not think the USAF/USSF could do it on its own. My own thought on this is that relying on industry, while seemingly a "no brainer" can simply get you "more of the same" rather than really revolutionary technology. The example I always think about is the invention of the gas turbine (jet), ramjet, and liquid rocket engines: neither the jet nor liquid rocket were invented in the established aero-engine companies. Instead, other manufacturers (for the United States, these included General Electric, Westinghouse, Marquardt, Reaction Motors, and Chrysler) appeared and only later did mainstream propulsion companies (Pratt-and-Whitney, Wright, Allison, etc.) get involved. The mainstream manufacturers were simply too invested in the combination of the propeller and piston engine, and were blind to a revolution that would transform both aeronautics and astronautics. We need to avoid that with DT.

I thought Rama Chellappa raised an important point by stressing that we can't afford a 20+ year effort here. Though he didn't mention Moore's Law (I may have missed it if he did), I would concur with him that with computational power doubling every 18 to 24 months or so, a 20+ year cycle for DT development makes no sense.

For my part, I think this is owing to changes in the decision-making environment. In World War II, you could have a major weapon system developed and fielded in about 2½ years (think P-80, the first U.S. combat-worthy jet fighter). A 20- to 25-year program runs over multiple Presidential administrations, differing Congressional Senators and Representatives, multiple service chiefs, multiple PEMs/corporate leaders, etc. as well as constantly changing external circumstances and advancing S&T. Is it any wonder you have little chance of continuity, focused change, or avoiding instant obsolescence? (See my later comment on perhaps returning to the era of Schriever, von Braun, Rickover and Kaminski.)

Rama's other comment—"Go big!"—illustrates the dichotomy between the Holmes evolutionary approach and his own revolutionary impulse. The merits (and flaws) of both approaches need to be well thought out.

Annie Green highlighted the mismatch of words, reality, and context, noting, "The gaping hole is architecture. We don't have the architecture we need so we can drive the strategy from top-down." She echoed as well a point raised by Julie, namely that you have no assurance that the qualifications listed on a resume actually match what the person really can do—what Julie termed the "charlatan" factor.

Cinco considers the "digital AF" as "eminently doable if done properly," stressing that it must begin with a compelling vision statement from the Chief, but noting that right now there is a distinct lack of doctrine, culture, strategy, TTPs, and methodology, too great a focus just on the technology elements, and the search for perfect centralized control and connectivity (which of course, leads to tremendous vulnerability as well).

Jay Santee asked, "What would a digital ecosystem look like for HQ, Engineering, and Operations?" and commented that "I think it is questionable whether this can get off the ground and overcome its own weight," adding, "We can't imagine the resulting change in culture and CONOPS."

In response, Deb Westphal pointed out that "culture is what we do every day," adding, "You can't change culture if you don't change what you do every day." She pointed out (quite rightly) that "the USAF talks a sense of urgency but hasn't created it," adding, "There is a lot of activity that looks urgent but isn't." My own thinking on this is that we need a "DT Czar," the kind of figure who, like Schriever and ballistic missiles, von Braun and space launch, Rickover and atomic subs, and Kaminski and low observables, has sweeping power and authority to affect change in DT across the USAF/USSF enterprise, and stays in place for some significant time—at least a decade—across changing Chiefs, PEMS, etc.

Last, Alden stressed like Julie and others "security-security-security," noting that the benefits and advantages we accrue from centralization are as well the vulnerabilities and deficits that endanger us. He felt there was too much focus on what the leadership over technology should be, and that the USAF/USSF should model commercial infrastructure and even employ commercial apps.

George Coyle, in his own follow-up rightly pointed out that our DT efforts might well offer a strategic offset against potential opponents and afford the USAF/USSF a means of strategic attack that could be decisive in any future cyber or kinetic encounter.